FUNNY BUSINESS

ALSO BY MATT SINGER

Opposable Thumbs:
How Siskel & Ebert Changed Movies Forever

FUNNY BUSINESS

The Old-School Wedding Crashers and Knocked-Up Virgins Who Changed Comedy Forever

MATT SINGER

G. P. Putnam's Sons
New York

PUTNAM
— EST. 1838 —
G. P. Putnam's Sons
Publishers Since 1838
An imprint of Penguin Random House LLC
1745 Broadway, New York, NY 10019
penguinrandomhouse.com

Book design by Laura K. Corless

ISBN 9798217047949
eBook ISBN 9798217047956

Printed in the United States of America
1st Printing

The authorized representative in the EU for product safety and compliance is Penguin Random House Ireland, Morrison Chambers, 32 Nassau Street, Dublin D02 YH68, Ireland, https://eu-contact.penguin.ie.

For Melissa,

who I never would have met

if not for a comedy movie

CONTENTS

CONTENTS

CONTENTS

FUNNY BUSINESS

INTRODUCTION

Leaders of the Pack

They're saying things that I can hardly believe
They really think we're getting out of control.

—Elvis Costello, "Radio, Radio"

It's kind of a funny story: One of the most consequential events in the history of twenty-first-century comedy happened on June 3, 1991, at a taping of the TV show *MTV Unplugged*.

The artist at Warner Hollywood Studios in Los Angeles that day was singer-songwriter Elvis Costello, who later compared his performance on *Unplugged* to "somebody literally putting a gun to the head of their career." (Producers wanted Costello to do an acoustic version of his classic ballad, "Alison." He refused and instead played a set of covers and obscurities while hiding his face behind dark sunglasses and a shaggy beard.)

Costello's set list and styling were impressively self-destructive, but the crucial event that day took place in the line to get into the show. That's where two future giants of American comedy met by chance for the first time.

Their names were Ben Stiller and Judd Apatow. Their paths had never crossed until that day in June of 1991, when Apatow and his friend and fellow comic Dana Gould spotted Stiller waiting in front of them in line. Gould and Stiller knew each other, and the three men struck up a conversation before the concert.

They had plenty to talk about. The twenty-five-year-old Stiller, the son of comedians Jerry Stiller and Anne Meara, had recently moved to Los Angeles from Manhattan following one of the shortest stints as a *Saturday Night Live* cast member in the history of the show. Apatow was just twenty-three and also an East Coast transplant, but he had been living and working in Hollywood ever since he dropped out of college several years prior. Since then, he'd scraped by performing stand-up and writing material for other comedians.

As Stiller and Apatow talked, they discovered they shared a common comedy language, cultivated over the course of childhoods spent obsessively studying the work of comedian Steve Martin, actor Bill Murray, the Canadian sketch series *SCTV*, and Albert Brooks's short films from the first season of *SNL*.

They had something else in common: They both needed a gig.

"We started chatting, and we'd both heard HBO wanted a sketch show," Apatow later recalled. "We said, 'Hey, maybe we should kick one around.'"

A few days after the concert, Stiller and Apatow met for a brainstorming session. They threw all their influences into a pot and came up with a proposal for a pilot that imagined Stiller as a film professor screening shorts made by his students. They took the pitch into HBO a few days later. The company loved the idea.

"Everyone thought that we were old, old friends but we had just met," Apatow remembered. "At the moment we sold the show we had known each other for two weeks."

The show they initially envisioned never aired. HBO sold their pitch to the upstart Fox network, and by the time *The Ben Stiller Show* premiered there on September 27, 1992, the series had evolved through three drastically different pilots—morphing from that initial film school concept to a show where Stiller introduced the sketches alongside a variety of celebrity guests.

The Ben Stiller Show got good reviews and terrible ratings. Fox yanked it from their schedule by mid-January 1993. But its impact lasted far beyond the sixteen weeks it spent on the air.

History is like a domino display that can only be comprehended after all of its pieces have fallen. Follow the trail of dominoes back to their origin and you'll find enormously important events that seemed utterly innocuous at the time.

That meeting outside an Elvis Costello concert, for example, did far more than spark one short-lived sketch TV show. Apatow used what he learned about making comedy on *The Ben Stiller Show* and applied it to everything he did after that, starting with a film that he and Stiller made together—one that became an even more notorious failure than *The Ben Stiller Show*, and effectively killed Stiller's nascent directing career for years.

But *that* failure was also one of the reasons Stiller took a chance on a role in a risqué romantic comedy about a man who gets his penis graphically caught in his zipper and a woman who mistakenly uses semen as hair gel. Grotesque as it sounds on paper, that film became one of the biggest hits of the 1990s. It helped kick-start a full-blown revolution in Hollywood that ultimately placed Stiller and Apatow at the forefront of a new generation of actors, writers, and directors. Empowered by techniques drawn from improvisational theater—and fueled by a spirit of collaboration instead of competition—they pioneered a wave of foulmouthed and filthy-minded films that made comedy one of the most bankable genres in Hollywood.

* * *

A few years and a few dominoes later, in June of 2004, *USA Today* sent entertainment reporter Susan Wloszczyna on an assignment to the Ellenborough estate in Easton, Maryland. The nine-bedroom, ten-thousand-square-foot mansion on Maryland's Eastern Shore had once been a vacation retreat for President Dwight D. Eisenhower. Now it served as the central location for an upcoming movie titled *The Wedding Crashers.*

Wloszczyna arrived on set to find one of the film's stars, shaggy-haired and crooked-nosed Owen Wilson, lounging in a rocking chair on Ellenborough's expansive porch. As Wilson glanced at a *New York Times*, his costar, the towering, fast-talking Vince Vaughn, endured one tackle after another as part of a scene where a touch football game gets wildly out of hand.

"I learned from working with Jackie Chan not to do any stunts," Wilson told Wloszczyna. "I think by the end, all my roles will just be playable from a chair."

USA Today published Wloszczyna's report from the *Wedding Crashers'* set on June 15, 2004, exactly one year to the day before the movie opened in theaters. It was extremely unusual then—or now—for a journalist to publish a story about a set visit so far in advance of its subject's opening weekend. (That sort of article typically gets saved for publication in the days leading up to a movie's release. That way, the outlet can capitalize on the curiosity surrounding the film, and the film can capitalize on a little free publicity.)

But in the summer of 2004, Owen Wilson and Vince Vaughn were about as hot as any actors in Hollywood. Wilson had just appeared in the hit comedy *Starsky & Hutch* with none other than Ben Stiller—their fifth such pairing in the previous six years. (A sixth, *Meet the Fockers*, was already set to open in theaters before the end of 2004.) And Vaughn, who also appeared in *Starsky & Hutch*, was on a meteoric rise of his own thanks to 2003's raucous college comedy *Old School.* When

Wloszczyna's piece appeared in *USA Today*, Vaughn was just days away from the premiere of the sports comedy *Dodgeball: A True Underdog Story*—which *also* featured Stiller, that time playing a ludicrously macho gym owner named White Goodman. (Spoiler alert: While he is white, he is not actually a good man.) That one became a sizable box-office smash, too.

Wloszczyna noted the strong chemistry between Wilson and Vaughn, and the fact that they (and Stiller and a handful of other actors) kept mixing and matching their talents in different combinations. Their projects often bore many of the same themes and motifs: immature men who refuse to grow up, heaping servings of outrageous humor, a fair amount of sex, and a dash of crowd-pleasing sentimentality.

Although Vaughn denied there was "any master plan of doing stuff together" he admitted to Wloszczyna that he loved working with guys like Wilson and his *Old School* costar Will Ferrell—who by that point had also appeared with Stiller and Wilson in a film set in the world of high fashion called *Zoolander*. ("You get comfortable with people, the people who you admire and think are funny, and so you naturally seek them out," Wilson confirmed. "A big part of comedies is being on the same wavelength.")

While the actors downplayed their relationships, Wloszczyna felt certain she'd stumbled upon the beginning of something big; she used her *Wedding Crashers* set visit to define this new wave in American comedy. Playing off the "Brat Pack" nickname given by *New York* magazine writer David Blum to the crew of young actors who burst onto the film scene in the 1980s (which was itself inspired by Frank Sinatra's swinging "Rat Pack" crew of the 1960s), Wloszczyna dubbed this chummy clique of like-minded performers the "Frat Pack."

Wloszczyna was not the first film journalist to observe the growing momentum generated by this brigade of interconnected comedians. A few months earlier, *Entertainment Weekly* had dubbed the same bunch the "Slacker Pack" in a short quiz about their combined filmographies. *USA Today*'s article, "Wilson and Vaughn: Leaders of the 'Frat Pack,'" wasn't even the first to use the term "Frat Pack" in print; *Variety*'s review of the Ferrell / Vaughn / Luke Wilson comedy *Old School* ran in the February 17, 2003, edition of *Variety* beneath the headline "Frat Pack Checks Zeitgeist."

But for whatever reason, Wloszczyna's article was the one that stuck the name to these men like glue, and that permanently linked these actors together for the rest of their careers. Later that same year, *Details* magazine unofficially added three filmmakers to the group when they dubbed Apatow, Adam McKay, and Todd Phillips the "Frat Packagers."

A new age of movie comedies was underway.

In a 2014 interview, Wloszczyna said that coining and popularizing the "Frat Pack" made her feel like she "contributed to the culture." ("I could have just quit then and I'd done my job," she joked.) For most of the 2000s, the Frat Pack and their numerous associates ruled the world of Hollywood comedies. For a while, it seemed like anything from any combination of its members was destined to become a hit.

But as the 2000s became the 2010s, the group's previously stellar track record at the box office weakened. Today, all the members of the so-called Frat Pack are still busy and successful—but almost none of them devote the majority of their time to movie comedies. Hell, almost *no one* devotes the majority of their time to movie comedies anymore. And the further the Frat Pack's heyday recedes into the past, the more it looks like the last great era for Hollywood's funny business.

To understand why, you need to follow the dominoes all the way back to the origins of R-rated movie comedies in the 1970s, then trace their slow decline through the 1980s, into their eventual resurrection in the late '90s, when this crew of boundary-pushing dudes—and they were pretty much *all* dudes—rewrote the rules of big-screen comedies for the twenty-first century.

All because two hilarious guys liked Elvis Costello. Can you imagine what the world would look like today if Ben Stiller was more of a Joe Jackson fan?

CHAPTER 1

The Less-Bad Guys

You can't hold a whole fraternity responsible for the behavior of a few, sick perverted individuals. For if you do, then shouldn't we blame the whole fraternity system?

—Otter, *Animal House*

You don't see too many gutters indoors. But the basement of the old brick house on East Wheelock Street had one. It ran the perimeter of the room along the base of the aged stone walls opposite the basement's other key feature: a well-stocked, U-shaped bar, which was frequented at all hours by the house's residents, the members of Dartmouth College's Alpha Delta Phi fraternity.

The frat's motto neatly encapsulated the activities in that basement: "Sickness Is Health, Blackness Is Truth, Drinking Is Strength."

All that strength came at a price, though. And the AD house's basement bathroom was tiny, maybe the size of a phone booth. So the residents would, when the urge struck, utilize the gutter to relieve themselves.

The gutter also came in handy during rush week, when new fraternity pledges were trained in the ways of "power booting"—AD's nickname for an upchuck so intense it flew ten feet through the air before striking its chosen target. Power booting was a skill much prized in the AD house. All pledges were expected to master it, along with its myriad variations: "spray booting," "nose booting," "sick booting," and the mythic "Technicolor yawn," a multi-chromatic spew that resulted from chugging food coloring prior to hurling.

Practicing these advanced techniques could get messy. Hence the gutter. Brothers joked about making pledges clean it with their tongues.

Through the decades, AD's basement was the site of countless acts of depravity and degeneracy. The members of the Adelphian Lodge, as its brothers affectionately called it, were known around campus as affable party hosts and perennial troublemakers—if not outright anarchists. During one particularly egregious incident, the frat got busted for simultaneous public urination, public masturbation, public defecation, *and* multiple acts of indecent exposure for mooning the Dartmouth Board of Trustees. Around town, AD's reputation was so noxious it became known as an animal house.

That was the reality at many American fraternities in the 1960s—a reality that might have remained hidden from wider view if not for the fact that one of AD's brothers was an aspiring writer. His name was Chris Miller, but his fellow AD brothers called him Pinto, a nickname he was given after another member of the frat sidled up to him while he was peeing (in the gutter) and observed that he had a two-toned penis. (A childhood accident involving tar and turpentine was to blame.) The sight so shocked the other Adelphians they dubbed him Pinto on the spot. (Well, *almost* on the spot; first they considered and rejected "Vanilla Fudge.") Miller always believed AD's shocking exploits deserved documentation, an instinct that eventually yielded a movie that reshaped the landscape of cinematic comedy in America.

After Miller (somehow) graduated from Dartmouth, he wound up in New York City. During the day, he worked at an ad agency; by night, he tinkered with a memoir about the animal house. One day in the fall of 1969, a friend recommended him for a side gig cranking out stories that could run between the nude pictures in one of the many porn magazines that sprouted up after the introduction of *Playboy*.

"The editor told me when the deadline was, and I came home from the ad agency, smoked some weed, and pumped out some piece of crap," Miller recalled. "He checked it to make sure it had enough sex and then I got a deal to write a dozen stories in a row for publication in a place where it didn't matter, without combat consequences. That was where I did my basic training."

Miller's outrageous stories began circulating among other magazine editors in New York; one found its way to an iconoclastic comedy writer named Doug Kenney. A few years earlier, Kenney and college buddies Henry Beard and Robert Hoffman had made the journey from an Ivy League school to New York City to pursue their own literary dreams. Inspired by the success they'd found writing in college—in particular, with a series of dead-on parodies of newsstand staples like *Mademoiselle*—the trio convinced a publishing executive named Matty Simmons to fund a new humor magazine. In honor of the *Harvard Lampoon*, the long-running publication they contributed to back at Harvard, Kenney, Beard, and Hoffman dubbed their creation *National Lampoon*.

"Doug really was brilliant," says *Animal House* director John Landis. "You read about the Algonquin Round Table, and the wit of Dorothy Parker and Robert Benchley, these people with these remarks that flow out of their mouths that are so smart and so funny and witty. Doug actually did that. He actually said things that were that smart and that funny, that had real wit. You never meet people like that. It's so rare."

Launched in April 1970, *National Lampoon* quickly exploded in popularity thanks to an unsparing approach to comedy that resonated with the deeply cynical generation that came of age amid the constant social and political upheavals of the 1960s. As the *Lampoon*'s P. J. O'Rourke put it in 1978, "It's a fair guess every one of the *Lampoon* editors was a member of the counter-culture back then, but look what happened: After all the folk songs and candlelit marches, it didn't change a thing."

As a result, no one was safe from the *Lampoon*, not even dogs. The magazine's most famous cover depicted an anxious pooch with a revolver pressed against its head beside the caption "If You Don't Buy This Magazine, We'll Kill This Dog." Kenney and his staff gleefully slaughtered every sacred cow (and dog) in sight. Early issues included features like "Children's Letters to the Gestapo," "The Joys of Wife Tasting," and "What Happened to the American Wet Dream?"

It was in that last area where Chris Miller was especially qualified to contribute. Fittingly, given his resume, Miller's first *Lampoon* piece appeared in the magazine's "Pornography" issue, dated July 1971. When the *Lampoon* wanted more, Miller dug through his drawers and found his unfinished book about Alpha Delta Phi. Turning each chapter into its own short story, he submitted several to the *Lampoon*, which published them with evocative titles like "The Night of the Seven Fires" and "Pinto's First Lay." Pretty soon the *National Lampoon* had a circulation of over a million copies a month, with Miller's "Tales from the Adelphian Lodge" regarded as one of the magazine's more popular recurring features.

By the middle of the 1970s, the *Lampoon* became so synonymous with edgy, pull-no-punches humor that Simmons—whose unorthodox career path included a stint helping launch the world's first credit card with the Diners Club—could freely grow the company into what he proudly called "the humor empire in the United States." A comedy album called *National Lampoon Radio Dinner* became a hit, and demand for a follow-up sparked the idea for a Woodstock parody filled with withering imitations of rock stars that concluded in an act of mass ritual suicide. The initial plan was to stage the concert in front of an audience and record it live. But the resulting show, *Lemmings*, proved so popular that the *Lampoon* kept it running for months. The positive response was fueled by its incredibly talented young cast, which included then-unknown actors like Chevy Chase, Christopher Guest, and John Belushi.

Belushi, a preternatural sketch performer with an appetite for illicit substances to rival anyone who passed through the basement at Alpha Delta Phi, also appeared on *The National Lampoon Radio Hour*, a syndicated program created by the magazine's staff and a cast of up-and-coming performers. Most of the *Radio Hour* cast, including Gilda Radner, brothers Bill Murray and Brian Doyle-Murray, and Harold Ramis, also worked on a *Lemmings* follow-up called *The National Lampoon Show*. That, too, became an off-Broadway hit—at least until Belushi and Radner were poached by a new late-night television show called *NBC's Saturday Night*.

Belushi served as *The National Lampoon Show*'s director, but the play was produced by a *Lampoon* newcomer; an enterprising Canadian named Ivan Reitman. The son of Hungarian Jewish refugees who had survived World War II, Reitman was a consummate hustler—and a fan of *National Lampoon*.

"I bought it every month," Reitman said in 2003. "It spoke to me and my generation. And I always felt that if that voice could be translated into films, it would have extraordinary national appeal."

By the mid-1970s, Reitman had produced some Canadian television and theater, and he'd also directed an exploitation film with the lurid title *Cannibal Girls*. (Its even more lurid tagline: "These girls do exactly what you think they do!") Reitman was so certain a *National Lampoon* movie would be a hit, and so convinced that he was the man to make it, that he scanned the magazine's masthead for the guy in charge and cold-called him.

"I said, 'Hey, let's do a comedy together.' And the publisher, Matty Simmons, said, 'We're not ready to do a movie yet, but we're interested in doing a sort of off-Broadway show called *The National Lampoon Show*. Would you want to produce it and put it together for us?' And I said, 'Alright.'"

Reitman's deal with the *Lampoon* gave him the right to produce any movie developed out of the stage show. So he offered Murray, Doyle-Murray, and Belushi $2,500 to turn some sketches from *The National Lampoon Show* into a film script. No dice, they said; they wanted $2,500 *each*.

Reitman's response: "I can get Ramis for $2,500."

That's exactly what he did. And although Simmons had previously hesitated to branch out into the world of movies, he now had a reason to rethink his cautiousness. Five years into the history of the *Lampoon*, Simmons's contract with its three other founders required him to buy out their share of the magazine. Once he did, Beard promptly retired. A year later, Kenney was ready to call it quits, too.

"I was faced with losing a key player," Simmons wrote in 2012. "I knew [Kenny] loved show business and without really thinking I snapped, 'You can't leave now! We're gonna make a movie!'"

Of course, there was no movie—except maybe the beginnings of one that Ivan Reitman and Harold Ramis were just starting to develop. So Reitman and Simmons paired up Ramis and Kenney. Their initial concept was set in a high school and featured a teenage Charles Manson as, in Ramis's words, "a strangely seductive, demented loner living in the white bread world of a typical midwestern suburb, corrupting the local youth and forming a depraved cult of flying saucer worshipping teenage zombies." They called it *Laser Orgy Girls*.

This idea, you might not be shocked to learn, was not approved.

Somewhat curiously, the Manson aspect *wasn't* the deal-breaker. Instead, Simmons objected to the high school setting, where the notion of orgies (much less *laser* orgies) was deemed a nonstarter. "Apparently," Landis explains, "it was so full of fucking and swearing that Matty said, 'You can't have high schoolers doing this! Make it college!'" From there, the creative team pivoted—and brought in Chris Miller, the *Lampoon*'s poet laureate of collegiate excess, as a third contributor.

The trio of Ramis, Kenney, and Miller spent the next three months locked in a room at the *Lampoon*'s Manhattan offices, swapping unspeakable acts they witnessed or heard about during their respective tours of academia. Many of their characters—along with the project's post–*Laser Orgy Girls* title—were informed by Miller's time at Dartmouth, which had its own smooth-talking Otter and awkward Flounder. Even Miller's own nickname wound up attached to the film's de facto protagonist, the shy Pinto. (Somewhat surprisingly, the final film never revealed the reason for Miller's moniker.)

The rest of the men who comprised the film's fictional frat, Delta House, were deliberate archetypes designed to remind the audience of guys present in every college: anxious Hoover, sarcastic Boon, eccentric D-Day, and, of course, wild man John "Bluto" Blutarsky, played with exuberant physical energy and an astonishing array of cartoonish facial expressions by John Belushi, who in the time it took Ramis and company to write *Animal House* had rocketed to stardom as a magnetic performer on the now named *Saturday Night Live*.

Kenney, Miller, and Ramis jammed every single story they could think of into the initial *Animal House* treatment, which ran 114 pages, at least four times the industry norm. (One studio executive who read it called it "*War and Peace* on speed.") After two more years of work, they whittled their epic saga of bacchanalian debauchery down to a manageable screenplay. Even then, Simmons and the *Animal House* script got rejected by almost every producer in Hollywood, until he found two young executives at Universal named Thom Mount and Sean Daniel.

Like Reitman, Mount and Daniel were *Lampoon* fans who felt the brand's acidic humor would connect with the new generation of moviegoers. Better still, they actually liked the *Animal House* script. There was just one problem: Their boss—Ned Tanen, the head of Universal—hated it.

"Tanen would say to Thom and me, 'Look, what is this?'" said Daniel. "'I mean, what the hell is this? This guy sleeps with the young kid's girlfriend and tries to sleep with every other girl on campus. The other guy is a Peeping Tom. And they're like downtown drunks, and *they're* the heroes?!'"

They were. *Animal House*'s plot was brilliantly simple. The troublemakers of Delta House, the so-called "worst fraternity on campus" at Faber College, get placed on "double secret probation" by the perpetually uptight Dean Wormer (John Vernon). The Deltas continue to escalate their war with the dean and his preppy allies from Omega Theta Pi until they're evicted from their house and expelled.

The names of the film's fraternities are telling. The villains are "the Omegas"—sniveling, sexually repressed bullies who represent humanity at its absolute nadir. But note that *Animal House*'s protagonists aren't "the Alphas." They're not the Omegas' polar opposites; they do not represent the shining pinnacle of empathy and human benevolence. In fact, Ned Tanen was correct; the Deltas *are* kind of terrible. They cheat on tests, lie to coeds to con them into bed, and kill at least one barnyard animal, although that one's sort of an accident. The Deltas aren't the good guys of *Animal House*; they're the *less*-bad guys.

Whether Tanen liked it, or even realized it, the amoral men of *Animal House*'s Delta Tau Chi made ideal protagonists in 1970s Hollywood, which had a long-running love affair with antiheroes. Although *Animal House* is rarely considered in those terms today, its lascivious rebels were cut from the same cloth as '60s and '70s movie icons like Bonnie and Clyde and Travis Bickle. Many of that era's biggest hits followed characters who would have qualified as villains in traditional Hollywood films; drug dealers, gangsters, and vigilantes. They were hailed for their subversive spirit and antiestablishment values, both of which the Deltas share.

Just a few years before *Animal House* got a green light from Universal, there had never been an R-rated comedy in history—for the simple reason that the R rating hadn't been invented yet. Until the mid-1960s the film industry was still subject to a draconian set of content standards informally known as "the Hays Code," named after the man, William Hays, who had been chosen to lead the predecessor of what eventually became the Motion Picture Association of America way back in 1922.

At the height of its power, the Hays Code, and its chief administrator Joseph Breen—a dictatorial moralist Dean Wormer would have *loved*—exerted enormous control over the content of American movies. No Hollywood film could be shown in America without his seal of approval. The Code's prohibitions were not only restrictive; they were often downright odd. The ban on "romantic partners without at least one foot on the floor in love scenes" makes a certain amount of sense, at least to a prude who wants to ensure moviegoers don't get too titillated by anything onscreen. But the Code also outlawed phrases like "hold your hat," and expressly forbade material that fell under the term "toilet gags." If those benign concepts were a no-go, one can only imagine what Breen would have thought of a Technicolor yawn.

Breen and Hays's rules stayed in place into the 1960s—an era that, not coincidentally, also marked a major decline in movie ticket sales as customers stayed home in droves to watch the upstart medium of television. Increasingly, if audiences did go to the theater, they were more inclined to seek out foreign films, which were not held to the same content standards as Hollywood movies, and could get away with far more in the realm of adult language and sexuality.

The need to compete with those more mature offerings was what finally burst the dam and inspired the MPAA's new administrator in the late 1960s, Jack Valenti, to launch the organization's first ratings system. That, in turn, led to the first wave of mainstream Hollywood movies with significant adult content—including, for the first time, R-rated comedies.

At last, Hollywood movies could talk about topics like sex—if not always fully depict the act, lest they cross over from the "restricted" R rating to the "adults only" X. Dyan Cannon joked about orgies in 1969's

Bob & Carol & Ted & Alice. 1970's *M*A*S*H* unleashed the first verbal "fuck" in a studio film—one whose anti-authority, antiestablishment attitude about American military intervention in Asia resonated with the same impulses behind the *National Lampoon.* ("I wasn't looking for anything subtle or clever," *M*A*S*H* director Robert Altman said of his film. "We were looking for basic bad taste.")

If *M*A*S*H* was basic bad taste, *Animal House* was advanced bad taste. Belushi's Bluto was possibly the first character in cinema history introduced while urinating on someone's shoes. (Technically, he urinates on *two* someones' shoes simultaneously.) The Deltas shoplift, start a riot in the middle of a parade, and lie to a dead student's friends in order to score dates with them—only to abandon the women at a bar after they're intimidated by a bunch of African American men who ask for a dance.

And yet somehow the original script was even more shocking. When Universal decided to hire high school dropout and lifelong movie obsessive John Landis to direct *Animal House*, he couldn't get over the extremity of its characters' behavior.

"I go to see Ned Tanen," Landis recalls. "He asked me, 'What do you think this script needs?' And I was very honest. I said, 'Well, I think it's truly funny. In fact, some of it's hilarious. But it's also truly offensive. . . . I said, 'I think it needs a revision.'" Tanen agreed, and sent Landis to New York to oversee the rewrite.

"I'll never forget going to Madison Avenue to the *Lampoon* offices," Landis continues. "And in a conference room, there sit three guys: Harold and Doug and Chris. And I walk into the most hostile room. They thought I was, like, 'the Hollywood guy,' and they just hated me."

For three days, Landis and the writing team butted heads over his suggestions. But eventually, Doug Kenney pulled Landis aside and asked to take him to dinner. When they sat down to eat, Kenney said, "I really want to make this movie and what you're saying makes sense. I'm gonna beat the other guys up, and we're gonna follow your lead."

Landis looked past all the Technicolor yawns in the original script (which he eventually nixed anyway) and recognized that beneath *Animal House*'s unprecedentedly crass exterior was actually a throwback to an earlier era. "There had always been college comedies," Landis explained. "In the silents there was Buster Keaton and Harold Lloyd. When I got the opportunity to make this picture—and this was me thinking, I don't know what anybody else's intention was—I set out to make a fairly classic college comedy." (That said, to this author's best recollection, Buster Keaton's *College* does not contain a scene where the Great Stone Face sleeps with the dean's wife.)

Landis's classical touch blended surprisingly well with the *Lampoon*'s ruthless sensibility. And Landis had a secret weapon up his sleeve: John Belushi, who could somehow spy on naked sorority sisters through their bedroom windows without losing the audience's support. With a naughty arch of his eyebrow, Belushi made it clear he was having a blast; every wink and smirk beckoned the viewer to join in the fun. That was particularly important because, as Reitman noted, "one of the tricky things about making a movie about fraternities is that for most of the world, a lot of what goes on at fraternities is not particularly likable." Clad in a sweater with the word "COLLEGE" emblazoned across his chest as if he were the walking, talking, belching, chugging embodiment of American higher learning, it was hard to dislike Belushi no matter what he did—and almost impossible to dislike *Animal House* as a result.

"Bluto, as written, is essentially all appetite. He's a pig," Landis admits. "But John was such an extraordinary performer, he made Bluto sympathetic. I told John: 'You play Bluto as a combination of Harpo Marx and the Cookie Monster,' because they're both all appetite. He totally understood. There's a scene at the toga party, where there's a folk singer on the stairs. And Bluto comes down in his toga and he listens, then he takes the guitar and violently smashes it. And what makes that scene is when he hands back the ruined guitar to the singer he says, 'Sorry.' It's an extraordinary performance. People loved him, but I don't think they realized how skilled it was."

Landis might have toned down the script's excesses slightly, but when *National Lampoon's Animal House* debuted in theaters in the summer of 1978, the characters' behavior shocked audiences—and the film's ticket sales shocked Hollywood when it became the top-grossing comedy in history against a budget of $2.3 million. Along with *Jaws*, *Star Wars*, and *Superman*, it was cited by *The New York Times* in an article about the movie industry's new era of "super-grossers." Today, we call them blockbusters.

While *Animal House* didn't look or sound like any other comedy at the time, Landis credits the film's record-breaking success to three simple facts: The script was funny, it featured John Belushi at the absolute zenith of his *Saturday Night Live* fame, and every single person who was in or had attended college recognized its characters.

"Over the past forty-five years, thousands of people have come up to me; senators, guys who work at gas stations. Tons of guys—and women—come up to me and say, 'That was my fraternity. I went to that college.' I think it was very relatable. Everyone knew someone like those guys. And I think that's the main reason."

Reitman had a different take. He argued that *Animal House* "really changed the comedic language. Before *Animal House* they were all watching Bob Hope and Phyllis Diller and Dean Martin and Jerry Lewis. . . . There really had been no film that had the language of *Animal House*, and even though it was set in 1962, it was made in the '70s and was more reflective of that kind of attitude and language and behavior."

Pinto himself, Chris Miller, felt it had something to do with why Ned Tanen and Universal almost didn't make the movie in the first place. "What *Animal House* did that was radical was it took all the characters who in earlier movies were the heroes and made them the bad guys," he said. "And it took all the crazies and the nuts and the Martians and the womanizers and the animals and raised them to some sort of mythic godhood of being the good guys. That was what people went crazy over."

In truth, *all* those elements played a role in *Animal House*'s success: the friction between its nostalgic milieu and its contemporary attitudes, between its protagonists' sometimes disgusting actions and the film's treatment of them as relatable underdogs. It bombarded the viewer with sexual content, but it didn't take sex—or anything else—seriously. It was staggering on first viewing, and endlessly quotable on the tenth.

Animal House's triumph was quickly replicated—in tone, if not creativity or quality—by every studio in Hollywood looking for the next comedic super-grosser. Some even came from *Animal House* alums. Kenney and Ramis reteamed on the similarly themed *Caddyshack*, starring *SNL* stars Chevy Chase and Bill Murray. The following year, Ramis and Murray partnered with Ivan Reitman on *Stripes*, in which a bunch of Delta-coded slobs set out to disrupt the ultimate symbols of order and authority: the U.S. military. Meanwhile, *National Lampoon* got Chase to appear in Ramis's adaptation of a popular *Lampoon* story by a writer named John Hughes. While the result, *National Lampoon's Vacation*, sounded on paper like family-friendly entertainment, the film contained elder abuse, intimations of incest, masturbation, kidnapping, and adultery. Like *Animal House*, it hit theaters carrying an R rating.

Other *Animal House* successors, like *Revenge of the Nerds*, came from creators outside the *Lampoon* umbrella looking to replicate its college milieu and underdog heroes. A few, like *Porky's*, even dared to try the one thing *National Lampoon* wouldn't: high school kids (or at least actors in their twenties portraying high school kids) in a story about horny teens trying to get laid.

There were so many *Animal House* knockoffs by the mid-'80s that what seemed novel in 1978 felt like a stale formula just a few years later. At the same time, studio executives began to realize that if they wanted a super-grosser, an R-rated film like *Animal House* put them at an immediate disadvantage. The R rating automatically barred younger audiences from buying tickets without parental supervision. No wonder R-rated comedy hits began to generate kid-friendly sequels. The *Police Academy* series, for example, started its life as an R-rated vulgarity set in a training camp for cops. It ultimately spawned six sequels—all of them rated PG-13 or PG.

Some of the *National Lampoon* generation died tragically young, including Doug Kenney, who fell from a cliff in Hawaii in 1980, and John Belushi, who passed away following a drug overdose in 1982. Those who survived saw which way the wind was blowing and followed it. After *Vacation*, Harold Ramis didn't direct an R-rated comedy for fifteen years. After *Stripes*, Ivan Reitman didn't make one for thirty years.

And so the R-rated comedy slipped to the Hollywood margins. It was too risky; not worth the trouble, given the limitations it seemed to place on a film's potential box office. But *Animal House* and its spiritual successors in the "slobs versus snobs" comedy subgenre made a huge impact on a generation of kids who saw those movies at a young age (arguably at *too* young an age) and grew up wanting to make similarly raunchy films of their own.

Two of those kids were a pair of siblings from Cumberland, Rhode Island, who later recounted the seismic impact *Animal House* had on their lives when it first hit theaters.

"*Animal House* is a tremendous landmark," said one of the brothers in 1998. "I remember seeing it as a kid and wondering, 'Isn't that illegal? Can they do that in movies?'" The other brother cited *Animal House* as the main film that spurred them to become a directing team. When they did, they created one of the few R-rated comedies in history to outgross—and out-*gross*—their inspiration.

CHAPTER 2

The Hustler of Money

See? Look at that. We just started out and already something almost funny happened.

—Ben Stiller, *The Ben Stiller Show*

Of the 139 shows aired by ABC, CBS, NBC, and Fox during the 1992–93 television season, the lowest-rated series wasn't *Likely Suspects*, the bizarre interactive cop drama where the lead actor spoke directly to the camera as if the viewer was their partner helping them solve mysteries. Somehow it wasn't the wacky sitcom about the last survivors of a nuclear apocalypse, either. (That show's title also doubled as a succinct review of its content: *Woops!*) No, the 1992 show watched by the fewest people around the country was an unusual sketch comedy series that spent years in development, and then just four months on the air. The ratings were so dismal Fox didn't even bother to air the final episode.

It was called *The Ben Stiller Show.*

Who was Ben Stiller? In 1992, few knew and fewer cared. When Stiller and his staff showed up at the Emmys to accept *The Ben Stiller Show*'s surprise award for Outstanding Writing for a Variety or Music Program long after the series' cancellation, he joked to the audience at the Pasadena Civic Auditorium that "not many of you probably know who the hell we are!" After rattling off a list of thank-yous, Stiller added "Fox Network, I think you missed, y'know, *something* here."

He wasn't wrong. Within five years of *The Ben Stiller Show*'s unceremonious conclusion, its creator and star headlined one of the most successful movie comedies in history, jump-starting a fifteen-year run of box office hits that grossed more than $6 billion in ticket sales worldwide.

In 1992, still reeling from the sting of *The Ben Stiller Show*'s collapse, that was not an outcome Stiller would have predicted—or even necessarily wanted. Although Stiller grew up in a showbiz family as the only son of a well-known comedy team, he didn't dream of becoming a famous comedian himself. From the time he was nine years old, he had his sights set on a different goal: directing. He would insist that if he had a future in front of the camera at all, it would be as a "serious" actor.

"I've always thought of myself as having a really good sense of humor, as opposed to being a really funny person," Stiller said. In another interview, he added, "When people tell me I'm funny, I think, Oh, really? What scene?"

Benjamin Edward Meara Stiller was born in New York City on November 30, 1965, to actors and comics Jerry Stiller and Anne Meara. Stiller and Meara and their comedy act were already regulars on *The Ed Sullivan Show* by the time Ben was born, and his childhood was anything but typical. Jerry and Anne, popular TV stars, were regularly recognized on the streets of New York and, as Ben put it, his father was "both loving and needy." If a fan approached him on the street, he would chat with them for as long as they wanted—or at least until Meara would grab him and insist, "Jerry, let's get the fuck out of here!"

Show business was an ever-present fact of life for young Ben Stiller.

He took a thrilling trip to the set of *The Partridge Family* and received swimming lessons in Las Vegas from Gladys Knight's backing group, the Pips. Thanksgiving dinner guests at the Stillers' apartment on Manhattan's Upper West Side included Rodney Dangerfield and Andy Kaufman, who ate peanut butter and jelly instead of turkey. And while the kids got to travel with their parents during the summers, they also spent a lot of time at home supervised by a housekeeper while Stiller and Meara toured their act around the country without them.

There was another important babysitter in the home: the television. Jerry Stiller remembered his son watching TV "for three, four hours at a time," absorbing shows like *Gilligan's Island*, *The Brady Bunch*, *Bewitched*, and reruns of the original *Star Trek*. ("All the colors were so rich and vivid, and that California back-lot reality seemed very comforting," Ben explained.) One late '90s profile of the actor described him as "quite literally a child of television."

Like most kids of his generation, the young Stiller loved the early years of *Saturday Night Live*—but it wasn't necessarily John Belushi and his bombastic characters who made the biggest impression on him. Instead, he was fascinated by Albert Brooks, who crafted witty shorts that aired between the live sketches. Stiller found himself drawn to Brooks's understated tone and his acerbic deconstructions of TV and film clichés. On the big screen, the young Stiller preferred disaster movies like *The Poseidon Adventure* and grand sci-fi dystopias like *Planet of the Apes*. He saw *Jaws* "20 trillion times" in the theater, not only reveling in the human drama and the aquatic thrills, but also studying the camera angles and patient editing deployed by director Steven Spielberg.

Those films began to rub off on Ben, and when Jerry Stiller gave his son a Super 8 camera, making his own became a passion. His first productions were much darker than you might expect from a future comedy legend. Inspired by his own experiences getting mugged on the Upper West Side, Stiller crafted a short film about a kid who gets robbed and then teams with a friend, tracks down the attacker, and beats him up.

The name of this early opus: *Murder in the Park*.

He may have enjoyed making his own shorts, especially the ones where he parodied big Hollywood movies like *The Exorcist* and *Airport 1975* (originally costarring one Jerry Stiller), but Ben quickly realized film school was not for him; he lasted just one year at UCLA before dropping out and moving back to New York City in 1984. For two years, Stiller waited tables around Manhattan while bombing one audition after another. Casting directors recognized him as Jerry Stiller's son, which only made it worse. ("People would say, 'Wow, Jerry Stiller's kid sucks.'") Even after he improved, he still needed a little help to get his foot in the door: Stiller landed his first Broadway role in a revival of *The House of Blue Leaves* after Meara, who had appeared in the original off-Broadway production, asked playwright John Guare to give her son a shot.

"I had rehearsed this monologue for two weeks with my acting teacher," Stiller recalled. "I thought, *These people know they're seeing me because of my mother.* But you meet people any way you can." He got the audition, and the job.

Stiller played Ronnie, the son of the main character, a zookeeper and aspiring songwriter named Artie, played by John Mahoney. The role suited Stiller; in his big monologue, Ronnie, a manic GI headed for Vietnam, cartwheels and spins around the stage with wild intensity as he recounts a failed Hollywood audition. When the audience in the theater chuckled at his antics, Stiller paused and asked, "You laughin' at me?" After they cracked up again, he replied, "Go ahead, laugh! Because you know what I think of you?" and blew the crowd a huge raspberry—and then, with perfect comic timing, apologized for spitting on everyone in the front row, getting an even bigger roar. Underestimated, rejected, not sure he wanted to generate laughs, and getting them anyway—in his first big role, Stiller was already carving out a niche.

Although he was finally making headway as an actor, Stiller still wanted a career behind the camera. So he started making films with his costars from *The House of Blue Leaves.* Their first short, *Portrait of the Artist as an Old Man*, was a fake documentary about Mahoney winning a Tony Award (and secretly being an alcoholic who hits on his fellow actors). On a lark, Stiller played it at his parents New Year's Eve party in 1986, where it killed in a room full of dozens of people. "It was one of the first times I saw people laughing at something I'd made and I thought, 'This is good,'" Stiller said.

That reception gave him the confidence to make an even more ambitious short, and to appear in it as well. Stiller's *The Hustler of Money* is a dead-on parody of Martin Scorsese's *The Color of Money*, with Mahoney as the Paul Newman stand-in and—in a role he would play several times over his career—Stiller in an uncanny impression of Tom Cruise. Instead of billiards, the characters hustle bowling; instead of cheap liquor, Mahoney's Fast Eddie Felson hawks Newman's Own salad dressing. ("This stuff tastes like moose sweat!" gripes the bowling alley bartender, played by Anne Meara.)

Stiller's fascination with the inner workings of moviemaking made him a crack parodist. Despite a meager budget and little experience, he managed to ape the look and feel of an ultra-stylish Scorsese thriller. A budding hustler himself, Stiller wasn't content with another amusing homemade spoof he could show his family and friends. After *Saturday Night Live* cast member Jon Lovitz showed up to watch *The House of Blue Leaves*, Stiller reached out to him to see if he would be willing to show *The Hustler of Money* to the higher-ups at *SNL.* Within a matter of days, Stiller met Lovitz in the lobby of 30 Rock and slipped him a VHS copy.

Despite the fact that it was made by a twenty-one-year-old kid and starred no one from the actual *SNL* cast, the show decided to air it on the March 28, 1987, episode. And after a series of other acting gigs—including a supporting role in Steven Spielberg's *Empire of the Sun*—

SNL hired Stiller to join the show. Just twenty-three years old, he had already achieved his dream: Barely a decade after he fell in love with Albert Brooks's *SNL* shorts, Stiller became a full-fledged cast member himself.

And then he quit after one month.

Once Stiller got to *SNL*, he realized he didn't fit in. He joined the show hoping to make more shorts like *The Hustler of Money*. Thanks to brilliant stars like Dana Carvey, Phil Hartman, and fellow newcomer Mike Myers, *Saturday Night Live* remained squarely focused on live sketches. By Stiller's own admission, that was not his strong suit. ("I got too nervous, I didn't enjoy it, and I wanted to be making short films," he later explained.)

So that's what he did. He left *SNL* and launched his own show on MTV. This first *Ben Stiller Show* was referred to at the network as a "Vid-Com": part sketch comedy and part music videos, with Stiller playing an unlikable version of himself in the wraparound segments. Unlike the pressure-cooker environment of *Saturday Night Live*, no one at MTV paid attention to what he and his tiny team did. As long as they stuck to the budget, they could basically make whatever they wanted. But that show didn't last, either.

In 1983, a fifteen-year-old kid from Syosset, New York, inadvertently invented the comedy podcast.

Obviously, that's not what Judd Apatow called it. But if he had been interested in a career in broadcasting, he could have evolved his high school radio show of granular interviews with stand-up comics into the first true comedy podcast, decades before a burned-out stand-up named Marc Maron launched *WTF*.

But Apatow was less interested in journalism than access. A self-described "comedy freak," Apatow later admitted the show was mostly just an excuse to pick his favorite comics' brains. By the time he was in high school, all Judd Apatow cared about was stand-up comedy. He came home from school, headed directly to the television, and watched until it was time to go to sleep. When Apatow's parents broke up while he was still in his early teens, it drove him even deeper into his comedy obsession. Rocked by the divorce, Apatow was determined to get an early start on becoming a comic.

"I thought, 'All right, maybe I'll just use this radio station,'" Apatow said. "And I would call [comedians'] publicists and ask them to do an interview on WKWZ Radio. But nobody knew what that was. They didn't know it was a high school radio station. So I was basically tricking everybody into speaking to me."

Born without whatever gene makes other people shy around their idols, Apatow was never intimidated meeting his heroes. While visiting his grandparents in Los Angeles as a twelve-year-old, he spotted Steve Martin outside his Los Angeles home and approached him to ask for an autograph. After Martin refused, Apatow wrote him a letter chastising him for treating his fans "like crap" and threatening to send his address to *Homes of the Stars* if he didn't apologize. A few months later, a copy of Martin's book *Cruel Shoes* arrived with the inscription "Dear Judd, I'm sorry. I didn't realize I was speaking to *the* Judd Apatow! Your Friend, Steve Martin."

Fueled by the insights he gleaned interviewing comics on the radio, Apatow began performing his own material by the time he was seventeen. After high school, he went to college at the University of Southern California, then dropped out to focus all of his energies on making it as a stand-up.

He also started spending time at "the Ranch," a San Fernando Valley home where comics would congregate after gigs to play poker and watch infomercials and underground VHS tapes. Apatow particularly liked one where a woman tried to mask her ineptitude at stand-up comedy with an obvious laugh track. Everyone else at the Ranch thought the tape was too weird (or maybe too sad) to be funny—except for another relatively recent L.A. transplant named Paul Feig. They both thought the woman was *hysterical*. An instant friendship was formed.

"Judd and I were like, 'It's funny *because* it's so terrible that it's almost like a piece of art," says Feig. "So that was where Judd and I went, 'God, we have the same sense of humor.' We bonded over that and stayed buddies." When Apatow first arrived at the Ranch, Feig adds, he couldn't get over how this "showbiz kid" was already working high-profile gigs.

"He was booking some club, and he also got on the *Young Comedians Special* on HBO. So it was kind of like, 'Wow. Who is this guy who's so hooked up?'"

But while the *Young Comedians Special* launched many up-and-coming comics, it didn't give Apatow the boost he'd desired, and he struggled to find a unique perspective on the world that would make his own act stand out in the burgeoning stand-up scene of the late '80s and early '90s.

"I worshipped guys like Bill Maher, Jay Leno, and Jerry Seinfeld, and was doing my variation of that. But as a young person with no political point of view or life experience, it was as funny as you can imagine," Apatow admitted. "When people would see me, they would think, 'Oh, that's a good writer.' No one would ever have said, 'Oh, that's a good performer.'"

So Apatow began to focus more on writing and helping other comedians with their material—including Garry Shandling, who hired him to brainstorm jokes for the 1991 Grammy Awards. Writing on awards shows, Apatow learned, was about helping the other talent "feel in the mood to write and spew and be creative . . . the vast majority of what came up, came out of them. But I was good at prodding them and knowing what areas they should think about."

Still in his early twenties, Apatow began to cultivate an innate gift more valuable than anything a comic could teach him while sitting around a beat-up tape recorder. Apatow was a decent stand-up, but he was a savant at finding the funny in other people. If there was untapped potential in someone, Apatow could find the best way to bring it out and present it to the world. He was like a comedy beachcomber—and he was about to find what he was looking for in the line outside an Elvis Costello concert.

The Ben Stiller Show, created by Stiller and Apatow, may not have been watched by a ton of people, but those who tuned in recognized that the series was something special—especially in the early 1990s, when television was still limited to four broadcast networks and a handful of cable channels, and formal experimentation was almost unheard of. Stiller and Apatow assembled a murderers' row of then-unknown talent who would go on to leave enormous marks on the comedy landscape, including Andy Dick, Janeane Garofalo, Bob Odenkirk, and David Cross, who later teamed with Odenkirk to create the classic HBO sketch series *Mr. Show*.

They were all undeniably green. Apatow, who had only produced a handful of comedy specials to that point, later copped to having so little managerial experience prior to *The Ben Stiller Show* that he hid in his office and read books about how to lead a staff. But the same determination that pushed Apatow to write Steve Martin a sternly worded letter about refusing to sign an autograph made him a great TV producer, one who would fight tooth and nail for what he believed in, even when executives tried to change his vision.

"The head of the network loved the pilot, but he quickly got a promotion and the new head hated the show," Apatow wrote in 2025. "I would get notes from the network and refuse to take them because my friend [*In Living Color* producer] Eric Gold told me, 'If you fail, they will never say it was because of their bad notes.' I would say to our young executive, 'I am not going to do any of them, now what happens?'"

"He burned bridges. He was not afraid," said Stiller. "He had the courage of his convictions. I don't know where he got that from. I was like, 'This is great, but maybe that sketch about the "Weird Tales of the

Dark Side" where I turn into a monster for eight minutes isn't the greatest thing in the world.' But he would be like, 'No. Come on. We're doing it.'"

Apatow and Stiller turned their inexperience into an advantage. Not knowing the "correct" way to make a TV show, they instead produced one that broke all of the medium's unwritten rules. When asked, Stiller would insist *The Ben Stiller Show* wasn't ahead of its time. He said they were "just sort of ripping off *SCTV*. We loved *SCTV* [and] we thought, 'Oh let's do something like that. . . .' Y'know, Albert Brooks, I wanted to be Albert Brooks. That was the influence really. We were just trying to get on the air."

Still, his collaborators were quick to credit him with his influence on *them*. For decades, Apatow would say he developed his own approach as a movie director after watching Stiller craft a series of recurring sketches about an appropriately named weasel of a Hollywood agent named Michael Pheret. The character himself wasn't necessarily revelatory, but the way Stiller shot the scenes was. He would have the celebrity guest—say, Howie Mandel—come in and film just his side of the scene.

"But then," Apatow explained, "Howie would leave and we'd do Ben's close ups and for two hours Ben would riff even more offensive pitches that you couldn't even say to Howie Mandel, but if Ben's in a clean shot and you have a clean shot of Howie Mandel and Howie looks annoyed you can really cut to anything from Ben." They would take Stiller's improvisations, figure out which bits worked best in the editing room, and stitch together the ultimate version of the sketch. Apatow was astounded with the results. In 2022, he told *Esquire*, "I learned how to shoot comedy watching Ben do those."

People around Hollywood were watching Ben's work, too, regardless of what the ratings said. Before *The Ben Stiller Show* was canceled, Stiller had already lined up his first gig directing a feature, after he received a script about postcollege malaise written by a former USC student named Helen Childress. Although the screenplay, which was titled *Reality Bites*, shared *The Ben Stiller Show*'s jaundiced view of popular culture, it otherwise bore little resemblance to the sketch show's absurd humor—which is precisely why Stiller wanted to do it.

"I was surprised it came my way, actually," Stiller said, "because it wasn't a broad comedy, which was most of the stuff I was getting sent to me at the time. That's why I was real excited. I didn't want to do a silly comedy. I wanted something that was different from my own experience."

Helen's characters were from Houston and included Lelaina, an aspiring documentarian who wants to make a free-flowing film about her friends, like Troy, a struggling musician. Before she can finish the project, she falls for a TV executive, Michael, who offers her the chance to turn her raw footage into a *Real World*–style reality show on his MTV-esque cable network. Stiller was initially brought in to direct the project based on the strength of his work behind the camera on *The Ben Stiller Show*. But as he and Childress developed the script, they began improvising the Michael character together, until it began to make sense for Stiller to play the part himself. After Winona Ryder, hot off a string of hits like *Edward Scissorhands* and *Bram Stoker's Dracula*, agreed to play Lelaina, Stiller had a go picture, along with a $12 million budget from Universal.

Like *The Ben Stiller Show*, *Reality Bites* was not a crossover commercial hit, but it struck a chord with young people of the age group that was just starting to be known as Generation X. They saw themselves reflected in its tale of disaffected twentysomethings searching for purpose and trying desperately not to sell out in the increasingly commercialized world of the early 1990s. The movie's cult popularity could have turned Stiller into the unofficial spokesperson for his generation—if he had any interest in such a position.

Instead, he said in 1994 that he "never felt a part of any Generation

X" and claimed he read the Douglas Coupland book and "didn't really connect with it." Even the film's comedic elements were less important to Stiller than the simple act of making a film.

"I really was thinking and always thought of it in terms of directing," Stiller explained. Asked what he wanted to do next in the winter of 1994, Stiller replied, "It's wide open now. Do I want comedy or drama? I guess I'd just like to work with something more plot driven, because I like strong stories. Funny or not. It doesn't matter. I'm not one of those people who say, 'Oh, I never want to be funny; I only want to be serious.' I want to do both."

With his next project as a director, Stiller did exactly that.

The first time Stiller was offered the chance to direct *The Cable Guy* he turned it down. Its initial screenplay, written on spec by Los Angeles lawyer Lou Holtz Jr. about "a needy cable guy you can't get rid of," was originally envisioned as a vehicle for up-and-coming comedian Chris Farley. Pitched as a buddy picture in which an uptight square is tormented (but eventually won over) by the bumbling, gregarious Farley, Stiller wasn't interested.

But then Farley dropped out, and the script caught the eye of Jim Carrey—at the time the hottest comedy star on the planet thanks to a trio of 1994 hits: *Ace Ventura: Pet Detective*, *The Mask*, and *Dumb and Dumber.* Carrey wanted an old friend from the stand-up circuit, Judd Apatow, to produce *The Cable Guy*, and to rewrite Holtz's script to his specifications. And Apatow and Carrey both wanted Stiller to direct it.

"I didn't think the script was very good," Stiller remembered. "I told Judd that I would want to go much darker with it, so it becomes more like a satiric *Fatal Attraction* or *Cape Fear.*" In fact, Stiller had already made a satiric *Cape Fear* once before—as a sketch on *The Ben Stiller*

Show called "Cape Munster," where he played a grown-up Eddie Munster seeking revenge on the TV executive who canceled his show years earlier. ("I don't know whether to look at him or go trick-or-treating!")

As it happened, "much darker" was exactly what Apatow and Carrey had in mind. As the trio reworked the premise, its tale of a cable installer who becomes obsessed with one of his clients took on weirder and more disturbing dimensions, like *Single White Female* starring one of Carrey's physics-defying goofballs from his sketch show, *In Living Color.* The object of the Cable Guy's obsession, played by Matthew Broderick, was named Steve. But the Cable Guy always calls him "Stevie!" a name that sounds an awful lot like "TV." It was as if Carrey's character had conflated the boob tube with his new buddy and was trying to replace one with the other.

Steve breaks up with his girlfriend and moves into a new apartment, then makes the disastrous mistake of asking Carrey's Cable Guy to give him free channels while hooking up his service. Using that innocuous request as leverage, the Cable Guy worms his way into every aspect of Steve's life. If he resists, the Cable Guy causes trouble—until the two are at each other's throats while dangling from the top of an enormous satellite dish.

Like Steve, Apatow and Stiller were both dealing with recent breakups—by Apatow's own admission on *The Cable Guy* DVD commentary, he was in such a lonely place when he was rewriting the script that getting into the mindset of this sad, desperate stalker "was not a big leap." He also gave the Cable Guy an origin that sounded a lot like his own: As kids, they both spent endless hours home alone in front of televisions while their parents were busy elsewhere.

The Cable Guy doesn't even have a name; throughout the film he goes by a series of aliases, all stolen from famous TV characters. He introduces himself as Chip Douglas (from *My Three Sons*), then claims he's actually Larry Tate (from *Bewitched*). After the final showdown on the satellite dish, Steve presses the Cable Guy to reveal his true self. "It's Ricardo," he chuckles, "Ricky Ricardo," before letting out an imitation of Desi Arnaz's distinctive laugh from *I Love Lucy*. The Cable Guy doesn't just love television; it's his entire identity.

This was already discomforting stuff for a mainstream Hollywood comedy, but Apatow, Stiller, and Carrey kept indulging their weirdest impulses. In a touch straight out of *The Ben Stiller Show*, Stiller cameoed as the defendant in a highly publicized murder trial that plays out on televisions sprinkled in the background throughout the film, a sly indictment of the coverage of the media circuses surrounding the O. J. Simpson and Menendez brothers cases. In perhaps the film's oddest beat, the Cable Guy takes Steve to the themed restaurant Medieval Times and then challenges him to a duel—only, instead of using the swords typical of a battle between knights, they fight with "lirpas," a bladed weapon from Stiller's childhood favorite, *Star Trek*. As Apatow put it, "We intended to disturb people—to be funny, but also a nightmare."

While their choices may have been nightmarish, Carrey had so much juice with the studio thanks to his recent trio of massive hits that he had the leverage to push their twisted vision past Sony's nervous executives. But Carrey's presence in the film was also something of a double-edged lirpa. Coming off all those box office hits, he was able to ask for a record-breaking $20 million salary, something that drew enormous press attention and placed enormous financial expectations on *The Cable Guy*. To be a hit, the film would need to attract huge numbers of Jim Carrey fans—most of whom would want to see the typical Carrey persona that Stiller, Apatow, and Carrey had deliberately set out to deconstruct with their offbeat, off-putting tale about the corrosive effect of television on emotionally stunted men.

The Cable Guy opened in theaters in June of 1996 as the number one movie in the country, but it quickly tumbled down the box office chart. The film wasn't a bomb—it grossed over $100 million in theaters against a reported budget of less than half that amount—but it was perceived as a major commercial disappointment, in part because of Carrey's exorbitant salary and his attempt to play against type as a creep. (*The New York Times* covered the film's underwhelming performance in an article headlined "How a Sure Summer Hit Missed.")

"The media's put this spin on it, 'Carrey's first straight role, can he pull it off?'" Stiller said. "There's a lot of expectations, and it does have edge. It's a dark comedy, it's meant to be funny, and if it isn't funny, my ass is more on the line than his."

He was right. Carrey immediately rebounded from *The Cable Guy* with *Liar Liar*, a $300 million hit. He followed it with the Academy Award–nominated *The Truman Show*. But Stiller didn't direct another movie for five years. For now, his childhood dream was on hold.

A month before *The Cable Guy* turned into a notorious misfire, Jim Carrey visited Stiller's old stomping grounds at *Saturday Night Live* to host the 1995–96 season finale, ostensibly as a way to promote the film's theatrical release. The appearance didn't do much to improve the *The Cable Guy*'s fortunes at the box office, but Carrey delivered one of the period's most memorable *SNL* episodes.

With his rubber-band physicality and years of work on *In Living Color*, Carrey made an ideal *SNL* host, and he appeared in six sketches across the episode. But despite Carrey's experience and high-wattage star power, he was nearly upstaged in five of the six sketches by a *Saturday Night Live* rookie, a failed stand-up turned improvisational wunderkind who matched Carrey note for manic note. In a sketch titled "Jimmy Tango's Fat Busters," where Carrey played a meth-addicted fitness guru who advised his clients to (spoiler alert) pound fistfuls of meth, this *SNL* cast member appeared in a vibrating heat-bead suit, howling about how losing sixty-five pounds in four days made him realize he was Satan incarnate.

Not quite. But as fake blood poured down his face while he hissed and screamed at Jim Carrey, it was clear that Will Ferrell deserved a mention in any conversation about who was the funniest person on the planet.

CHAPTER 3

The Silent Assassin

So you've been showing off for the Taylors, huh? Well, I'm gonna put on a little show of my own!

—Frank Henderson, *Saturday Night Live*

Even by the standards of live television, the mood in Studio 8H was tense on the night of September 30, 1995. It was the twenty-first-season premiere for *Saturday Night Live*, and if things didn't turn around fast, the show might not survive to see a twenty-second.

The 1994–95 season of *SNL* had been among the rockiest in the series' two-decade history. Ratings were bad. The reviews were radioactive. (One *Newsweek* headline read simply "Dear Saturday Night Live: It's Over. Please Die.") Nervous NBC executives began breathing down longtime *SNL* producer Lorne Michaels's neck, demanding major changes to the late-night sketch show—or else. By May of 1995, a dozen cast members had quit or been fired, including famous stars Mike Myers, Chris Farley, and Adam Sandler.

When *SNL* returned in late September, the show looked completely different. Only a handful of veterans returned, and the dozen departed actors were replaced by ten newcomers with little to no television experience. That included twenty-eight-year-old Will Ferrell, who received the honor of being the first person to appear on camera during the season premiere. The cold-open sketch was a TV show called *O.J. Today*, a spoof on the media's all-consuming obsession with the O.J. Simpson murder trial. Ferrell played the news program's anchor.

The role wasn't an entirely unfamiliar one for Ferrell. Just a few years earlier, he had been pursuing a career in broadcast journalism when he had an epiphany on the air. Covering the local sports scene on a cable-access show back home in Orange County, he cracked a joke that got a laugh.

"I realized," he later said, "I didn't want to be Jim Lampley. I wanted to be Chevy Chase."

In the very first minute of his very first sketch on *Saturday Night Live* he got his shot to do exactly that. Moments before the show went live, Ferrell took his position on set and waited to perform on national television for the very first time. That's when Michaels approached.

"No pressure," he whispered, "but the whole show's riding on you." Then he walked away.

"It cracked me up," Ferrell recalled. "It really made me laugh. But I'm sitting there. They're counting the show down. And then all of a sudden I felt the enormity of this moment. Being on live television. And I'm like, 'Oh no. This is crazy!' And so I totally garbled the lines."

Not the most auspicious debut for a new cast member—and an uncharacteristically nervous moment for Will Ferrell, an actor who, by all accounts, is one of the least anxious, most well-adjusted comedians in the history of film and television. The word that comes up in interviews with Ferrell's colleagues and friends, over and over, is *normal*.

"I have watched him," said Judd Apatow. "I have watched his lovely wife. I'm looking for the cracks. I've met his parents. They're very nice people. . . . The real Will Ferrell is so normal. Other than his comedy, he's uninteresting. In the best possible way."

Lorne Michaels once said Ferrell was so normal "that you can forget how talented he is." His *SNL* costar Chris Kattan got so flustered by

Ferrell's pervasive normalcy that he flat-out asked him, "'Don't you have any problems? Weren't you ever abused as a child?' How can he be so funny and have come from a good childhood? Isn't that wrong?" And Ferrell himself claimed he felt like he was "continuously letting people down by being normal."

With a mop of sandy curls and a slightly doughy physique, Ferrell *looked* pretty ordinary, too. In fact, when he first arrived at *SNL* in the fall of 1995, writers who weren't familiar with his earlier stage work assumed he'd been hired to play the new cast's straight man; the latest target for the show's never-ending parade of wacky recurring characters.

Those writers were mistaken.

Former *Saturday Night Live* head writer and longtime Ferrell collaborator Adam McKay, who was hired at *SNL* on the same day in 1995 that Ferrell joined the cast, recalled the season's very first table read, where the unassuming Ferrell stunned the room with a torrent of bizarre characters. "We all walked away going, 'Where did that come from?'"

The blindsided writers soon gave Ferrell a nickname: "The Silent Assassin." Ferrell may have looked "normal," but his fevered commitment to every character and sketch no matter how absurd or extreme was anything but.

By his own account, Ferrell was never the class clown, and he rarely sought out opportunities to make people laugh. But he loved to write and do comedy bits whenever an opportunity emerged. When his high school sold T-shirts as a fundraiser, Ferrell got on the school's public-address system, used jokes to pitch the shirts to the entire school, and sold them out. Sometimes he showed up for class in his pajamas just to see if he could get away with it. Then there was the time he started a Reptile Club, even though no one in school owned a reptile. ("We only had two meetings," Ferrell said, shrugging.)

Ferrell's parents divorced when he was eight; his mom, Betty Kay, held down the fort at home while his father, Lee, toured with the Righteous Brothers as a keyboard player. Work wasn't always steady and money was sometimes tight, instilling in young Will a hunger for stability.

"The stereotype you made fun of as a kid was 'the job in the bank,'" Ferrell said. "But to me that sounded all right. Nine to five and you know where you're going. You get a decent salary and vacations and get to carry a briefcase. I was fine with that idea."

Ferrell loved watching the news as a kid, so his desire for a steady job that encouraged his exhibitionist tendencies led him to the University of Southern California to study sports information as a prelude to a job as a broadcaster. But he still felt too intimidated to try his hand at comedy. He'd come home from college on weekends, hang out at the Irvine Improv, and try to talk himself into taking the stage. He chickened out every time.

Instead, he joined the Delta Tau Delta fraternity, where he sometimes struggled to fit in. At one house meeting, he stood in front of the entire frat and proposed with deadpan sincerity that they should all become gay. After all: The only reason they threw parties was to attract women. Think of all the money they would save! Plus, they would no longer have to worry about accusations of sexual assault.

"Half the guys thought I was really funny," said Ferrell. "The other half were like, 'What's *his* problem?'"

Ferrell's *real* problem: He was resisting his true nature. He didn't have a reporter's instinct for tracking down a big story. Then, at last, came his epiphany while cracking jokes on a cable-access telecast. He was only using broadcasting as the "safe" outlet for what he really wanted to do. Ferrell shifted his focus to comedy.

His mom let him move back home for what she dubbed his "theatrical graduate school"; as long as he worked toward his ultimate goal, he could stay without paying rent. First, Ferrell tried his hand at stand-up, enrolling in a workshop taught by a local comic. Thirty people showed up for the first class. By the second week, twenty remained. By the fourth class, just eight aspiring comedians were left. Ferrell did well enough at a student showcase singing a bad a cappella rendition of the *Star Trek* theme that the instructor recruited him to perform at local clubs with him—unpaid. The teacher kept all the money.

Ferrell also took classes at Orange County's South Coast Repertory, but the school that changed his life was the one affiliated with a Los Angeles sketch and improv group known as the Groundlings. Founded in 1974 by an actor named Gary Austin, who previously belonged to San Francisco's famed improv group the Committee and then left to start his own school and theater in L.A., the Groundlings had not only become a fixture in the Southern California comedy scene; they were widely known in showbiz as an incubator of talent for places like *Saturday Night Live.* By the time Ferrell discovered the Groundlings in the late 1980s, its main company had already produced *SNL* stars like Jon Lovitz and Phil Hartman.

That wasn't what attracted Ferrell to the Groundlings' school, though; it was the sense of teamwork and camaraderie. As much as he enjoyed stand-up when he got laughs, he hated stand-up when he didn't—which, given his shaky material and his prankster's love of rambling stories with little to no punch line, was not uncommon. Improv had its own share of pitfalls, but they were shared by the group.

"That's when I realized, 'Oh, I'd rather work in the ensemble and fail up onstage with a bunch of people than just by myself,'" Ferrell recalled.

Ferrell didn't fail for long. He first enrolled in the Groundlings' school in 1991. In a matter of months, he graduated from student to performer with the group's main company, where he worked with the likes of Chris Kattan and Cheri Oteri. When *SNL* scouted the Groundlings in 1995—less than five years after Ferrell tried improv for the very first time—producers invited Ferrell to audition.

Comedians trying out for *SNL* were expected to prepare five minutes of their best material, including a celebrity impression, a political impression, and an original character. In a choice that foreshadowed Ferrell's eclectic sensibilities (and underscored his disinterest in current events), his celebrity was eighty-one-year-old Chicago Cubs announcer Harry Caray. In a meta-touch, he played Caray struggling to fake his way through an audition for a play. Likewise, his political impression was sixty-three-year-old Ted Kennedy as he bombed a standup set.

Ferrell's original character was a "normal" suburban dad named Frank Henderson working the grill at a family barbecue. As he mimed flipping some burgers, Frank became psychotically fixated on a group of unseen kids who won't get off his shed. "GET OFF THE DAMN SHED!" Ferrell howled over and over, never once explaining why anyone would get on a shed, or what was so important inside the shed that it required such frenzied protection.

For the grand finale of his *SNL* audition, Ferrell became a businessman who tells his assistant he should not be disturbed because he has a lot of "paperwork" to do. Ferrell then lay on the stage of Studio 8H and fiddled with cat toys. Although that final bit played to pin-drop silence, Ferrell's quirky sensibilities (and his undeniably hilarious Harry Caray impression) earned him a spot in the subsequent six-week gauntlet of callbacks and meetings with Lorne Michaels.

Ferrell had heard that Michaels had a soft spot for big gestures; according to Hollywood legend, he hired Adam Sandler after he humped a chair like a dog in his *SNL* audition. So Ferrell hatched a scheme. He grabbed a briefcase, filled it with fake cash he bought at a toy store, and brought it to his next meeting with Michaels. When the moment was right, he'd take out the case, open it, dump the toy money on the desk in front of Michaels, and say, "You know what, Lorne, you can talk all you want, but I'm going to walk out of this room, I'm not going to know what happened to this money, you either take it or leave it." Ferrell had fulfilled his childhood dream of being a dude with a briefcase—only, he was doing it while auditioning for the biggest sketch show in television history.

That was the plan, anyway. When Ferrell had his big meeting, he chickened out. At the next audition, he chickened out again. Called in for another meeting with Michaels, Ferrell summoned his courage and brought the briefcase a third time—only to be told by Michaels's assistant to leave it in the waiting room when he entered Lorne's office. After Michaels announced Ferrell would be hired at *SNL*, Ferrell left, grabbed the briefcase, and awkwardly began handing the phony cash to Michaels's assistants.

"Would you just give Lorne some of this fake money?" he sheepishly asked. "I've tried to do this twice now and I never could pull the trigger."

Ferrell's early days at *SNL* were similarly rocky. He impressed the writing staff, but not the show's critics. Two weeks after the season premiere, *Entertainment Weekly* gave the new-look *SNL* a C+ grade—and bestowed Ferrell with the title "Most Annoying Newcomer." Unfazed, Ferrell stuck a "Most Annoying Newcomer" sign on his office door and soldiered on.

He brought that same defiant energy to his onscreen performances. Supremely confident in his own sense of what was funny and unafraid to perform to total silence, Ferrell sometimes derived more pleasure from sketches that bombed than ones that killed. "If something wasn't working," he told one interviewer, "the tendency would be to speed up and get through it. . . . But I would slow way down, and I would have this thing—I don't know why, I love the audience, I want them to laugh, and yet something would kick in like, 'Okay, you don't like it, I'm going to make sure you really hate it,' so I would just take my time. I don't know, it was like a perverse joy in the agony of it being so painful."

"The spirit of it is that he likes to fuck with people," explained Adam McKay. "He's a crank-phone-call guy at heart." In other words, Ferrell was going to keep yelling until you got off his damn shed—comedically speaking.

Soon, the archetypal Will Ferrell comedy character was established: an ordinary-looking dude whose pleasant exterior masks a boiling caldera of inner turmoil that occasionally erupts in futile fury. While Ferrell copped to an interest in writing and portraying characters with anger issues, he always insisted it wasn't necessarily a way to work out any hidden personal demons. "I don't feel like I have a lot of deep-seated rage pent up somewhere," he said in 2003. "I just find yelling and inappropriate behavior really funny."

SNL audiences found Ferrell really funny, too. He appeared in many of *Saturday Night Live*'s most popular sketches in the late '90s, from the excitable Spartan Cheerleader squad with Cheri Oteri to the musician teacher duo the Culps, where Ferrell and Ana Gasteyer performed deeply unhip covers of pop songs at school assemblies. He played a strange beardo who canoodled with Rachel Dratch in hot tubs, and did a hard-charging spoof of Attorney General Janet Reno. His beloved Harry Caray made several surreal appearances as the host of his own space-themed talk show, where he asked guests baffling questions like "We all know that the moon is *not* made of green cheese . . . but what if it were made of barbecue spare ribs, would you eat it then?"

"Here's what's special about Ferrell, and why I would put him above Phil Hartman and Eddie Murphy as the best *SNL* cast member ever," says television critic Alan Sepinwall. "Eddie Murphy was the star of the show. He's literally the only reason you're watching in his period. You do not put Eddie Murphy in a sketch to be a supporting character; you put Eddie Murphy in a sketch because it's about Eddie Murphy. Phil Hartman is the ultimate glue guy. The best Phil Hartman moments are almost always Phil as straight man or Phil reacting to someone else and making sure the sketch that's not about him works. Ferrell does *both* of those things. . . . There's almost no one else in the run of the show who does both of those things as well as he did."

Not surprisingly, the *SNL* writing staff began to capitalize on Ferrell's range, building sketch after sketch around his unique comic tool kit—to the point that Lorne Michaels once reminded the staff, "Don't forget to write for other people in the cast." Of course, since Michaels himself referred to Ferrell in the press as "the center pillar . . . as good as anyone who's ever done the show," and he was the one choosing which sketches aired each week, it's hard to fault the writers for increasing their chances by emphasizing the show's center pillar as much as possible.

As the years passed and *SNL*'s ratings rebounded, Ferrell began to attract interest from Hollywood. In May of 1997 he appeared in a small but memorable role in *Austin Powers: International Man of Mystery*, starring, written, and produced by *SNL* alum Mike Myers. The success of Myers's earlier *Wayne's World* movies, based on one of his recurring *SNL* sketches, inspired Lorne Michaels to produce a whole slew of *SNL* films; of the eleven *Saturday Night Live* films made over the show's half century on NBC, nine were released from 1992 to 2000. Of those, three featured Ferrell: *Superstar*, *The Ladies Man*, and *A Night at the Roxbury*, based on Ferrell's own "Roxbury Guys" sketches with Chris Kattan as a pair of obnoxious clubbers who perpetually bob their heads to music in matching suits.

The Roxbury Guys, with their exaggerated physicality and boorish manners, made great *SNL* characters in four-minute doses. They were less well-suited to the demands of a ninety-minute movie, even one anchored by Ferrell's surprisingly committed performance as Steve Butabi, complete with an appropriately dim Southern Californian surfer dude accent. The film's first few minutes dutifully replicated the contours of a Roxbury Guys sketch, then limped along for the next seventy-five minutes, rehashing jokes and leaning heavily on celebrity cameos (Richard Grieco showed up to play famous actor Richard Grieco and, it must be said, he made an exceptional Richard Grieco, easily one of the two or three best Richard Griecos in cinema history).

Week in and week out, Ferrell was the star of *Saturday Night Live*—but all of his *Saturday Night Live* movies were critical and commercial flops. In interviews, Ferrell noted that despite his success on television, breaking through in movies was a whole different ball game. "It's like you're starting over again," he said. "I got into one club and now I'm trying to get into another club."

The main issue: While Ferrell could headline a film based on an *SNL* sketch or appear in a small supporting role for some other comedian, Hollywood was skeptical that he could make the transition from TV star to full-fledged leading man. And they were *very* skeptical about any of Ferrell's own ideas.

To break through in the movie business, Ferrell would need to somehow prove his box office bona fides *and* write something so funny it couldn't be denied. As the '90s dragged on, he had no luck with either one. But at *Saturday Night Live*, he kept getting closer and closer with writer Adam McKay.

"You'd always look forward to seeing a McKay sketch 'cause it was gonna be funny and weird and anything you hadn't heard before," Ferrell explained. "We both shared the same strategy in terms of writing quickly. We wouldn't overthink. It would just take a couple hours, write something, look at it later, and that was it."

After *A Night at the Roxbury*, Ferrell was contractually obligated to star in another movie for Paramount Pictures. He asked McKay to write it with him. They began to imagine something fueled by their mutual love of mocking pathetic white guys and the hubris that comes with unearned confidence. They just needed a producer with the confidence to back them.

CHAPTER 4

Through a Constant Regimen of Activities We Begin to Learn a Craft

Wow.
—Dignan, *Bottle Rocket*

Owen Wilson had had enough. He was going to join the Marines.

Never mind that before the age of twenty-seven, with almost no prior experience and very little ambition, he had already cowritten and headlined a Hollywood studio movie. By late 1995, the film—a humble crime comedy called *Bottle Rocket* he'd made with his siblings and a college buddy—wasn't performing to his expectations. For one thing, the Sundance Film Festival had rejected it . . . even though Sundance had previously screened the *Bottle Rocket* short film that helped bring Wilson and his collaborators to Hollywood's attention in the first place.

Perhaps the festival had gotten wind of the movie's test-screening scores, which, according to the filmmakers, were the worst in the seventy-year history of Columbia Pictures. No matter where the studio tested *Bottle Rocket* or what the producers did to the film to appease preview audiences, the response never improved. The highest *Bottle Rocket* ever scored with a test audience was a 24. (This number is measured out of 100, mind you.) Wes Anderson, *Bottle Rocket*'s director and cowriter, estimated that eighty-five people walked out of a single screening. Those who remained left incredibly harsh comments on their post-screening surveys. A sampling:

- *This wasn't a James Caan comedy.*
- *This sucks.*
- *This is shit.*

That just confirmed what Owen Wilson already thought: His film career was over. With no other fallback plan, he decided to look into the Marines.

It wasn't as if Wilson was walking away from a lifelong dream. A few years prior, Wilson had never even considered a career in front of the camera. He described himself as a "serious" child growing up in Dallas with two rambunctious brothers, Andrew and Luke. Wilson never studied theater before Anderson began casting him in his projects, first onstage, then in short films, and finally in their feature, *Bottle Rocket.* And even the biggest *Bottle Rocket* fan on the planet would have to concede that Owen Wilson did not appear to have the makings of a classic movie star. For one thing, he had an unbelievably crooked nose, broken once in ninth grade and then a second time at the University of Texas in an intramural football game.

In *Bottle Rocket*, Wilson played Dignan, a wannabe thief who helps his best friend, Anthony (played by Owen's brother Luke) "break out" of a voluntary mental institution so the duo can embark on a life of crime. Dignan is so determined to become a master thief that he writes out an elaborate "75-year Plan" and then presents it to Anthony on the bus ride home from the hospital. Page after page lays out Dignan's vision for their future in meticulous detail. The "Initial Five Years" section, for example, declares that "through a constant regimen of activities we begin to learn a craft."

That's not quite how it happened for Anderson and Wilson. When they first crossed paths in a playwriting class at the University of Texas in 1990, they did not get along. Wilson and Anderson had both been educated at private schools in Texas. (Unlike Wilson, Wes didn't get expelled from his.) Like Ben Stiller, Anderson got his hands on his first 8mm camera before the age of ten and, like Stiller, he rarely went a day without thinking about making a movie from that day forward—although, unlike Stiller, Anderson also enjoyed staging wildly ambitious plays, most based on epics like *The Alamo* and *Star Wars*.

The class where Wilson and Anderson first met was a small seminar; less than a dozen people sitting around a table. Wilson took one look at Anderson in his L.L.Bean boots and long shorts, sitting in a corner apart from the rest of the class, and immediately decided he was uninterested in associating with such an "obnoxious" person. Anderson reciprocated Wilson's distaste. He couldn't stand the fact that Wilson spent most of the seminar openly reading a newspaper instead of engaging with the other students.

Eventually, a mutual friend thawed their icy relationship and formally introduced the pair—at which point they realized they shared a slew of interests, including a love of filmmakers like John Cassavetes and Martin Scorsese. The duo became regulars at U of T's on-campus cinema. (Wes even worked in the projection booth.) In their playwriting class, Anderson wrote a piece called *A Night in Tunisia*, his personal riff on Sam Shepard's *True West*. Despite Wilson's total lack of experience, Anderson cast him in one of the lead roles. After the play, the pair became roommates.

Living and working together, they began making short films they would air on local public access. Wilson's on-camera work in these shorts may have been borne out of necessity, but it quickly became clear (to Anderson, if not to Wilson himself) that Owen was a natural performer, utterly at ease in front of the camera. Wilson eventually dropped out of college, but after Anderson graduated from U of T, the pair moved into an apartment on Throckmorton Street in Dallas with Wilson's two brothers. There, Wes and Owen began collaborating on their first feature-length script, one drawn, somewhat elliptically, from their mutual love of Scorsese crime pictures.

Although Anderson and Wilson wrote *Bottle Rocket* as a feature, they didn't have the resources to make a full-length movie. They were able to scrounge a few thousand dollars from their families, and then shot what they could, which only amounted to about a dozen minutes of footage. They submitted the meager results to Sundance—which accepted *Bottle Rocket* as a short film.

Anderson and Wilson's little firework did its job; it got Hollywood's attention. Veteran producer and production designer Polly Platt, who had worked on films like *The Last Picture Show*, *Terms of Endearment*, and *Say Anything* . . . , loved the short and showed it to James L. Brooks, one of the creators of *Taxi* and the director of *Broadcast News*. Brooks was "dazzled" by the "language and rhythms" of Anderson and Wilson's dialogue and, intrigued by their potential, offered his professional guidance as the duo set out turning their short into a feature.

They needed it. Although *Bottle Rocket* was the story of a group of bumbling crooks, their inept crimes shared a certain metaphorical symmetry with the filmmakers' own fumbling foray into the Hollywood studio system. When Brooks suggested they perform a script reading, they looked at him like he was speaking another language. ("Wes and Owen figured you write it, you sell it, and then make it or die. Reading it aloud was froufrou," Brooks quipped.) Luke Wilson later recalled that they were such novices when they started shooting the feature, they didn't know what essential crew members like the focus puller did.

After a year of work with Brooks, Anderson and Wilson completed their script and secured a $5 million budget for the *Bottle Rocket* feature. Despite the boost in financial resources, the Wilson brothers remained the project's leads. (Andrew Wilson played the role of the disapproving brother of the third member of their crew.) Owen went along with the plan—but said he never stopped thinking, even as they launched into preproduction on the movie, that he might be replaced at any moment by a more experienced actor.

"I thought that if we got somebody like, I don't know, Keanu Reeves or somebody, that it would make it kind of a more legitimate movie," Wilson said a few years later.

Modesty aside, it is difficult to imagine Keanu Reeves—or any other actor—replacing Owen Wilson in *Bottle Rocket*. While he relied on his quirky comic timing and instinctual line readings as Dignan, he also drew upon surprising depths of feeling when Anderson required it. Near the end of the film, as Dignan realizes all of his well-laid plans are about to land him in jail, Anderson cut to a lingering close-up of Wilson's face as he suppresses a lifetime of disappointment while the cops drag him away. It's a devastating, star-making moment.

"He's not Daniel Day-Lewis, but chops-wise, he's as good as anyone," notes director John Hamburg, who's worked with Owen Wilson on multiple films and television shows. "Not only is he extraordinarily funny, but he has amazing dramatic chops, too."

A few months later, when test audiences and Sundance united in their rejection of *Bottle Rocket*, Wilson could relate to Dignan's wide-eyed *What do I do now?* stare. Things didn't get much better when *Bottle Rocket* finally opened in theaters; according to the box office website The Numbers, the film earned a pitiful $407,488 in a few dozen theaters around the country. Even on its tiny $5 million budget, *Bottle Rocket* was a significant flop.

But before Owen Wilson could formally enlist, a funny thing happened: People around Hollywood started to talk about *Bottle Rocket* and its unknown leading men. Two of those people were Ben Stiller and Judd Apatow, then in the process of casting *The Cable Guy.*

"We saw footage of *Bottle Rocket* before the movie came out, and we loved the movie, and Owen was instantly one of our favorite comedy people of all time," producer Judd Apatow said. He and Stiller cast Wilson as a sleazy jerk who takes the hero's ex-girlfriend out on a date and then gets attacked in the bathroom by Jim Carrey's Cable Guy. Wilson lands a few amusingly obnoxious moments as a type he'd come to play often, especially in his early career: the overconfident, excessively handsome man whose obvious charms threaten a nebbish's hold on a beautiful woman.

"It was really exciting having him in the movie," Apatow said, immediately clocking that Wilson was "someone really special" and a unique talent. But a couple of sly come-ons aside, Wilson was mostly used as an amusingly unlikely punching bag for Carrey's character. At one point the Cable Guy even gives Wilson a swirly in the men's room toilet—which Stiller shot from inside the bowl looking up at Wilson as his face is dunked into the dirty water. In that moment, gagging on toilet filth as Jim Carrey cackles like a lunatic, Owen Wilson did not necessarily look like a star in the making.

And for a few years, he *wasn't* a star, especially when the vehicle Judd Apatow wrote with him next, a Cameron Crowe–esque dramedy called *Making Amends* about a recovering alcoholic who sets out to apologize to every single person he's ever wronged, couldn't find a studio willing to green-light it. But as Apatow shopped the project around, Wilson began picking up steady work as a character actor; popping up for small but important roles that jolted otherwise staid Hollywood productions to life with his unique energy.

For the time being, at least, the Marines could wait.

CHAPTER 5

Beans Before Franks

He doesn't flog the dolphin before a big date. Are you crazy? That's like going out there with a loaded gun!

—Dom Woganowski, *There's Something About Mary*

In 1996, Ben Stiller was a talent on the rise. He appeared in three comedies, including an uncredited role in Adam Sandler's *Happy Gilmore*, the surprise hit about a temperamental hockey player turned pro golfer. (Stiller played an orderly at a retirement home who forces the elderly residents to work in his sweatshop.) On top of all his acting work that year, Stiller also wrote, directed, and cameoed in another film.

Unfortunately for him, that other film was *The Cable Guy*.

Sizing up *The Cable Guy*'s toxic reputation and its impact on Stiller's career, his agent told him flat-out: "You're in movie jail."

Fortunately for Stiller, his sentence got commuted slightly. Three months before *The Cable Guy* hit theaters, he appeared in a dark indie comedy called *Flirting with Disaster*, director David O. Russell's breakthrough about an adopted man who goes searching for his biological parents. The film grossed a fraction of what *The Cable Guy* earned in theaters, but it got great reviews and, more importantly, generated interest in Stiller's work in front of the camera.

One of the scripts that came Stiller's way during his doghouse period was from a pair of filmmaking brothers from Rhode Island who had adored *Animal House* growing up, and had begun getting attention in the 1990s thanks to a series of unapologetically raunchy comedies made in its image.

Peter and Bobby Farrelly never went to film school and would be the first to admit: When they started out, they had no clue what they were doing. Baffled studio executives would watch their dailies and ask *why* they made their idiosyncratic filmmaking choices. Their response, per Bobby Farrelly: "'Because it makes us laugh and when we showed it to people, it made them laugh too.' We were making it for audiences and not studio executives." For the Farrellys, it was as simple as that.

Audiences showed up to the Farrellys' work right out of the gate. Their first movie was Jim Carrey's *Dumb and Dumber*, which cost less than $20 million to make and grossed more than ten times that amount. But their follow-up, the bawdy bowling romp *Kingpin*, was a comparative flop, grossing only $32 million. Suddenly, Peter Farrelly recalled, "the phone stopped ringing. . . . It was like, 'Shit. What are we going to do here?'"

Scrambling for a plan, they remembered a script they had read years earlier, written by Ed Decter and John J. Strauss, with a somewhat tawdry origin. Decter and Strauss were struggling with a script when they happened to glance out the window of their rent-controlled Santa Monica apartment and caught a glimpse of a beautiful neighbor getting undressed after coming home from her job as an aerobics instructor.

"It was either me or John who said to the other one, 'This is sick. We're being stalkers,'" Decter explained. "And the other one said, 'No. Don't think of it as being stalkers. Think of it as being detectives.' . . . It occurred to us what a great idea for a film [that is]; if you sent a private eye to look for a girl and she was incredibly beautiful, if the private eye fell for her he would lie to you and tell you that he didn't find her so he could have her for himself."

From that initial spark grew *There's Something About Mary.* Decter and Strauss wrote it on spec and then sold it to a producer. But the project never went anywhere—the producer unsuccessfully tried to turn it into an action comedy with lots of villains and guns—and the rights to the material returned to the duo around the same time the Farrellys were looking for a new project. So the foursome teamed up, with the Farrellys rewriting Decter and Strauss's concept.

Some filmmakers might have been wary of a project that started with two men spying on a woman through an open window. For the Farrellys, the project's leering origins and edgy content was a feature, not a bug. In the years since the heyday of *Animal House* and its loutish brethren, movie comedies had grown more timid and cartoonish. That gave the Farrellys a market gap they could exploit.

"There hadn't been an R-rated comedy in a long time," Bobby Farrelly said. "We wanted to do something more for adults. We weren't going to hold back. *Animal House* was a movie we loved growing up. The jokes those guys were willing to attempt is what motivated us."

To that end, they took what Decter and Strauss had written and amplified it, sometimes drawing on absurd episodes from their own lives. When the Farrellys were kids, for instance, their sister had thrown a party where one of the guests got into a pickle with his, uh, pickle.

"The poor kid was in [the bathroom] for a long time trying to figure out how to untangle himself," Bobby said. The Farrellys' parents eventually had to go into the bathroom to help dislodge him. The brothers turned their memories of the toothy entanglement into *There's Something About Mary*'s tone-setting opening set piece, an adolescent trial by fire (and zipper) for the film's hero, Ted.

He arrives at the home of his dream girl, Mary, to escort her to the prom. While using the restroom, Ted gets distracted by a pair of birds cooing on a nearby tree branch. Then the birds fly away, and it suddenly looks like Ted is spying on Mary as she's putting on her prom dress. Ted's in such a rush to clear up the confusion that he's not careful zipping up his pants.

What follows are four full minutes of comedically excruciating humiliation. Ted can't free himself and refuses to come out of the bathroom. So Mary's father goes in to help. When Mary's dad sees what Ted's done to his genitals he screams in horror like he's just stumbled upon a corpse—and then drags his wife into the room to inspect the damage. ("She's a dental hygienist, she'll know exactly what to do," Mary's dad reassures him.) Ted's so badly mangled himself that Mary's mom can't even discern what she's looking at.

The scene grows increasingly nightmarish. While Mary's mom searches for some Bactine, a cop appears from the bathroom window. ("Neighbors said they heard a lady scream!" he explains.) Then a firefighter walks in. Through all of these indignities, characters keep recoiling in horror at the sight of Ted's mashed member. Occasionally, they describe ghastly details of the gruesome sight. ("How the hell did you get the beans above the frank?!?") But the Farrellys never show the injured phallus to the audience, and because they go so long without showing it, the viewer becomes convinced that they're not going to see it—which is precisely when, out of nowhere, *Mary* cut to an extreme close-up of said frank and beans (technically said beans and frank if we're listing from top to bottom)—a moment that sent moviegoers into hysterics. The scene made an especially huge impression on a sixteen-year-old aspiring Canadian screenwriter named Seth Rogen. He would later call *There's Something About Mary*, and particularly that scene, one of the most revelatory experiences he had in a movie theater in his entire life.

"It's like in a horror movie when you do something really scary upfront," Rogen explained. "And you go, 'Oh, the stakes are set. Anyone could die in any minute.'" By showing Ted's nuts in a proverbial vice, the Farrellys signaled to the audience that their movie could show or do anything. The audience spends the remaining one hundred minutes tingling with anticipation of what might come next. (Uh, no pun intended.)

The Farrellys needed an actor who could capture that unpredictable quality, who could get his dick caught in a zipper, hire a private detective to hunt down his old flame, follow her to Florida, fight off a crazed dog that bites down on what's left of his genitals, and still come across like a likable guy.

Enter Ben Stiller.

"Ben, he had done some real hipster movies before this—*Reality Bites*, that kind of stuff. It was really about being cool. And so he really did throw the ego out the window with this one," noted Peter Farrelly. "He was very easy to work with. And he made himself look as dumb as we asked him to, and I think that's why people fell so much in love with this character—because he really was just ego free."

An actor would need to be ego free to perform *There's Something About Mary*'s most infamous and most R-rated sequence, where an anxious Ted masturbates in preparation for a date and then, after he climaxes, cannot locate what the Farrelly's script delicately described as "the Load." Mary arrives and discovers said load dangling ever so precariously from Ted's left ear. Mistaking it for hair gel, she applies it to her head, and the pair proceed on their date, with Mary unaware that the offending substance has styled her hair into an enormous, gravity-defying wave.

The studio not only hated the scene, they were terrified of it. According to Decter, they "absolutely forbid" the Farrellys from shooting it. They didn't want to see Ben Stiller masturbating, they didn't want to see sperm dangling from his ear, they didn't want to see any bodily fluids anywhere *near* the actress playing Mary, Cameron Diaz—who had understandable concerns of her own about the whole situation. After initially agreeing to the sequence, Diaz began having second thoughts. Jizz in her hair? She had only broken into the movie business a few years earlier, opposite Jim Carrey in the superhero comedy *The Mask*. *There's Something About Mary* was her biggest role to date. She told the Farrellys she was terrified it could derail her career.

The Farrellys ignored the studio and convinced Diaz the joke would work. Ever the meticulous filmmaker, Stiller wasn't offended by the gag on moral grounds, but he did struggle to convince himself of the scene's internal logic. In an interview after *Mary*'s release, he refused any responsibility for the bit and claimed he "always had a problem with that scene. I thought a person would feel it. I was like, 'Should we set up earlier in the movie that I have a numbness in my ear?' Turns out, nobody cared."

They sure didn't. And when the studio, Fox, saw how test audiences lost their minds over the hair gel scene, they didn't just allow it to remain in the film, they began emphasizing it in *There's Something About Mary*'s marketing campaign. They even handed out tiny promotional samples of hair gel at preview screenings; the packets encouraged moviegoers to visit the website www.clean-pipes.com and instructed them to "squirt a wad into wet or dry hair and work with hands as desired. Results will come naturally. Drying time may vary as each packet is individually loaded."

Hair gel and all, *There's Something About Mary* was that rarest of things: an R-rated comedy that critics loved. ("*There's Something About Mary* is sensational, sicko fun," raved *Rolling Stone*'s Peter Travers.) For braving Ted's advances (among other things) with such exuberant good cheer, Cameron Diaz won the New York Film Critics Circle Award for Best Supporting Actress.

More importantly, audiences adored the movie. If they had any qualms about a film that mined stalking for laughs—if they were bothered by the jokes about Mary's intellectually disabled brother, or the scene where the private eye, played by Matt Dillon, nearly murders a dog and then has to shock it back to life with a makeshift defibrillator—

you wouldn't know it from the film's massive $370 million worldwide gross.

"The Farrelly brothers changed modern comedy," says *Wedding Crashers* director David Dobkin. "I was in the theater for *Something About Mary* when [Stiller] zips his balls in the zipper. It was hands down the funniest comedy moment I've ever seen. I remember at one point it was so loud and then it started getting quieter, and I looked over, and nobody could breathe. It's literally getting quieter because people had lost it *that* hard. I've been chasing that my whole career."

Like the Farrellys' beloved *Animal House*, *There's Something About Mary* reveled in the antics of poorly behaved men, and then leavened their lascivious and often amoral behavior with underdog warmth. After the ensnared schlong and the most alarmingly literal hair spray in all of film history, *There's Something About Mary* ended with Mary choosing Ted out of all her potential suitors. Admittedly, their long-awaited embrace gets interrupted by Mary's neighbor's boyfriend trying to shoot Ted out of jealousy and accidentally killing a bystander instead. Otherwise, it's a very sweet moment.

Mary marked quite a reversal of fortune for Ben Stiller. A guy who never dreamed of comedy stardom suddenly found himself at the center of the biggest comedy movie of the decade, one that firmly reestablished audiences' hunger for outrageously filthy humor. He had executed about as successful a break from movie jail as humanly possible.

Stiller's life changed almost overnight. He was billed third on *There's Something About Mary*'s poster, below Cameron Diaz and Matt Dillon. But within days of the movie's debut in theaters, he couldn't walk down the street in New York without someone yelling at him, "That's the guy who got his dick caught in a zipper!" He found the whole situation bewildering. "I never had the experience of being in a movie that so many people found funny. I'm used to doing stuff that only a specific group of people find funny," he admitted.

Stiller enjoyed some of the perks that came with celebrity, and he liked that *Mary*'s success enabled him to get other projects made. But he often talked about the runaway success of *There's Something About Mary* and the sharp fork in the road it created in his career—from subversive cult-comedy darling to bumbling leading man with splooge dripping from his ear—with a fair amount of ambivalence. Within a few months of the movie's release, Stiller told *The New York Times*, "I'm not running out to play that character again," and added, "On the other hand, I realize the role has opened up opportunities for me. So that's a good thing, I guess."

He didn't sound especially convinced. When a reporter asked Stiller where he thought comedy might head next in the wake of *There's Something About Mary*'s seismic impact on Hollywood he replied, "I hope we'll return to good old solid funny situations and characters. And not having to shock people. It's gotten out of control, and it's not funny. I know *There's Something About Mary* kind of put it in the forefront, but I mean, what else can you do?"

A lot, as it turned out.

CHAPTER 6

The Most Personal Thing You've Ever Done

Is it just me, or does the whole world suck?

—Lindsay Weir, *Freaks and Geeks*

By the mid-1990s, Judd Apatow was used to professional failure. Fox kneecapped *The Ben Stiller Show* after only thirteen episodes. His first-produced screenplays—*Heavyweights*, a kids' comedy about a fat camp with Ben Stiller in a supporting role, and *Celtic Pride*, a basketball comedy featuring Dan Aykroyd and Damon Wayans—performed poorly at the box office.

But Apatow had a good feeling about *The Cable Guy*. He knew the film was strange and even a little confrontational, but he loved making it. It was largely the movie he, Stiller, and Jim Carrey set out to make. Then *The Cable Guy* hit theaters and proved to be a major financial disappointment, grossing a fraction of what Carrey's *The Mask* and the *Ace Ventura* sequel had made. Even more unexpectedly, critics hated it. They'd never supported Jim Carrey's cartoonish schtick, and yet when he tried something different, it seemed to make them genuinely angry. *The New York Times* called *The Cable Guy* "the true disaster movie of the summer," whose "only unifying attitudes are misanthropy and contempt." (To be fair, that last part might not be inaccurate.)

"When we shot it, we laughed so hard every day," Apatow explained. "When the movie came out, the fact that it got a weird reception totally blindsided us. We didn't see that coming at all. We just thought the movie was a weird roller-coaster ride. . . . We were so proud of the fact that we were trying to break new ground and take chances."

That last part proved especially frustrating for Apatow, because *The Cable Guy* was the film where Apatow channeled everything he had learned about comedy in the years since *The Ben Stiller Show*'s cancellation—including lessons from his mentor, Garry Shandling. After stints as an adman and sitcom writer, Shandling rose to prominence in the early 1980s as a regular guest, and then a frequent guest host, on *The Tonight Show Starring Johnny Carson*. Shandling's popularity on the talk show circuit meant he could have easily landed his own late-night series; instead, he created and starred in *The Larry Sanders Show* for HBO, a sitcom set backstage of a fictional talk show hosted by a neurotic, self-obsessed comic.

Onstage and on *The Larry Sanders Show*, Shandling became known for his brutally honest and painfully personal approach to comedy, something that rubbed off on everyone who worked with him—especially Apatow, after Shandling offered him a job as a consulting producer on *Larry Sanders* after *The Ben Stiller Show* ended.

"Garry said writing is a way to figure out who you are," Apatow said. "It's all about self-exploration. I didn't think that. I just thought I was writing a funny wife joke for Rodney Dangerfield. I didn't think spiritually about any of it. It was like, comedy is about knowing yourself? What? I thought it was just punching the horse in *Blazing Saddles*."

At the same time Apatow was absorbing lessons about confessional comedy from Shandling, he also worked part-time at *The Critic*, a short-lived animated series from several of the producers behind *The Simpsons* about the life of an irritable film critic. (There is no other kind.)

The Critic embraced a different style of comedy than *Larry Sanders*, one based on a machine-gun spray of jokes aimed at the viewer. Bouncing between the two shows, Apatow said, left him with a "weird education" in screenwriting.

"I feel like what I do is a combination of what I learned on those two shows," Apatow noted. "I was learning about very grounded emotional comedy. I was also learning about more imaginative, broader comedy." But infusing that combination into *The Cable Guy* didn't land with audiences in the way Apatow had hoped. He'd made something genuinely different . . . and had little to show for it.

Things got worse before they got better. Apatow wrote and wrote and wrote, and most of the things he wrote never saw the light of day, including the *Making Amends* script for Owen Wilson. He also made a pilot for Fox called *Sick in the Head*, about a young therapist played by David Krumholtz who begins treating a new patient played by Amy Poehler. After Fox passed, network president Doug Herzog consoled Apatow by telling him, "Judd, ninety percent of everything fails. Don't worry, I'll probably be fired in a year anyway." (Herzog resigned from Fox ten months later.) But while *Sick in the Head* wasted away in development hell, Apatow received a script from Paul Feig, his old buddy on the L.A. stand-up scene, that reshaped both of their careers.

Feig's professional life was at a similarly low ebb in the mid-1990s. He finally landed a solid gig playing a teacher on *Sabrina the Teenage Witch*, and then he was dropped from the show after one season. He spent $30,000 of his savings to write, direct, produce, and star in his own independent movie, *Life Sold Separately*. It went nowhere. With nothing left to lose, Feig decided to indulge one of his lifelong dreams: writing a high school show that reflected his own experiences growing up as teenage outsider in Michigan.

"I'd seen so many [high school films and shows] where it was like, 'Who are these people?' I felt like they weren't honest at all," Feig later explained. "My friends and I weren't popular in high school, we weren't dating all the time, and we were just trying to get through our lives. It was important to me to show that side."

Feig bumped into Apatow, who had recently signed a deal with DreamWorks Television. Apatow told him if he ever came up with an idea for a TV show to let him know. Feig poured all of his most embarrassing memories into a script, which he called *Freaks and Geeks*, and sent it to Apatow.

"I didn't think he would hand me a finished script a few months later, and I certainly didn't expect it to be the best thing I have ever worked on. That just never happens," Apatow said. Within hours of reading the script, Apatow called Feig on the phone. He was going to get DreamWorks to buy it.

Feig's teleplay followed the ups and downs (okay, mostly the downs) in the lives of a pair of teenage siblings living in early 1980s Michigan. Like Apatow, whose whole world tilted off its axis when his parents got divorced, Feig's protagonist, Lindsay Weir, faces an existential crisis in high school after a family tragedy. In her case, Lindsay visits her grandmother on her deathbed and is shaken to her core when her grandma says she sees "nothing" waiting for her on the other side. No God, no heaven, no white light. Nothing. Losing interest in academics and her old friends, Lindsay falls in with a group of burnouts. Like both Feig and Apatow, Lindsay's younger brother, Sam, is a diminutive gym-class pariah who loves Steve Martin records, Harold Ramis movies, and *Saturday Night Live*.

The idea of focusing on the ordinary problems of two social outcasts and their respective friend groups stood in stark contrast to the other high school shows in that era, almost all of which were built around beautiful "teenagers" portrayed by men and women many years past their own high school graduations. Other '90s TV teens were full-blown superheroes, like Buffy the Vampire Slayer. No one on *Freaks and Geeks* was ever going to slay a vampire—except maybe in a particularly imaginative game of Dungeons & Dragons.

Apatow instantly wanted to work on *Freaks and Geeks*, and to make it the rare high school TV show steeped in authentic teen experiences—pain, anxiety, and heartache. He also wanted to make sure it didn't look like *Beverly Hills, 90210*, so the show held casting sessions all over the U.S. and Canada in search of "'normal'-looking kids." ("Most beautiful people never develop a funny bone as a defense mechanism because good looks and breasts usually are enough," he once complained.) Shockingly, NBC loved Feig's script and not only wanted to make it, they signed off on Feig and Apatow's realistic approach to casting and story.

When they assembled their writers' room for the show, Feig and Apatow asked everyone to fill out questionnaires that detailed all their most painful experiences in their teenage years, a Shandling-esque touch that yielded a massive document of true-to-life high school horrors. All the most brutal stories got written into the show. (The episode where Sam gets talked into buying a denim jumpsuit at the mall that he thinks will make him look cool, only to realize once he arrives at school that he has made a terrible mistake? That one happened to Feig in real life.)

Apatow and Feig broke almost every long-standing rule of television production. Comedies were thirty minutes; *Freaks and Geeks* was an hour. Comedies were filmed with multiple cameras in front of live studio audiences; theirs was shot with a single camera, often on location, like a little forty-five-minute movie every single week. There was no laugh track, no catchphrases, and very few happy endings.

"I just love underdogs. I felt like an underdog for the first thirty-five years of my life," Feig says. "I never responded to stories about the coolest lawyer in town. Or 'He has it all and then he loses it.' I don't really care about that guy! I just think it's a great way to tell a story, because those are the stories I know."

As Apatow put it, "Paul wanted a realistic tone. He was very passionate about the show being about kids who failed at the things they were attempting to do during high school. It was an argument against wish-fulfillment television. We agreed that we weren't gonna water it down."

That made NBC nervous. So did *Freaks and Geeks*' ratings, which started off okay, but kept sinking lower and lower as NBC shuffled the series off and on its schedule. The series received some of the best reviews of the 1999 television season, but it couldn't stay on the air for more than a couple weeks at a time, and it got lower ratings than everything from the American Music Awards to a *Mary Tyler Moore Show* reunion.

Undeterred, Apatow kept pushing *Freaks and Geeks*' writers to go further, burrow deeper, even into themselves. Apatow himself cowrote and directed an episode that included a subplot about mega-geek Bill Haverchuck (Martin Starr) grappling with his parents' divorce and his mother's first tentative steps back into the dating world. One scene followed Bill step-by-step through his after-school routine. Home alone, he makes himself a grilled cheese and laughs his head off while watching an episode of *Dinah!*

The scene contained no jokes. It had no dialogue, period. It was ripped directly from Apatow's memories of his own teenage years; he even chose a *Dinah!* episode featuring Garry Shandling as a tribute to the mentor who taught him "people connect more when they know you're telling them the truth or some aspect of your story, some mutated version of how you are experiencing this life." When they assembled the sequence in the editing room, *Freaks and Geeks* producer and director Jake Kasdan turned to Apatow and told him, "That's the most personal thing you've ever done, and it's the best thing."

It was a lightning-bolt moment for Apatow, who had quit stand-up because he felt he didn't have the sort of piercing point of view that made his peers special. *The Cable Guy* might have contained some of Apatow's feelings about being a solitary outsider and pop culture junkie, but it couched those feelings in a *Hand That Rocks the Cradle* spoof loaded with Jim Carrey's manic antics. Working on *Freaks and Geeks* crystallized Apatow's belief in telling his *own* stories—even one as simple as a lonely kid from a divorced family escaping from his troubles through stand-up comedy. After years of writing in the voices of other comedians, he had finally found his own.

But no one ever saw Apatow's best stuff on NBC. The network canceled *Freaks and Geeks* in March, before they had finished broadcasting the entirety of its eighteen-episode season. From a dollars-and-cents perspective, that decision made sense; *Freaks and Geeks*' ratings placed it ninety-third out of all the shows on television that year; a slight improvement over *The Ben Stiller Show*, but still so unpopular that NBC didn't even bother to air the final three episodes, including the one with Apatow's intimate re-creation of his after-school ritual. The unaired installments would first see the light of day on cable, where *Freaks and Geeks* quickly found an appreciative, if never enormous, cult fan base.

But even in truncated form, a case could be made that *Freaks and Geeks* is the most important television show in recent movie history. Many of the best comedy films released in the twenty-first century were made by people who worked on the show—not just Apatow and Feig, but writers like *School of Rock*'s Mike White and directors like *Freaks and Geeks* star John Francis Daley, who transitioned from playing Sam to writing and directing hit comedies like *Horrible Bosses* and *Game Night*. (In a peculiar bit of life imitating art, Daley went from pretending to play Dungeons & Dragons on *Freaks and Geeks* to directing 2023's big-budget Dungeons & Dragons movie, *Honor Among Thieves*.) The show's cast was arguably even more successful; almost every young actor the show discovered through its extensive casting calls found long-running success in Hollywood, including Linda Cardellini, James Franco, Jason Segel, Busy Philipps, and seventeen-year-old high school dropout Seth Rogen.

In 2000, though, *Freaks and Geeks*' swift collapse gave Apatow what he would later describe as "a complete nervous breakdown."

"It tapped into all my issues from when I was a kid about families separating," he explained. "Like, 'Oh no, we must keep this together at all costs.'" Because he saw *Freaks and Geeks* as a family, he couldn't help but see the show as a home—one all of the young talents that he and Feig had found and supported were now getting kicked out of.

So Apatow kept fighting for the show and for the chosen family who made it, even after *Freaks and Geeks* itself could not be saved. Reeling from the sting of NBC taking away the best thing he had made in his career so far, he thought to himself, "Oh, you think this show is over and that we're never going to work together again?" and determined that one way or another, he would prove them wrong. To really do that, though, he'd need a hit. Not a critical darling; not a cult favorite. A full-blown, mainstream blockbuster.

CHAPTER 7

Mr. Creepy

Unleash the fury!!
—Barry Manilow, *Road Trip*

Something splashed the back of Todd Phillips's head. It took a second for the smell to hit him. Stale beer. Maybe some cigarette ashes? Oh, and tobacco spit.

Yeah, definitely tobacco spit.

Phillips had to guess the liquid by smell because he couldn't see what was getting poured on his back. The guys in the fraternity house had shoved him inside a tiny dog cage before they started dumping the contents of their red plastic cups on him, and the cage was too cramped for Phillips to do anything but hunch over, cover his eyes, and hope the brothers got bored before the nauseating stench made him puke.

Most people in Phillips's position would be desperate to escape. They'd cry, or scream, or beg to be released. But as one college kid after another emptied the contents of their cups through the top of the dog cage, Phillips felt only one thing: *pure elation*.

As a general rule, you should never believe any man in a frat house whose excuse for their bad behavior is "They asked for it." Except in this one case—Todd Phillips had *literally* asked for it.

He'd arrived at Allentown, Pennsylvania's Muhlenberg College along with his friend and filmmaking partner Andrew Gurland desperate to salvage a documentary they were making about fraternity hazing rituals. They had already gotten thrown out of one college campus—not by the authorities, but by their subjects, who had turned on Phillips and Gurland after they showed up unannounced at one of their initiations. The small crew wandered the Northeast looking for alternative locations until they found Alpha Tau Omega at Muhlenberg.

ATO was the only frat that would agree to let Phillips and Garland make a film about "Hell Night," the final, cruelest stage of the pledges' gauntlet of torture. But they only agreed to participate under certain conditions: The documentary couldn't name the school or the fraternity, and Phillips and Garland could only film the hazing if the directors participated in the hazing themselves. That's how Phillips wound up crammed into a dog cage, covered in beer, cigarette butts, and who knows what else—quietly delighted at his own degradation.

"It's funny," Phillips said, looking back on the experience, "you feel excited because you're getting exactly the footage you wanted. That's why I was there. I wasn't upset in any way because this is why I came, and the fact that it was happening meant it would only be over sooner, which was a good thing. Better than waiting around for it to happen."

Above all, Todd Philip Bunzl was a guy who refused to wait around for things to happen. A consummate go-getter, Phillips had directed his first feature documentary while he was still a college student. Back in high school, when he and his buddies needed cash, they started a shoplifting ring for profit. By that point, Phillips's parents were already divorced. A mostly fatherless childhood, along with a mother who drilled into him from a very early age that "the last thing you want to do is belong to a group," instilled in Phillips a fascination with men and their need to fit in.

"I never had a real male influence in my life," he said. "I never really understood heterosexual male relationships. It's like, what do you get out of that relationship? I never understood that bonding that happens."

Phillips first got into movies through photography; when he and his buddies weren't shoplifting, Phillips was taking pictures of them goofing off and getting into trouble. He sent the pictures as part of his application to New York University. Like most of his peers at NYU, Phillips wanted to make movies. Unlike his peers, he recognized that he didn't have the life experiences to draw upon for a worthwhile screenplay at that age. So he decided to make documentaries instead.

"Filmmaking is all storytelling to me," Phillips said in a 2000 interview. "Whether you're doing it with real people or not, you're still telling a story, you're still creating characters, still creating a beginning, middle, and an end. . . . The techniques are the same—at least mine are."

Phillips was not going to wait until he graduated to put those techniques into action. (Good thing, too; Phillips never graduated from NYU.) He had been going to punk shows in New York City since he was a teenager; he loved the take-no-prisoners energy of extreme punk rocker GG Allin, who often assaulted his audience, and sometimes shit onstage as part of his act. Phillips had once arrived for an Allin show at the Lismar Lounge on First Avenue, only to find the musician shooting heroin at the bar.

"Eventually," Phillips recalled, "he got up and turned around and just tumbled down the stairs and had a violent fit, and that was it. There was no show—that *was* the show. So when I was looking for documentary subjects at NYU, I thought of him."

Unfortunately, Allin was sitting in a Michigan jail at the time. Phillips wrote Allin a letter anyway, pitching him on the idea of a documentary about his life. Allin wrote him back and said that if Phillips sent him a bus ticket he would break his parole, come to New York, and let Phillips film him.

Some might have turned down that deal. Some might second-guess serving as an accessory to an ex-con's parole violation. Phillips sent the ticket. To raise the $14,000 he needed to fund the production, he struck a deal with a friend of Allin's: serial killer John Wayne Gacy, who agreed to paint the poster for Phillips's documentary from prison in exchange for $50, art supplies, and a picture of Phillips.

Most people would have turned down *that* deal. Phillips gladly sent every item on Gacy's wish list, along with a bio he wanted ("which was sort of sexual and weird," Phillips admitted). Gacy made good on his promise and painted the poster. Phillips printed a thousand copies, got Gacy to sign them, and then sold them to GG Allin fans for $15 apiece. In six months, he raised $15,000.

The movie was on—at least until Allin got arrested again and was extradited back to Michigan, where he served another year in prison. He was released just in time to attend the New York premiere of Phillips's documentary, *Hated: GG Allin & the Murder Junkies*, although the night was cut short after Allin threw a bottle of alcohol and hit a woman in the head. A few months later, Allin was dead of a drug overdose—which only brought more attention to Phillips and his film, which wound up grossing in the neighborhood of $1 million, a huge sum for a film that cost only $14,000 (and a photo to John Wayne Gacy).

"My whole life, even now, I'm attracted to mayhem," Phillips said.

A vice president at HBO loved *Hated*, but the film's content was so intense it couldn't even air on the cable channel known for racy reality shows like *Real Sex* and *Taxicab Confessions*. Invited to pitch the network on a follow-up project, Phillips and Gurland, a buddy from NYU, suggested a documentary inspired by *National Lampoon's Animal House* about real fraternity culture in America. HBO liked the idea. *Frat House* was a go.

They knew it wouldn't be easy. Fraternities were notoriously private about their traditions, especially the ones around the rituals of pledging and rushing. But Phillips also knew if he could earn a frat's trust and capture some of those secret moments on camera, the footage would be very juicy—and it would speak to his curiosity about the lengths men would go to in order to belong.

Phillips himself only had to go about 170 miles north of New York City to SUNY Oneonta, where he and his small crew began documenting the goings-on at the Beta Chi fraternity, a house with the fitting motto "Only the Strong Survive." Early scenes in *Frat House* depict typical college debauchery, supplemented by drunken interviews with undergraduates who happily offer their inebriated outlook on life. ("Alcohol is the most important thing in fucking college, because people come here, sure, to get an education, but this is where you develop your social skills, mostly," says one heavily intoxicated frat bro.)

Then Phillips and Gurland ran afoul of a Beta Chi brother named Blossom. One day he might tell the filmmakers to stick with him because he enjoys their company; the next, he warns Phillips over the phone, "If you come to my fucking house I'm gonna take your fucking head and throw it against the fucking wall, you understand me? Hang up the fucking phone and be smart, otherwise I'm gonna come to your fucking house and kick the living shit out of you!" In the film, a small smile creeps across Phillips's face as he listens to Blossom's threats. He does not hang up the phone.

Eventually, though, Blossom does indeed attack Gurland (on camera!), and the crew decamps to Muhlenberg College. There, the directors spend agonizing hours in Alpha Tau Omega's basement, where a brother nicknamed "the Dragon" barks orders as young men stand on their heads, perform endless push-ups, and get covered in a swill that Phillips says smelled like "a mixture of ravioli and vomit." (If this basement had a gutter like Dartmouth's animal house, it's not shown on camera.) Later, Phillips and the pledges participate in a ritual called "the Tabasco Run." A victim fills their mouth with hot sauce, runs around the house at top speed, then drops to the ground to make imaginary snow angels on the grimy ATO bathroom floor.

The abuse became so brutal Gurland went to the hospital complaining of extreme stomach pain. Phillips had to endure Hell Night, along with a "final baptism"—getting drenched in alternating buckets of boiling-hot and freezing-cold water while blindfolded—alone. After an endless series of humiliations, he and the other candidates must answer one last question before induction into the fraternity: "Would you ever dick a brother?" (The correct answer to the question, should you ever find yourself forced to answer it: No.)

The footage was shocking, disgusting, and sensational. When the completed *Frat House* debuted at the Sundance Film Festival in January of 1998, it was instantly the talk of Park City, Utah. No one had seen anything like it before. The documentary captured men at their absolute worst; callously degrading women, physically and mentally torturing one another in the name of brotherhood. *Frat House* won the festival's Grand Jury Prize for documentaries. HBO set the premiere for August 12.

But in early August HBO delayed the broadcast until at least October, after some of *Frat House*'s subjects and a few national fraternity leaders complained that the film was not an accurate portrayal of campus life. At first, HBO claimed the pause was simply so its staff could reexamine the footage and ensure it was up to their standards. "This is *nothing* unusual. We have extremely high criteria for airing documentaries," a spokesperson told *Entertainment Weekly*.

By the end of December, HBO could no longer claim everything was proceeding as planned. ATO's national leadership took depositions from students, who told them that the documentary was staged, sometimes by full frat brothers playing the roles of pledges. They also claimed they thought they were helping student filmmakers work on a fictional college comedy as part of a class project, not a documentary for a major network like HBO. The executive director of Alpha Tau Omega's national office, Wynn R. Smiley, told *The Chronicle of Higher Education*, "I have never heard of anything close to what those young men were subjected to."

Those comments directly contradicted an ATO brother quoted in the same article, who conceded that many of *Frat House*'s most grueling scenes, like the nonstop push-ups and the hot- and cold-water baths, were based on real rituals. But that same brother also insisted shoving Phillips into a dog cage was not a "tradition" at the frat, as Phillips himself says in his *Frat House* voice-over narration. He claimed that was Phillips's own idea.

After the fraternity and its lawyers confronted HBO, the network decided to shelve *Frat House* indefinitely. "It would be great if all the questions went away and we could run this film. But it doesn't look like that will happen," HBO's Sheila Nevins told *Entertainment Weekly* in 1999. "It's beyond *Rashomon*. There's not three or four stories at odds. There's a hundred and five," she added.

Phillips and Gurland stood by the movie and alleged HBO was looking for "excuses" not to air it. The only purposeful misstep they conceded was getting their subjects to sign their releases while they were inebriated. ("How else are you supposed to make this shit? Of course you get kids to sign releases when they're drunk," Phillips said in 2010—although by 2016 he conceded to *Rolling Stone* that "acquiring those releases in a fucked-up way was a fucked-up thing to do.")

Once you actually watch *Frat House*, it's harder to believe that Phillips scripted its horrifying content. Indeed, if these frat brothers were pretending to haze Phillips at his direction, *they* were the ones who should have gone on to big Hollywood careers. Their "performances" as they berate and torture their pledges are chillingly intense and authentic.

Phillips later said the movie's subjects weren't upset the film was fake; they were worried that if the movie aired it would ruin their reputations and affect their ability to find jobs after graduation. "When you turn your cameras on the sons and daughters of rich white Americans, you're going to get heat for it," Phillips explained. However much of *Frat House* was massaged into reality by the crew, this much is undeniable: Less than three years after *Frat House*'s Sundance premiere, Muhlenberg College revoked ATO's charter due to "allegations of hazing, fights, and underage drinking."

In some ways, it worked out better for everyone that *Frat House* never aired. The scandalous nature of the film—a documentary not even HBO would broadcast!—lent its nascent director a reputation as a punk rock provocateur. More importantly, by the time HBO pulled *Frat House* from its schedule, Phillips had already parlayed it into his first gig directing a mainstream Hollywood production.

In his first big Hollywood role after *The Cable Guy*, Owen Wilson played a filmmaker who made Todd Phillips's grueling Hell Night gauntlet look like a walk in the park.

In 1997's *Anaconda*, Wilson's Gary Dixon is a documentary soundman who gets eaten by a giant snake—but only after he delivers the immortal line "Is it just me or does the jungle make you really, really horny?" The next year, he appeared in *Armageddon* as a "spacey but absolutely brilliant geologist" who joins Bruce Willis to drill a hole in an asteroid and save the planet. He made an early exit in that film as well, but yet again Wilson made the most out of every line of dialogue he got. ("This is space! And we're just in the beginning part of space, we haven't even gotten to *outer* space yet!") In most of his late '90s movies, Owen Wilson was like the tantalizing side dish on a plate of food with a really bland protein. Every time you got a little taste of what he was doing, it made everything around him look even more boring in comparison.

As he kept making inroads as a comedic character actor, he also began collaborating with Wes Anderson on their follow-up to *Bottle*

Rocket. On one of their road trips from Dallas to L.A., the pair decided it would be wise to have another project to pitch to interested agents or studio executives. Over the course of a single drive, they fleshed out the character of Max Fischer, who Wilson described as "a megalomaniacal kid who doesn't have much irony or self-awareness—kind of like a Donald Trump book on tape. Max loves school but is a terrible student." That school is tony Rushmore Academy, a fictional institution that drew on Anderson's and Wilson's own teenage experiences. (The film was shot at Anderson's alma mater, St. John's, and included a storyline where, like Wilson, precocious Max gets expelled.)

In *Rushmore*, Max (Jason Schwartzman) becomes obsessed with a beautiful young professor named Rosemary Cross (Olivia Williams), and then competes for her affections (if only in his mind) with Herman Blume, the father of some of his classmates. Even as they feud over the right to court the lovely Ms. Cross, Blume also becomes something of a mentor to Max.

Anderson and Wilson partly based the character of Blume on Wilson's own father. Blume's disgusted comment about his pair of failsons—"Never in my wildest imagination did I dream I'd have children like this"—was a direct quote from Robert Wilson. And despite *Bottle Rocket*'s struggles at the box office, the duo managed to convince a major star to play him: Bill Murray, who gave a quietly melancholic and dryly hilarious performance that earned him some of the best reviews of his entire career.

More importantly, *Rushmore* was a hit—at least on the scale of an arthouse picture made on a relatively frugal $10 million budget. It became an almost immediate cult film and turned Anderson and Wilson into even hotter commodities as a screenwriting duo.

As an actor, though, Wilson was still muddling through a series of undistinguished projects, like Jan de Bont's dreadful remake of Robert Wise's psychological horror film *The Haunting*. Luckily, Wilson still had Ben Stiller in his corner. Around the same time *The Haunting* opened to reviews that made *The Cable Guy* look like *Broadcast News*, Stiller cast Wilson in an offbeat pilot for Fox called *Heat Vision and Jack*.

Viewed with modern eyes, it boasts a creative pedigree that is almost impossible to fathom: In addition to Stiller as director, it was cowritten by future *Community* and *Rick and Morty* creator Dan Harmon and cult comic book legend Rob Schrab, and it costarred Wilson and a young Jack Black. If Fox had picked up *Heat Vision and Jack* for a series, they could have had all of those massive talents locked up for years.

Naturally, they passed.

During the Q&A after *Frat House*'s Sundance premiere, Todd Phillips fielded a question from a twentysomething guy in the audience. He wanted to know what inspired Phillips to make the film. Phillips proceeded to explain the entire backstory: how he wanted to use *Animal House* as the inspiration for a documentary on the same subject. A few days later, the same kid walked up to Phillips with a middle-aged man.

"Hey, Dad," he said, "this is the guy I was telling you about."

The kid was twenty-year-old Jason Reitman, later an Oscar-nominated director, but in 1998 still a film student at the University of Southern California. His dad was Ivan Reitman, the producer of *Animal House*.

Reitman took an immediate liking to Phillips, and when HBO started getting nervous about *Frat House*, he never cared. ("I actually thought it was kind of funny," Reitman confessed.) He mentioned to Phillips that he'd always wanted to make a movie set entirely on a college road trip.

Phillips had recently hit it off with a comedy-obsessed adman—Scot Armstrong, who had grown up listening to Steve Martin comedy albums and watching films like Ivan Reitman's *Stripes*. Armstrong liked Phillips's documentaries and hired him to shoot some beer commercials.

"We took a budget of whatever it was to shoot three commercials, and we shot like ten," Armstrong says. "We just kept making stuff and staying up all night and talking about comedy." After Phillips's meeting with Reitman, he and Armstrong threw together a treatment for a college comedy called *Road Trip*, filled with the sort of outlandish behavior Phillips documented in *Frat House*. Reitman was sold; Phillips had his first studio feature.

The scenario Phillips and Armstrong devised wore its influences on its sleeve. Several moments bear an unmistakable resemblance to *Animal House*. Armstrong calls working with Reitman on the script a "mini film school" that involved a "really intense rewrite process," where the veteran director showed them how to crack a story and build out characters the audience actually would care about.

"Movies are delicate," Armstrong adds. "You think it's like, 'Oh, just put as many great jokes in there as you can and make sure there's a story there. But it's so much more fragile than that, to build something that really works. And he was able to share that with us. It wasn't like 'Have some funny parts and then have a story.' It was making sure the story beats *were* the funny parts."

Phillips also cannily cast his film with young talent from other recent hits. He grabbed Seann William Scott, hot off of a star-making turn in the massive R-rated high school comedy hit *American Pie*. For the role of the film's narrator, Phillips signed Tom Green, at the time one of the most talked-about comics on the planet thanks to his surreal series on MTV.

Road Trip's script wasn't revolutionary and sometimes it was shockingly crass—something Phillips himself mocked in the film. In one sequence, he cut from a conversation between a group of topless coeds in a locker room to a woman questioning Green about his breathless retelling of this salacious story. ("Girls don't just stand around naked!") Green resumed the story and Phillips cut back to the buxom, half-naked women, one of whom quips, "All men are dirty pigs. All they think about, all they really care about, really all they think about, is sex." A Todd Phillips movie was about having your cake and eating it, too. Phillips felt absolutely no shame about that. In fact, he was proud of it.

"When I was 15 years old, I saw *Fast Times at Ridgemont High*. Phoebe Cates took her top off and it changed my life," Phillips said around the time of *Road Trip*'s release. "I feel like I owe that to other 15-year-olds."

Phillips also joined in the action himself. In one scene, a young college student played by Amy Smart gets accosted on a Greyhound bus by a stranger who tries to suck on her feet. The toe sucker was played by none other than Todd Phillips. *Road Trip*'s closing credits call him "Foot Lover." But after Phillips began to reprise his Foot Lover in his other films, the character acquired another name: "Mr. Creepy."

DJ Qualls, who played the nebbishy dork who joins the road trip mostly because the other characters need his car, recalled an instance when his female costar did not perform her half of a love scene to Phillips's liking. Phillips leapt on top of Qualls and pretended to ride the actor, exclaiming: "You need to do *this*!" Summing up Phillips's hands-on approach and lewd ideas, *Road Trip* star Breckin Meyer told *Entertainment Weekly*, "Todd's either got the makings of a brilliant director or a serial killer. He's either Jonathan Demme or Buffalo Bill from *The Silence of the Lambs*."

The secret to Phillips's success might lie in the fact that he combined both of those impulses; an uncanny gift for sniffing out scenarios for shock and extreme humor, and the slightly sadistic quality that made him want to exploit those moments for maximum impact. With *Road Trip*, he created an appealing package by mixing shameless sexuality, big comic set pieces, and nauseating gross-out humor. (The things done to a plate of French toast in *Road Trip* make the apple pie from *American Pie* almost look appetizing in comparison.) Powered by that combination, *Road Trip* became a surprisingly big hit when it opened in theaters in May of 2000, grossing almost $120 million at the box office against a $15 million budget.

For Phillips, the film's success was a validation—and a huge reversal of fortune from just eighteen months earlier, when HBO shelved a documentary about basically the same subject, to say nothing of the time he had spent a couple years prior getting covered in spit and ashes in a dog cage.

Even before *Road Trip* opened in theaters, Reitman signed Phillips to a deal that ensured he got first crack at whatever wild idea he cooked up next. Phillips already had a very old-school concept in mind.

CHAPTER 8

So Hot Right Now

> ***Who cares about Derek Zoolander anyway? The man has only one look, for Christ's sake! Blue Steel? Ferrari? Le Tigre? They're the same face! Doesn't anyone notice this? I feel like I'm taking crazy pills!***
>
> —Jacobim Mugatu, *Zoolander*

The stars came out for the 1996 VH1 Fashion Awards. Heather Locklear hosted. Jimmy Smits and Stephanie Seymour presented. Miuccia Prada won the award for Best Second Collection. A parade of supermodels strutted across the stage of the Paramount Theater at Madison Square Garden to the sounds of Bryan Adams's "The Only Thing That Looks Good on Me Is You." Fashion and rock icon David Bowie even played a couple of songs.

But the evening's most important moment would only become clear a few years later. It was a three-minute comedy sketch conceived as part of Fashion Awards executive producer Joel Gallen's plan to poke fun at the self-important fashion world with a series of shorts spoofing various industry archetypes: the agent, the photographer, the model.

For extra oomph, they made the model male.

Stand-up comedian and writer Drake Sather was assigned to write the sketch. Looking for a name for the character, he drew inspiration from two real-world male models: Johnny Zander and Mark Vanderloo.

"I think it was originally 'Zanderloo,' which was just too close to Vanderloo," Sather later recalled. "So we constructed Zoolander out of that."

Derek Zoolander was born.

"I wanted to do a twist on the dumb male model and have it be kind of how . . . fashion forces us to accept that someone's beautiful. So we took this odd-looking character with the conceit that he was the most beautiful man in the world," Sather explained. To play the odd-looking yet strangely beautiful Zoolander, VH1 recruited an actor eager for a win after the summer of *The Cable Guy*: Ben Stiller.

The Zoolander VH1 viewers saw that night in the fall of 1996 was not quite the really, really, really good-looking guy who would headline the 2001 film that bears his name. Stiller had not quite perfected the character's soft-spoken speech pattern or his pursed-lips expression of wide-eyed innocence. (Innocence, abject stupidity, same difference.) Still, even in this primordial state, the basic concept was there, along with some of the character's best-known gags—like the fact that Zoolander is so dumb he cannot will his body to turn left, or that each of his signature facial expressions from "Ferrari" to "Blue Steel" look exactly the same.

With the benefit of hindsight, it's easy to see the building blocks of a great comedy character. But initially, Stiller wasn't so certain. According to Gallen, he had second thoughts about the whole concept a few days before the Fashion Awards.

"He was concerned maybe it wasn't funny enough," Gallen said in 2021. "I told him, 'Look, this [broadcast] is not going out for another few days. Let me put it on the big screens tonight and let's see what kind of reaction we get. If it doesn't get a great reaction, only a couple thousand people will see it. That's it. It won't air.'"

Stiller agreed, and the bit got huge laughs in the Paramount Theater. Zoolander lived—and then returned one year later in a second short for the 1997 VH1 Fashion Awards. At that point, Stiller—taking stock of the Hollywood comedy scene, and Mike Myers's enormous success that year with the broad James Bond parody *Austin Powers: International Man of Mystery*—realized Zoolander could have potential headlining a film spoofing the world of fashion and celebrity.

If *The Cable Guy* had sent Ben Stiller to movie jail, *There's Something About Mary* was his Get Out of Movie Jail Free card. As the star of the third-highest-grossing film of 1998, Stiller was suddenly in demand. While *Zoolander* slowly evolved through various script drafts, he took on another project that landed in his lap only because his *Cable Guy* star, Jim Carrey, passed on it first. The film, *Meet the Parents*, began its life as a totally different movie under the exact same title by Chicago comedian Greg Glienna.

"I had an idea inspired by the Peter Sellers movie *The Party*," Glienna said. "The entire premise is he goes to a party and wrecks it. I thought why couldn't it just be a guy goes and spends the weekend with his girlfriend's parents and everything goes wrong. . . . We did it very cheap: For like $30,000."

Glienna signed a distribution deal with *National Lampoon*, but the comedy juggernaut's best days were well behind it by that point and the original *Meet the Parents* never went into wide release. But *Sex, Lies, and Videotape* director Steven Soderbergh saw Glienna's film and sensed its enormous potential as fodder for a remake. He developed the material for a while, then left the project. At one point, Steven Spielberg took an interest in *Meet the Parents*; he was the one that thought Jim Carrey would make a good fit for a big-budget Hollywood version. Eventually, they both departed as well. Nobody was going to meet any more parents, at least for a while.

* * *

In June of 1998, Ben Stiller attended the third annual Nantucket Film Festival, where he saw a comedy called *Safe Men* about a pair of musicians mistaken for safecrackers. Stiller liked the film, and got to meet its twenty-eight-year-old writer/director, John Hamburg.

"*Safe Men*'s a true cult film," Hamburg says. "It's not for everyone. But people who like it *really* like it. It just clicks with them. Thankfully [Stiller] was one of those people for whom it clicked. We met that weekend in Nantucket and he was like, 'I think this movie is amazing. Would you ever want to work on stuff together?' And the first thing we did—it ended up being the second movie we made—but the first project we worked on was *Zoolander*."

After attending a reading of the current draft of Sather and Stiller's *Zoolander* script, Hamburg—a self-described "comedy nerd kid" who, like Stiller, began making films as a kid when he was given a camera as a gift—set to work making Derek a more likable hero.

"When John wrote his draft, that was sort of what crystalized it," Stiller said. "Like, *Oh yeah. Now the movie actually works.* He gave it this emotional heart in terms of really caring about Derek."

Stiller might have been convinced that the movie would work, but Paramount still wasn't sold. After several drafts, Hamburg says, the movie "fell apart, because people were like, 'Who wants to see a movie about a male model?'"

Meanwhile, *Meet the Parents* began to gain momentum at Universal, thanks to a new script draft by writer Jim Herzfeld and a new director: Jay Roach, the same man who helmed Mike Myers's *Austin Powers*. And Roach wanted Stiller to play the new Greg.

"I think Ben Stiller is a complete leading man and he also is one of the great comedians," Roach said. "He's got such an earnest sincere appeal in his eyes. And yet underneath there's a kind of worry that he can't cover up. And a lot of times we found ourselves cutting the film to emphasize that aspect."

Meet the Parents would give Stiller plenty to worry about. His Greg, a nurse who works in a Chicago hospital, wants to propose to his girlfriend Pam (Teri Polo). He just has to meet her parents at Pam's sister's wedding first. Greg believes Pam's dad, Jack, is a retired florist, but that's a cover for his real identity: former CIA agent and master interrogator. Most intimidating of all: Jack is played by Robert De Niro.

"This whole movie, to me, was an anxiety dream," explained Roach. "It connected with my own sense of always wanting to please the [in-laws] and trying too hard and always having it go wrong."

When Stiller joined the project, he recruited Hamburg to contribute to the script, who used suggestions from Roach, De Niro, and Stiller to tailor the film to their particular skills. The film's most famous sequence involves De Niro's character administering an excruciating lie detector test to an anxious Stiller, and then peppering him with all sorts of personal questions he has to answer truthfully—an idea that resonated as a nightmarish extension of the premise, and a perfect use of Stiller's gifts as a comedian—to be, in Hamburg's words, "the most incredibly reactive actor he's ever seen."

"I don't think he gets enough credit for it, because he makes it look effortless," Hamburg adds. "All you really want when you're directing actors are actors who listen to their scene partner. And Ben is so good at that. He doesn't need to say a lot. His expressions are gonna be just right."

As part of the film's escalating series of humiliations, Greg winds up spending time with Pam's ex-boyfriend Kevin, who is everything Greg is not: wealthy, confident, charismatic, chummy with Jack, and inexplicably good at woodworking. (He fashions Pam's sister's wedding canopy by hand from wood he salvaged from an old seaman's chapel in Nantucket.) And who better to play the anti–Ben Stiller than Owen Wilson?

Stiller had cast Wilson in a small role in *The Cable Guy*, but they never shared the screen in the film. They also worked together on the dark showbiz biopic *Permanent Midnight*. But *Meet the Parents* was the first time Stiller and Wilson got to go toe-to-toe in a comedy, and exploit their mismatched energies—Stiller with his reactive insecurity, Wilson with his easygoing confidence. Like the great comedy teams of old, even their physicalities were at odds; the lanky Wilson with his flowing blond locks versus Stiller, coiled and tense with his short brown hair. They looked funny just standing next to each other—and that was before they began improvising their dialogue. (Kevin's line about the wood from the old seaman's chapel in Nantucket was cooked up by Wilson.)

Jay Roach's *Meet the Parents* is the sort of movie Hollywood doesn't make anymore; mainstream comedies with big stars that play in theaters aren't allowed to be rooted in such small, relatable problems. The combination of a great cast, a smart script, a universal concept, and inspired comic set pieces made *Meet the Parents* a massive hit—with over $166 million in U.S. theaters, it was the seventh-highest-grossing film of 2000. Two years after *There's Something About Mary*, it confirmed Stiller as one of the biggest comedic actors of his generation, the sort of A-list talent whose name alone could get a movie made—even one about a male model.

Building off their work in *Meet the Parents*, the part of Hansel, Zoolander's upstart rival in the modeling world, was tailored specifically for Owen Wilson. The part of Mugatu was written for Stiller's *Ben Stiller Show* castmate Andy Dick. But Dick eventually had to turn the role down because he was already committed to a TV show.

That's when Stiller turned to Will Ferrell, who was still central to the action every week on *Saturday Night Live*. Despite his small-screen success, Ferrell was still looking for his first breakout role in a movie. Mugatu, a cruel fashion designer whose "Derelicte" clothing line is actually made out of garbage, gave Ferrell exactly what he needed. He threw himself into the role, screaming at Mugatu's subordinates, and dyeing and styling his own hair into Mugatu's distinctive U-shaped do rather than relying on a wig.

As the director of *Zoolander*, Stiller took his own commitment to the bit to new heights. The script called for Derek to endure a humiliating defeat at the VH1 Fashion Awards at the hands and rugged good looks of Hansel. Instead of creating a fake awards broadcast, Stiller shot the sequence at the 2000 edition of the show, snagging interviews with real celebrities on the red carpet, and then shooting scenes for his film during the commercial breaks.

The sheer number of cameos in the film was staggering: from Garry Shandling to Donald Trump; from Paris Hilton to Tommy Hilfiger; from Fred Durst to David Bowie, who officiated the "Walk Off" between Zoolander and Hansel after their rivalry for the title of Best Male Model reaches a boiling point. The enormous list of guest stars certainly yielded some surprise laughs. But more importantly, they grounded the movie's absurd story about a male model brainwashed into murdering the prime minister of Malaysia in the real world, or something close to it.

As if in response, the real world repeatedly intruded on *Zoolander*. The Motion Picture Association of America objected to a scene where Zoolander receives a massage from a hideous masseuse (played by Andy Dick under a mountain of prosthetic makeup) and the outline of Derek's erect penis is visible under a sheet. They also disapproved of a comically over-the-top orgy between Derek, Hansel, a journalist (played by Stiller's wife, Christine Taylor), a little person, a Sherpa, and several other unexpected participants.

Instead of removing the scenes, Stiller went to the MPAA ratings board and appealed their decision to rate *Zoolander* R. And because there are no hard-and-fast rules about what is or isn't allowed, Stiller tried to negotiate with the raters—a process he compared to a hitter arguing about the strike zone with a baseball umpire. When the raters insisted that the orgy scene alone deserved an R, he responded, "Listen, would I ever put my wife in a scene that would be compromising or anything worse than PG-esque?" In the end, the MPAA forced him to trim the scenes, but both survived—with a PG-13 rating. ("That was one victory," he said.)

But even bigger problems lay ahead. Paramount slated the film for release in late September, which should have been a prime spot for a sharp comedy. But that all changed on September 11, 2001. With the country gripped by anguish and fear in the early days after the 9/11 attacks, it wasn't clear what was or wasn't appropriate; whether audiences would want to laugh, or if they were even capable of laughing. To make matters worse, Stiller's movie cracked jokes about political assassinations in New York City—one where the now-destroyed World Trade Center was still visible in the city's skyline.

"It was such a surreal experience to even be sort of considering what to do. Everybody was so thrown off by 9/11 and so affected by it, that there was no context for it," Stiller said in 2021.

Paramount released the movie as planned—with the Twin Towers digitally erased from several shots, something Stiller later claimed to regret. (He eventually restored the World Trade Center to the shots in later DVD releases.) At the press junket, he fielded questions about whether anyone should release a comedy in the days after a national tragedy—to which he responded that he believed the film was an opportunity for an escape from reality for ninety minutes for those who wanted it.

That was a nice sentiment, but the public didn't take him up on it. *Zoolander*'s budget was low enough to ensure the film wasn't a disaster, but it wasn't exactly a blockbuster, either—it earned less than half of what the supposedly disappointing *Cable Guy* had grossed in theaters a few years earlier.

But Stiller soon noticed that the people who did see *Zoolander*—first in theaters, but then in larger numbers on home video and cable—really responded to it. Just months after the film premiered, Stiller was on vacation in Hawaii, trying to learn how to boogie board, when several kids swam up beside him.

"Do Blue Steel! Do Blue Steel!" they screamed.

For Stiller, *Zoolander* represented a validation of his meticulous approach, and a revelation, too. After growing up with dreams of becoming a serious auteur, *Zoolander* was the moment he realized he could do everything he wanted to do *in* comedies. ("People can be critical of them," he explained, "but I think they're worth it.") He believed so strongly in the film that when the shoot went over budget, Stiller paid a million-dollar penalty in order to complete it—something he said he did not regret. ("I do regret the end-title sequence they wouldn't let me do," he added, "even though it was only sixty thousand dollars—this great thing of Will Ferrell dancing. God, do I regret that.")

In hindsight, *Zoolander* endures because it far exceeded its origins as an *Austin Powers*–esque spoof of the fashion world. Stiller's sharp directorial eye supported a script that delivered one quotable line after another. ("It's that damn Hansel! He's so hot right now!" Mugatu hisses after the two male models bury the hatchet and team up to stop the designer's evil scheme.) Derek Zoolander is ridiculously good-looking, but at his core he's like most of us: someone who desperately wants to look cool but, despite his best efforts, comes across like a total idiot.

Maybe most important, *Zoolander* contains the combined brilliance of three comedy stars—Stiller, Wilson, and Ferrell—who were all funny enough to headline movies on their own. In *Zoolander*, they all split screen time for the benefit of the whole; the comedy equivalent of putting Robert Downey Jr., Samuel L. Jackson, and Scarlett Johansson together in *The Avengers*. Derek and Hansel are fanatically competitive throughout most of *Zoolander*, but in the end they can only succeed by working together. In other words, *Zoolander* celebrates precisely the sort of collaboration that made it so entertaining.

In *Zoolander*, a new funny person pops up in almost every scene. David Duchovny has a small role as a hand model who offers Derek evidence of Mugatu's conspiracy; Justin Theroux plays a Mugatu henchman who breakdance fights Hansel during the big climax. When Derek suffers a crisis of confidence following his loss to Hansel at the VH1 Fashion Awards, he briefly retires from male modeling and returns to his ancestral home in the coal mines of Southern New Jersey. (Don't look for them on a map; they're there, just trust me.) Back with his family for the first time in years, he tries to reconnect with his father and two brothers, who all boast identical spiky haircuts to Derek.

Derek's dad, Larry, was played by Academy Award–winning actor Jon Voight, who infused a surprising amount of pathos into his role as a coal miner who cannot relate to his glamorous son. Zoolander's brothers get less screen time—so little, in fact, that some people might not catch that one of them was played by another famous actor with several huge credits already to his name.

When Stiller recorded the DVD commentary for *Zoolander* and Derek's brothers appeared on the screen, he chuckled at the absurdity of it all.

"I don't think people can believe that's Vince Vaughn."

CHAPTER 9

The Movie Star Superstar Guy

This is a very big idea, my friends. We're talking about a non-exclusive egalitarian brotherhood where community status and, more importantly, age have no bearing whatsoever.

—Beanie, *Old School*

Todd Phillips was looking for a *Road Trip* follow-up when one found him. While directing a commercial between bigger projects, he worked with an advertising executive named Court Crandall. One day on set, Crandall sidled up to Phillips and said, "You know, I have this interesting idea for a movie."

His idea was called *Frat Men*. Crandall later said it came to him at a fancy Hollywood party thrown by some of his agency's creative directors. Surrounded by a harpist and fancy hors d'oeuvres, Crandall started pining for the good old days of a college kegger. Which got him thinking . . . What if someone went back to college in middle age?

For Phillips, it seemed like the perfect jumping-off point for an R-rated comedy. Directing *Frat House* had taught him fraternities were inherently ridiculous places, especially when you stick someone who doesn't belong—like, say, an HBO documentarian—into the middle of one. How much *more* ridiculous would it get if you threw a bunch of thirtysomething losers into the chaos?

Phillips brought the concept to *Road Trip* producer Ivan Reitman, who liked it, too. But Crandall's script, Phillips later said, was "an amazing idea" with an execution that "wasn't really great." Eventually, Phillips and his *Road Trip* writing partner, Scot Armstrong, got the go-ahead to take Crandall's concept and rewrite it from the ground up. *Frat Men* became *Old School*.

"It's never easy to do your second thing, the sophomore album or movie or book," Scot Armstrong says. "So we put a lot of thought into what we wanted to do next. . . . Me and Todd, we always just thought guys are funny. What guys do is funny, the way they hang out. And a fraternity . . . it's just so dumb the way guys can't talk to each other, so they do weird stuff to connect."

DreamWorks concurred—but they did not immediately sign off on Phillips's big casting idea. For the role of Beanie, the speaker salesman with a wife and two kids who convinces his aging buddies that they should start their own college fraternity, Phillips wanted an actor he loved but had never met: thirty-year-old Vince Vaughn.

DreamWorks' response: That guy? Can he even *do* comedy?

It's true that Vincent Anthony Vaughn had never worked on a sketch show like Ben Stiller or Will Ferrell had. But Vaughn was a natural-born talker and improviser, and by the time he was in junior high, he had already played Daddy Warbucks in a student production of *Annie* and hosted a few local variety shows.

But Vaughn also talked back to teachers and struggled in school, and around that same age he was sent to the school psychologist, who suggested a prescription for Ritalin. One of the seminal experiences of his life, Vaughn would later say, came when his poor grades and hyperactive behavior landed him in a class for students with learning disabilities and emotional problems.

"When I first went into that class, I thought, 'These kids are wackos. What the hell am I doing in here with them?' Well, slowly but surely, I really started to like these kids. And then I became very protective of them. If there was a game on the playground, I'd go grab the tall girl and make sure she played. And the other kids would say, 'She can't play!' and I'd say, 'Dammit, she's gonna play!'"

Vaughn eventually left that special-needs class, but his grades remained so low that he ran for class president on the assumption that his high school wouldn't flunk the senior who held the highest office in the student government. He won, and he graduated. Along the way, Vaughn played baseball, football, and wrestled—at least until he was the passenger in a one-car accident at the age of seventeen.

"A Jeep flipped, and I hurt my back a little bit," Vaughn recalled. "I'm fine now, but I had to take it slow for a while, so I wasn't able to go out for any sports. There was a high school play going on, and I got one of the leads. I just found acting again. After that I wanted to get involved professionally."

Vaughn's mother and father—a stockbroker and a manufacturer's rep for toys, including the Teenage Mutant Ninja Turtles—weren't so sure that was a good idea. But a friend of Vaughn's had a more agreeable parent who took him into Chicago for auditions; one day Vaughn cut school and tagged along to a reading for an industrial film. The casting director spotted Vaughn in the waiting room and asked if he wanted to give it a try. He did, and landed his first job.

Pretty soon, Vaughn had an agent and began taking acting classes, where a fellow student suggested he look into the ImprovOlympic. Founded in 1981 by Charna Halpern and Del Close, "iO" became a Chicago institution, and a home to comedians and actors like Mike Myers and Chris Farley. Vaughn took a six-week summer course with Close, and then he continued studying and performing at iO for several more months. Vaughn credited his training with helping him understand something critical to his success onscreen: "Improv is writing."

By the time Vaughn had graduated high school he started booking television commercials, including one for Chevy that played during the Super Bowl and paid him well enough that he could afford to move out to California at the age of eighteen. Then early success collided with the harsh reality of show business. In Chicago, Vaughn was a big fish in a little pond. (Like, a *literal* big fish. Vaughn is six foot five.) In Los Angeles, he was one of countless struggling actors, and it took a year for him to get cast in anything. Eventually, he eked out a meager living taking whatever roles came his way, including guest spots on *Doogie Howser, M.D.* and *21 Jump Street.*

Then Vaughn caught a break. A sports movie based on the life of famed Notre Dame walk-on football player Rudy Ruettiger was looking for young actors who could pass for football players. Vaughn, with his towering frame, looked the part. Without ever having to audition, he got cast as one of the members of the Fighting Irish.

Vaughn only had a handful of lines in *Rudy*. But while he was on location shooting the movie in Indiana, he connected with another young member of the ensemble. Twenty-six-year-old Jon Favreau grew up in New York, but while visiting a Chicago friend studying at Second City, he had fallen in love with improv. Favreau spent the next four years at Second City bartending, washing dishes, taking classes, and trying to earn a spot in the theater's exclusive main company. He was still there when he got cast in *Rudy*.

Favreau moved to Los Angeles after *Rudy* wrapped, and he and Vaughn started spending a lot of time together. They toured the city's burgeoning neo-swing club scene, where the duo spent endless nights venting their frustrations about their stalled careers, while Vaughn jokingly adopted exaggerated lounge lizard affectations. Convinced they needed to take charge of their own Hollywood destinies, they began talking about writing their own material. Favreau got a copy of the Final Draft screenwriting software as a Christmas gift and pounded out a script based on his own misery as a transplanted out-of-work actor in Los Angeles. He gave his fictional avatar a fast-talking buddy named Trent inspired by Vaughn, even lifting some of the dialogue directly from Vaughn's most outlandish late-night quips.

"It was amazing how much it looked like a screenplay," Favreau recalled. "Next thing you know, I've got eight to ten pages, twenty pages. You're showing it to people, and they're laughing. So I wrote the whole thing."

After just a week and a half of writing, the thing became *Swingers*. Favreau gave it to Vaughn, who loved it and wanted to make it. But when Favreau and Vaughn pitched the film, potential investors asked questions like "Who listens to swing music? Can you make it grunge music?" Others doubted the film could work without a strong female lead as a member of the central group of friends. Vaughn's response to that suggestion: "This isn't a fucking health video. This is about a bunch of guys who don't really know what they're doing trying to figure it out. If there was a girl hanging out there wouldn't be a fucking movie."

Of course, if Favreau and Vaughn couldn't find the funds they needed, there wouldn't be a movie at all. One potential deal after another fell through: One producer wanted big-name actors involved; another wanted the movie to be more violent. Then Vaughn showed the *Swingers* script to a young filmmaker friend named Doug Liman, who would supply the money they needed—his father, high-powered attorney Arthur Liman, sourced $200,000 from a wealthy client—if Favreau allowed Liman himself to direct the movie. With no other options available, Favreau agreed. Once installed as director, Liman made Vaughn audition for the part of Trent—even though Favreau had *based* the character on Vaughn—but after a search for a movie star went nowhere, Liman finally gave him the role.

Favreau, Vaughn, and Liman made the entire film in just twenty-two days, on such a shoestring budget that while they were able to convince many of their favorite bars to let them shoot inside, they couldn't afford to pay them to close down during production. Favreau and Vaughn would recite their lines while actual paying customers were getting drunk just out of frame.

But maybe that's what gave *Swingers* the right touch of lived-in authenticity. After all, *Swingers* was a movie all about appearances. Favreau's Mike and Vaughn's Trent are barely scraping by at the Hollywood margins, but they show up in Las Vegas in snappy suits acting like a bunch of high rollers. "The trick is," Mike explains, "we gotta look like we don't need the shit, then they give us the shit for free." The parallels to Favreau and Vaughn, who made *Swingers* to prove to Hollywood that they didn't need their help to break into the movie business, spoke for themselves.

The film did that and more. *Swingers* forever froze in amber the world of mid-'90s L.A. nightlife and the single guys who populated it, while Vaughn and his endless array of pseudo-suave catchphrases and pickup lines became part of an entire generation of dudes' everyday lexicon. His memorable lines included the ubiquitous "Vegas, baby! Vegas!" an exclamation that is being uttered by someone in Las Vegas right this very second as you read these words, whether that is in 2026 or 3026.

Miramax eventually bought the rights to distribute *Swingers* for $5.5 million. Most of that money went to Liman, but Vaughn got something even more valuable: a star-making role in a cult indie hit. By the time *Swingers* arrived on home video, teens and twentysomethings around the country were telling each other they were "so money and they don't even know it" in Vaughn's distinctive cadence. (In a curious bit of foreshadowing, as Mike and Trent stroll into an ancient, empty Las Vegas casino, Vaughn notes, "Guys like me and you gotta kick it here, old-school.")

Swingers benefited Vaughn's career in other ways. Liman wanted to use John Williams's famous score from *Jaws* in a scene where Trent gets cornered by a woman at a party. Steven Spielberg had to sign off on the use of the music, and before he did, he wanted to see the movie—and when Spielberg watched *Swingers*, he took one look at Vaughn and realized he was perfect for his next project, the massive sequel to *Jurassic Park*.

"I knew nothing of Vince until I saw *Swingers*," Spielberg said. "That made me interested in meeting him for *Lost World*. I found him to be so different from Trent that immediately I was struck by his ability to play character parts."

After years of struggle, Vaughn was an overnight sensation. Favreau dubbed his buddy "the movie star superstar guy."

In the wake of *Swingers*, Vaughn got offered a ton of roles in Hollywood comedies. Underwhelmed by their scripts and afraid of being typecast as the fast-talking ladies' man, he turned them all down. "I didn't want to do these studio films," Vaughn said. "When I started, I was happy just to be working. And then after *Swingers* I felt like, 'Well, gosh, I want to do movies that are about something.'"

After his one taste of big-budget filmmaking with Spielberg on *The Lost World*, Vaughn spent the rest of the '90s working in smaller, darker projects. He played serials killers in *Clay Pigeons* and the remake of Alfred Hitchcock's *Psycho*. He hunted a deranged criminal in the imaginative sci-fi film *The Cell*. John Travolta electrocuted him in the very silly thriller *Domestic Disturbance*. Vaughn didn't make a single comedy after *Swingers* until he reunited with Favreau for 2001's *Made*, a movie designed as a deconstruction of the collaborators' feel-good chemistry on *Swingers*. *Made* opened with the two buddies in a heated boxing match, and then cut to the duo driving together, their faces bloody and bruised after the fight, an elegant metaphor for the way Hollywood had beaten the shit out of them in the five years since *Swingers*.

Which is why Todd Phillips had such a hard time selling DreamWorks on Vaughn as his star. But Phillips was insistent; Vaughn was his guy. "What he did in *Swingers* and then in *Made* blew me away," Phillips explained. "He's funny in a grounded and real way. He shows pain in such a unique way—it's amazing. For me there are certain people where I feel like, 'If I can make them laugh, fuck that would be the best.' Vince is the top of that list."

Unlike so many of the comedy scripts Vaughn got offered in the wake of *Swingers*, the script for *Old School* made him laugh. And he *really* wanted to work with Phillips.

"Talking with Todd and hearing his thoughts [convinced me]," he explained. "I could tell that he was a very unique and a defiant voice. Also, that he was very funny and built a great atmosphere to create in."

"I'm not sure if the studio really thought Vince was funny enough, but we just sort of laid it down that this was our specialty, not theirs, and they went with it," producer Ivan Reitman later recalled.

With Vaughn on board to play Beanie, Phillips began the search for his other leads. The film would live or die on Beanie's relationship with his two best friends: Frank, a domesticated newlywed who in his younger days was a local partying legend known as Frank "the Tank," and straightlaced Mitch, who initiates *Old School*'s plot when he moves into a house near the local college after he walks in on his girlfriend hosting an orgy in their home. (The guests include Phillips's alter ego, Mr. Creepy, who knocks on the door just after Mitch breaks up the party and declares, "I'm here for the gang bang!") After Beanie coaxes Mitch to launch a fraternity out of his new bachelor pad, Frank's old persona reemerges, threatening his marriage—and providing most of the film's biggest laughs.

For Mitch, Phillips and Reitman picked Luke Wilson, brother of Owen, costar of *Bottle Rocket* and, more recently, the Reese Witherspoon rom-com *Legally Blonde.* Wilson didn't know Phillips but, like

Vaughn, he loved *Old School*'s script and was thrilled to be a part of the movie. So was Will Ferrell, who, despite his stellar turn in *Zoolander* and his high-profile gig on *Saturday Night Live*, remained on the hunt for a big box office hit.

"As for Todd trying to persuade me to do the movie, it was quite the opposite. He actually had to convince some of those at the studio to hire me, so I've always felt indebted to Todd," Ferrell noted.

Reitman backed Phillips over the film's cast. But after *Road Trip* became a surprise smash, he and Phillips sparred more on *Old School* over their diverging visions for the film.

"In success, everyone thinks it was them that did it," Scot Armstrong notes. "We stood up and fought for our vision even more [after *Road Trip*]. We were empowered. Especially Todd, he knew what he wanted to do. Ivan, if he was around, he'd be the first to admit he's tough to work with. He just wants you to succeed, but his version of you succeeding is doing things the way he thinks will be successful."

Reitman, for example, wanted *Old School* to focus more on the romance between Mitch and his love interest, Nicole (a pre–*Grey's Anatomy* Ellen Pompeo); Phillips and Armstrong disagreed. Reitman also wanted Ferrell's Frank the Tank to see the error of his hard-partying ways and return to his wife at the end of the film; Phillips and Armstrong refused.

"That was something we fought for," Armstrong says. "'Cause there's no romantic comedy where the person starts off in love and then ends up getting divorced. Usually they break up and they get back together. The idea that Frank the Tank's arc [ends with him] more lost, I love. That was a bit of a fight." Still, Armstrong adds, "Ivan's a smart guy. In the end, he helped us fight for that. And we ended up being a great team again. But it wasn't easy in the beginning."

Old School's title proved to be very fitting. The movie really was a throwback to vintage R-rated comedies like the Reitman-produced

Animal House. Both feature libidinous parties, casual nudity, excessive alcohol consumption, and tasteless humor—and both culminate with a battle between a bunch of charming reprobates and a cruel dean (played in *Old School* by Jeremy Piven). The "heroes," whose fraternity becomes home to all of the campus's misfits rejected by traditional social groups, revel in their misbehavior. When the dean threatens to eject them from campus, they rally together and fight back in the name of brotherhood—the supposed purpose of a fraternity, after all.

At times, the fictional debauchery bled through into the real world, especially when Snoop Dogg showed up to film a cameo as the guest of honor at the movie's big house-party scene. During a break between takes to adjust the lighting, Snoop retired to his trailer—along with some of the more attractive extras who were there to appear as partygoers.

"When it was time to shoot again, a PA goes to his trailer, but there's a long line of people waiting to get into this club that Snoop had created," Armstrong recalls. "And it turns out Snoop Dogg had invited all the hot girls into his trailer and was, like, DJing. The PA's supposed to escort him back to set, but he couldn't get in; there was a bouncer at the door not letting him inside."

Hours passed while Vaughn entertained the hundreds of extras who couldn't get into Snoop's trailer. Finally, Todd Phillips had enough. He arrived at Snoop's trailer and found him asleep. He grabbed him by the shoulder and shook him awake.

"Hey, Snoop," Phillips said.

"What's up, man?" Snoop replied.

"We're ready," Phillips shot back.

Snoop's response: "Oh, we're doing that now?"

Snoop's big musical number at the house party leads directly into *Old School*'s most memorable sequence, when Frank the Tank reemerges after he drinks a single beer. By the time Snoop concludes his song, Frank's ripped off all his clothes and declares to the crowd that it's time to go streaking. Frank races off into the night, while the partygoers recoil at the sight of Frank's pasty, hairy body. ("Skinny is not funny," Ferrell once said. "When I take my clothes off, it's not to show off. It wouldn't be funny if I was ripped.")

The fearless Ferrell, who claimed he thought the streaking gag was hilarious in the script without quite realizing he would actually be asked to run around naked in front of hundreds of extras, performed the sequence with only a sock covering his genitals.

"Will is a lot of things, but he's mostly brave, and he just doesn't give a shit," Phillips said, laughing. "I thought it was going to be a whole thing, like, 'Here, put this robe on.' But Will was so comfortable—I was amazed." Not only did Ferrell not want a robe, he barely cared about the sock. ("He never wanted to wear the thing," Phillips marvels on the *Old School* DVD commentary.)

"If it's funny, Will will go for it," Armstrong says. "Anything for the bit. He is as committed as an artist. It sounds funny to say it, but he is truly a comedy artist."

The comic chemistry between the three core stars, the heavily R-rated humor, and the satisfying, *Animal House*–esque underdog storyline—complete with a reshot final act featuring the frat squaring off with the evil dean's cronies in a series of absurd competitions like debate, dancing, and "school spirit," in which Frank the Tank sets himself ablaze while attempting to leap through a ring of fire—all proved to be a winning combination. *Old School* wasn't an immediate blockbuster; it didn't win its opening weekend (it came in second to Ben Affleck's superhero movie *Daredevil*), and it only wound up grossing a respectable $87 million worldwide in theaters, about $30 million less than Phillips's own *Road Trip*.

But *Old School* became a massive hit on home video and television, watched and rewatched, quoted and re-quoted endlessly by fans. It helped solidify Ferrell's movie star status, and it proved to Hollywood once and for all that Vince Vaughn could do comedy. And this time, he wasn't going to wait for five years to make another one. In fact, by the time *Old School* hit theaters, Vaughn had multiple comedies in development—including another with Todd Phillips that would pair him with two more hot comedy stars as a classic '70s cop duo.

CHAPTER 10

A Bold Strategy

Thanks for pointing out something that I couldn't notice on my own. You're a real benefit to have.

—Reese Feldman, *Starsky & Hutch*

A case could be made that no actor has had a better single year in the twenty-first century than Ben Stiller's 2004.

From the audience's perspective, it came out of nowhere. After *Zoolander* and a strong supporting turn in Wes Anderson's *The Royal Tenenbaums*, Stiller all but vanished from movie theaters for the next two years. In 2002 and 2003, he made a handful of cameo appearances and headlined just one movie: Danny DeVito's *Duplex*, a dark comedy opposite Drew Barrymore about a young couple who buy a Brooklyn brownstone and then contemplate murdering their annoying rent-controlled tenant. It bombed at the box office.

Things worked out differently in 2004. Stiller didn't have one $100 million hit, or two, or even three. He had *four*—including one that grossed more than half a billion dollars worldwide all by itself. Jim Carrey's 1994—the one so massive it earned him that $20 million payday for *The Cable Guy*—included three hits that earned a total $705.9 million at the box office. Stiller's 2004 blew both of those numbers out of the water. He starred in five movies with a combined worldwide box office of $1.05 billion. That's a twelve-month span with basically no equal in history for a comedian.

Ben Stiller would not be going back to movie jail anytime soon.

His year got off to a very fast start. Despite Stiller's vocal complaints that he did not want to repeat his enfeebled character from *There's Something About Mary*, he essentially did just that in the January 2004 release *Along Came Polly*.

Written and directed by John Hamburg, who Stiller had leaned on to punch up the scripts for *Meet the Parents* and *Zoolander*, the movie was awash in *Something About Mary* parallels, with Stiller playing a nebbishy control freak—his job is to assess risk for a life insurance company, the most Ben Stiller job imaginable—who falls for a free-spirited beauty who should be way out of his league, played by Jennifer Aniston at the very height of her fame and *Friends*' popularity.

As in *There's Something About Mary*, Stiller's character must endure a series of brutal embarrassments. Instead of fighting with a dog, he tangles with a blind ferret, who bit Stiller on the chin so badly he needed to get a rabies shot. ("Their teeth are sharp, like razors," Stiller told the *New York Post.*) Instead of getting his dick caught in his zipper, Stiller's Reuben accidentally clogs and overflows Aniston's character's toilet during a date, sending him into a panic to stop the spill and hide the evidence. Instead of jizz dangling from his ear, Stiller had another man's belly sweat smeared all over his face in slow motion during a pickup basketball game, a moment so revolting it prompted the star to ask Hamburg, "Really? Really, I have to do it?"

Stiller may not have liked it, but once he went for it, he did it well. Hamburg, who calls Stiller his "cinematic alter ego," says that the key to writing one of his characters involves imagining "what he'll react to—so usually he's in a scene with someone who's kind of the most extreme character, taking control, making him uncomfortable." *Along*

Came Polly was basically ninety minutes of uncomfortable Ben Stiller—and audiences loved it.

Despite middling reviews from critics, the film exceeded all of its distributor's expectations. *Along Came Polly* wound up grossing $178 million worldwide and helped popularize a new cornerstone of bathroom slang: "the shart," uttered by a hysterically blunt Philip Seymour Hoffman as Reuben's buddy Sandy, who begs to leave an art show early because he just had an accident in his pants. ("I tried to fart and a little shit came out. I just sharted. Now let's go," he mutters.)

Stiller's 2004 was off to a shitty start in the best possible way. His next project started with a five-word pitch, spoken by Stiller to his agent:

"Owen Wilson. *Starsky & Hutch*."

In days, Warner Bros.—which owned the rights to make a movie version of the mid-'70s television series about a pair of mismatched Bay City cops—had bought the concept. A cop comedy about unlikely partners offered plenty of potential for another Stiller and Wilson team-up. Stiller played the uptight, by-the-book David Starsky, while Wilson was cast as the easygoing (and sometimes lawbreaking) Ken "Hutch" Hutchinson. (In a strange bit of synchronicity, the very first *Bottle Rocket* short Wilson made with Wes Anderson included a Tarantino-esque scene where the characters discussed Huggy Bear, the pimp character from *Starsky & Hutch*.)

For Stiller, it was the perfect venue to satirize vapid TV culture à la *The Cable Guy*, and to craft another one of his carefully observed pop culture parodies in the vein of *The Ben Stiller Show*—only, this one would be feature-length and produced on a $60 million budget. It also gave him the opportunity to make his fifth big-screen pairing with Owen Wilson in a span of six years, and a chance to team up with one of Hollywood's buzzy young comedy directors: Todd Phillips.

Shortly after *Road Trip*, Stiller and Phillips had a general meeting and hit it off. A few weeks later Stiller called Phillips back with that same bare-bones pitch: him and Owen Wilson as Starsky and Hutch. Phillips and cowriter Scot Armstrong didn't need to hear any more than that.

"There's all these fun things about it," Armstrong explains. "It's a period piece. It's a cop procedural. It's a mystery thriller, but at the same time it's really about this friendship. That's the main thing me and Todd are interested in: What makes these guys tick? Male friendships are funny because guys will go play golf together, and they'll come back and someone will go, 'How's their family?' And they didn't ask. It's only through osmosis that guys become really close."

Rather than simply poke fun at the old *Starsky & Hutch* television series, Phillips proposed making a "love letter to the show" that also functioned as a prequel, revealing how the title characters first met and became partners. That choice not only gave the film a narrative spine; it added a surprisingly sweet undercurrent to the story.

"I viewed this movie as a romantic comedy between two straight guys," Phillips said. "Meaning it went through a lot of the beats a typical romantic comedy goes through. At first they're forced together and they don't like each other. Then they learn to get along. Then they really like each other. Then something pulls them apart. . . . And then of course something brings them back together to form an even greater union than they were before. And in a weird way *Starsky & Hutch* the movie follows those same beats."

Phillips's goal to pay homage to *Starsky & Hutch* without losing his comedic edge was aided by the fact that the vintage show had aged into a surreal time capsule of questionable '70s fashions and macho cop clichés. Some of the film's most bizarre moments came directly from the series, like Starsky and Hutch brandishing their firearms while wearing nothing but tiny towels and shoulder holsters, something Phillips had spotted on a vintage *Starsky & Hutch* poster and thought, "We have to make that a scene."

True to that philosophy, the movie alternated big action scenes—with shootouts and elaborate car chases involving the duo's famous red-and-white "Striped Tomato" Ford Gran Torino—with big comic set pieces, although those had to be calibrated just right. In a break from Phillips's typical approach, *Starsky & Hutch* was his first PG-13 movie—although he still managed to sneak in rampant cocaine use, pony murder, and even a threesome.

At the heart of it all was Stiller. "Especially at that time, he was the best comedy actor," says Armstrong. "I love writing for Vince, I love writing for Will, but there's no better straight man that you can put all the anxiety of trying to get through something on. You just feel all that tension, all his wanting to succeed, his sweaty attempt to be liked. It's just on his face." Always committed to the authenticity of whatever he was making, Stiller took driving lessons in order to perform as many of his own stunts as possible—much to costar Owen Wilson's dismay, since he had to be seated next to him in Starsky's Striped Tomato during the action. ("He was terrified for his life," Armstrong says, laughing.)

Phillips, who got to make yet another film on the subject of male bonding, brought in several members of his *Old School* team, including Armstrong, Vince Vaughn as the film's villain, Will Ferrell (who showed up for an uncredited day of work to play Vaughn's jailed fixer Big Earl), and Snoop Dogg—who took over the role of Starsky and Hutch's underworld informant Huggy Bear on the promise that there would be no delays while he got high in his trailer. When Phillips pressed Snoop to make sure he took this role seriously, the rapper replied, "No, no, no—you don't get it. On *Old School*, you hired Snoop to play Snoop Dogg. With Snoop Dogg, you get all this other shit. But as Calvin [Broadus], I'm going to be a professional." ("And by the way, he *was*—he was a fucking dream to work with," Phillips added.)

When *Starsky & Hutch* opened in theaters on March 5, it grossed $170 million, another big hit for Stiller and Wilson's duo act. The pair leaned into their growing image as a full-fledged comedy team by doing most of the publicity for the movie together. In a joint appearance on *Late Night with Conan O'Brien*, they joked about a contract they signed to *only* work together in the future, and presented posters for some of their upcoming projects, like the evocatively titled *Magnet Crotch and Iron Face*. They also presented the Best Short Film award for 2004 together at the Academy Awards that month, with Wilson dressed in dapper black tie and Stiller wearing his full David Starsky costume—complete with belted cardigan, sunglasses, curly wig—a gag predicated on once again embarrassing Stiller in front of a worldwide audience of hundreds of millions of people.

Significantly fewer people saw Stiller's next 2004 release, his only misstep of the year. Like *Starsky & Hutch*, *Envy* focused on a tenuous friendship, this one between a pair of neighbors played by Stiller and Jack Black, whose power dynamics get thrown out of whack after Black's hapless inventor actually creates a billion-dollar product (a spray that dissolves dog poop) after Stiller turns down an opportunity to invest in his business. That leaves Stiller's Tim on the outside looking in at his neighbor's burgeoning affluence.

Stiller was still in very familiar territory in *Envy* as another put-upon loser, and the movie did include a very funny, very strange supporting turn from Christopher Walken as a drifter who gets mixed up in the escalating war between the two leads and offers inspired pearls of wisdom like "If a pretzel is a quality pretzel, you don't need salt! It's just a fact." But the film never quite settled on a tone between the two extremes of dark satire and broad physical comedy, and it flopped with critics and audiences.

Stiller's next 2004 hit started as a 154-page spec script that combined a young USC grad named Rawson Marshall Thurber's two loves: sports and comedy. Driven by painful childhood memories, Thurber imagined a ludicrous film about adults playing the quintessential gym-class game: *Dodgeball.*

As Thurber sent the script around Hollywood, he kept hearing variations of the same response: "It's really funny. We don't want to make it." Then he managed to get the screenplay to Stiller's production company, Red Hour Films, which had recently signed a first-look deal with DreamWorks. Thurber spent over a year working and reworking his screenplay; he eventually convinced Vince Vaughn to play his hero, humble gym owner Peter LaFleur, while Stiller signed on for the part of the film's over-the-top villain, fitness guru White Goodman. And yet when it was time for DreamWorks to decide once and for all whether to proceed, they said no. Their explanation, according to Thurber: "We don't make dodgeball movies at DreamWorks. We make Academy Award–winning movies at DreamWorks."

It took a while to find a new home—one studio asked Thurber to change the movie from a dodgeball comedy to a soccer comedy, which is certainly an unorthodox subject for a film titled *Dodgeball: A True Underdog Story.* Eventually, the project landed at Fox, thanks to a new executive at the company, Debbie Liebling, who had recently joined the studio from Comedy Central and wanted to get into business with Stiller. There were a few hiccups along the way—as with *Old School*, which hadn't opened in theaters at this point, the studio was initially wary about Vaughn as a comedic lead—but eventually Fox agreed to put the movie into production.

Dodgeball cast Vaughn as a fictional variation of the figure he served in that special-needs class he attended in high school: as the fast-talking leader of a group of outcasts. When the Globo Gym fitness chain—owned by Stiller's White Goodman—threatens to close Peter's Average Joe's gym, he and his customers need to raise $50,000 in a month to pay off their mortgage and save their beloved hangout. To do it, they decide to enter a pro dodgeball tournament with a convenient $50,000 cash prize. In response, White—who is so committed to his militant diet that he shoves a slice of pizza down his pants rather than take a bite of it—hires a bunch of dodgeball ringers to oppose the Average Joes in the tournament, setting up an epic winner-take-all showdown in the finals.

Rather than attempt to rationalize the fate of a gym resting on a pro dodgeball tournament, Thurber leaned into the absurdity of his premise. Peter's team includes a man who thinks he is a pirate (played with impressive dedication by Alan Tudyk) and they battle teams like a German squad that prays to a picture of David Hasselhoff before they take the field. (Hasselhoff shows up after they lose to scream, "You are all swine!" at them in subtitled German.)

The production sourced three different types of dodgeballs to use on camera: real ones like those you'd find in a brutal high school gym class; a second, softer alternative; and a third variation that Thurber compared to "a pillow." Unfortunately, to make dodgeball look competitive on camera, the cast needed to play it for real. Just throwing dozens of heavy dodgeballs in take after take took its toll; Vaughn tweaked his shoulder at one point from overthrowing.

But that was nothing compared to the pain endured by the recipients of those balls, many of which were launched by Thurber himself via an off-camera pitching machine. ("When you get hit with one of those balls, the slow-motion memories of my childhood in my gym uniform came back," said Christine Taylor, Ben Stiller's *Zoolander* costar and real-life wife, who played one of *Dodgeball*'s Average Joes.) The actor most often at the receiving end of the rubbery fury was Justin Long, playing the rookie of the Average Joe's squad. Eager to prove he could hang with the cast's big names, and uncannily adept at playing physical agony for laughs, Long agreed to get pelted by dodgeball after dodgeball hurled at top speed. One deleted scene among the *Dodgeball* DVD bonus features is comprised of Long receiving twenty-five consecutive dodgeball shots to the face, back, and groin.

While Vaughn and Stiller both starred in *Starsky & Hutch*, their scenes together were limited. *Dodgeball* gave them far more interactions, where the physical mismatch between the tall, breezy Vaughn and the diminutive, intense Stiller made them charming onscreen opponents.

"I was a little bit concerned that I was doing this ridiculous, over-the-top character that might've been in a totally different universe," Stiller said. "I had moments of insecurity. I was like, 'Oh man, Vince is being really serious and cool, and I'm really going *here*.' That was kind of the undercurrent of what was going on, but it worked."

As funny as Vaughn and Stiller were playing off each other, *Dodgeball*'s longest tail came from its dodgeball tournament's TV announcers, who supposedly worked for the sub-sub-sub-sub-sub-sports network ESPN8: The Ocho. Gary Cole played the straightlaced play-by-play man Cotton McKnight; Jason Bateman was his spiky-haired color commentator, Pepper Brooks. Cole and Bateman's back-and-forth banter, sending up the tropes of staid live-sports coverage, became a font of popular quotes and later, in the age of social media, the source of one of the most repeated GIFs in all of the internet, in response to the Joes being forced to forfeit in a key game due to a lack of eligible players: "It's a bold strategy, Cotton! Let's see if it pays off for them!"

Dodgeball wound up paying off for all involved—except perhaps for the DreamWorks executives who passed on the project only to see it trounce their own comedy, Steven Spielberg's *The Terminal*, at the weekend box office in June of 2004, $30 million to $19 million. The sports comedy wound up grossing $168 million worldwide, making it Stiller's third film to earn at least that much in a five-month span.

His hot streak only got hotter in December of 2004, when he closed out the year with the *Meet the Parents* sequel *Meet the Fockers*. The movie reunited almost all of the first film's cast and creative team for the obvious continuation of the story: with Stiller's Greg introducing

Robert De Niro's Jack and the rest of the Byrnes family to his own parents—played by Dustin Hoffman and Barbra Streisand. *Meet the Fockers* did not contain the same relatable zing as *Meet the Parents*; some of the jokes were so outlandish they made a cat peeing on a dead woman's ashes in the first movie look like something out of a documentary.

Audiences didn't care. *Meet the Fockers* was a wild success; the fourth-biggest film in America that year behind only *Shrek 2*, *Spider-Man 2*, and *The Passion of the Christ*. Its $522.6 million worldwide remains one of the largest totals for a comedy film in history, and an incredible capper to a monumental year for Stiller.

But with a monumental year came an equally large amount of scrutiny from the media. *The Cable Guy* notwithstanding, Stiller had mostly gotten good reviews throughout his career. All that changed in 2004. Suddenly Ben Stiller was everywhere, and critics began to grow weary of his cinema of male mortification. The *New York Post* found him guilty of "overexposure" and picking "threadbare scripts" that allowed him to remain in a "comfortable, remunerative rut." In *The New York Times*, David Edelstein called Stiller "America's favorite seething man-child" and tossed off a series of backhanded compliments (or front-handed insults) about his work and his persona; he was "an odd-looking man" with "Alfred E. Neuman ears," a "compulsively pumped-up clown" whose schtick "grows increasingly reflexive and self-indulgent."

Shortly after *Meet the Fockers*, *The New Yorker*'s David Denby penned a fifteen-hundred-word consideration of Stiller's work titled "The Contender." Like Edelstein, Denby called Stiller "odd-looking." But then he went even further. He claimed he was "not a natural comic," described him as "the latest, and crudest, version of the urban Jewish male on the make," and compared him to a child performing in a summer camp show, "cutting up for his relatives and friends, [a] boy-man [who] wants the camera." Denby's barbs were so fierce they inspired Owen Wilson to write a letter to *The New Yorker* defending his frequent costar and friend, and calling Denby a "bully" and a "jerk."

Even the Razzie Awards—the annual alternative to the Oscars that "honors" the worst films released each year—targeted Stiller, nominating him for Worst Actor for his collective performances across all of his 2004 movies. (He lost to, of all people, President George W. Bush in Michael Moore's *Fahrenheit 9/11.*)

Pressed by *New York* magazine to respond to both his massive financial success and the increasing criticism of his work, Stiller evaded the question like White Goodman leaping out of the way of a dodgeball. "I don't really get into the whole meta aspect of the thing," he insisted. He also claimed that the "cold, hard bottom line of moviemaking" meant he still couldn't convince studios to take a chance on him in anything except a broad comedy. Despite all that success, Stiller said, getting studios to bankroll his filmmaking ambitions behind the camera was "still like pushing a boulder up a hill."

Still, if audiences saw every 2004 film Stiller appeared in, they caught him stretching himself a little. In July of that year he made an uncredited cameo in yet another comedy, this one produced by his old buddy Judd Apatow and cowritten and starring Will Ferrell. In their latest film, Stiller showed up as a Spanish-language newsman who brandishes a whip while vowing to make the sewers run red with the blood of Ferrell's character, an arrogant anchorman by the name of Ron Burgundy.

CHAPTER 11

Keep Going, Only Bigger

The following is based on actual events. Only the names, locations and events have been changed.

—Opening titles, *Anchorman: The Legend of Ron Burgundy*

It was decided: Adam McKay was going to commit suicide.

He even printed up flyers. They read:

Attention: On Feb. 28, 1992 Adam McKay, age 23, will kill himself during the performance of Virtual Reality *. . . No Joke.*

Virtual Reality was a regular show performed by members of a comedy troupe named the Upright Citizens Brigade. So the flyers, which McKay and his UCB colleagues pasted up all over Chicago, advertised a comedy show with the promise of a real suicide and a vow of no comedy. As marketing tactics go, it was a bold strategy (See: Cotton).

It worked, too. On February 28, a large crowd converged on the ImprovOlympic to see Adam McKay, age twenty-three, kill himself. When the time was right, the assembled throng spilled out of the theater and congregated outside a nearby five-story building, where McKay was perched on the roof.

"Is this what you want?! Is this why you came here?!" McKay screamed to the crowd.

From somewhere below, McKay heard a voice yell back, "Jump! Jump!" He immediately recognized it: Del Close, one of the key pioneers of improv comedies and cofounder of the ImprovOlympic, urging him to leap from the building. Close, who always pushed his students to experiment and explore the boundaries of what improvisation could do, was overjoyed by McKay's outlandish stunt.

Suddenly, somconc fell over the side of the building. The crowd gasped.

Before anyone realized that a CPR dummy had been tossed from the roof, the real Adam McKay was racing downstairs. Meanwhile, an actor dressed as the Grim Reaper appeared to drag the "dead" McKay away—until other members of the Upright Citizens Brigade offered the Angel of Death a bribe to look the other way in this one unfortunate instance. With the audience distracted by the otherworldly spectacle, McKay snuck into the crowd, replaced the dummy, and rose from the proverbial dead. The audience went wild.

That's Adam McKay's comedy in a nutshell: simultaneously shocking and silly, with a smidge of transgressive confrontation. Working with the original incarnation of the Upright Citizens Brigade and later at Second City, McKay's best improvisations were as much spontaneous sketches as Andy Kaufman–esque provocations. McKay was onstage during one Second City revue when future *30 Rock* cast member Scott Adsit interrupted the show to announce that President Bill Clinton had been assassinated.

"Scott's a really good actor and he played it very real," McKay recalled. "The whole crowd completely believed it. We then wheeled out a television to watch the most up-to-date news coverage. We turned it on, and NFL bloopers came on—we had already inserted a VHS tape. One of us yelled, 'Wait, don't change it!' The whole cast came out and hunkered down and just started laughing at these football bloopers.

The people in the audience slowly began to file out, dazed. That was the end of our show."

That was an extreme example, but not entirely out of character for McKay, who once said he was never as proud of any of his accomplishments in the worlds of film or television as he was of the time in 1989 that he called the Philadelphia Phillies, impersonated Boston Red Sox general manager Lou Gorman, and nearly engineered a trade for infielder Randy Ready.

The Phillies were not a random choice. Although Adam McKay was born in Denver, and spent some of his childhood in Worcester, Massachusetts, in his teen years his family moved to Malvern, Pennsylvania. The son of a waitress and a bass player (and, later, the product of divorce), his life changed forever when he saw the Zucker brothers' spoof *Airplane!* He particularly loved the joke inspired by the moment from countless films and TV shows where a newspaper spins into focus, highlighting a story central to a movie's plot. Only because this was *Airplane!*, one of the silliest movies ever made, the headline read "BOY TRAPPED IN REFRIGERATOR EATS OWN FOOT." The utter randomness of the headline, along with the violence it suggested (not to mention the sheer stupidity of the joke, the boy in the fridge with a mouthful of foot meat has nothing to do with *Airplane!*'s story), unlocked something in McKay's brain. He never forgot it.

McKay stayed close to home for college, first at Penn State. He liked making a comedy show for the school's radio station, but he struggled to "assimilate into the frat world" in Happy Valley. So he transferred to Temple, where he majored in English and started getting into stand-up comedy. That's when he reconnected with a buddy who had recently moved to Chicago and studied with Del Close.

"He came back and he said, 'There's this old hipster teaching this form where you get onstage, and you can do whatever you want,'" McKay remembered. "Like, you improvise plays and anything you say happens . . . and literally, I was just like, 'I'm coming out there, hold on.'"

Months from graduation, McKay dropped out, sold his comic book collection, used the proceeds to buy a used Chrysler New Yorker, and headed to Chicago. Studying under Close taught McKay several key lessons of comedy, none more important than the directive to always go with your third thought in any situation.

"When you're onstage, your first thought is knee-jerk," McKay explained. "Your second thought is usually okay, but not great. Del would make you stay in a scene until you found your third thought, which was a little above and beyond what most other teachers would suggest."

Close also counseled his students to always play to the top of their intelligence. "If you treat the audience like poets and geniuses," McKay noted, "that's what they will become"—and in his experience, that was true. The smarter the material, the smarter the audience. Stupid jokes were fine. But a *brilliant* stupid joke (like, say, a newspaper headline that reads "BOY TRAPPED IN REFRIGERATOR EATS OWN FOOT") was something truly special.

When *Saturday Night Live* scouts came to Second City and saw McKay in a show called *Piñata Full of Bees* (which included a recurring bit where he demanded the audience hand over their Blockbuster Video membership cards for ritual destruction), he earned himself a tryout. But McKay recognized that he did not have the kinds of performing skills prized by *SNL*; he didn't do impressions, and his characters tended to be willfully alienating. So he brought some of his sketch scripts with him to the audition and handed them over to a producer, landing a spot with *SNL* on his first try—as a writer. He joined the staff in the fall of 1995, the same year the cast was almost entirely overhauled with new recruits like Will Ferrell.

Although McKay was among the many *SNL* writers who underestimated Ferrell at first glance, he quickly realized the actor could sell any concept McKay hatched up, no matter how ridiculous. "That was sort of the power of Will Ferrell," McKay confirmed. "And that's why all the writers loved him and wrote for him endlessly. 'Cause he broke that barrier between funny strange and funny ha-ha."

The feeling was mutual; Ferrell loved collaborating with McKay on weird skits like "Wake Up and Smile," about a morning news program whose hosts descend into murder and cannibalism after a teleprompter malfunction leaves them fumbling for things to say. ("We can't wait! If we wait we die! I'm the dominant one here, so I'll be the leader!" Ferrell's previously amiable host roars shortly before he rips the weatherman's head off and feasts on his entrails.)

As their partnership deepened, they began thinking about working together beyond *Saturday Night Live.* Their first serious attempt coalesced at the end of the 1990s. Titled *August Blowout*, Ferrell described it as "*Glengarry Glen Ross* meets a car dealership, meets *Used Cars.* It was about weird, horrible, eccentric car dealership guys."

The subjects of *August Blowout* were perhaps a bit too weird, horrible, and eccentric for Hollywood—the script never got produced—but it did get passed around the studios, attracting a fair amount of attention for Ferrell and McKay as a writing team. One of the film's unlikely fans was *Boogie Nights* director Paul Thomas Anderson, who loved *Saturday Night Live* so much he actually joined the show for a brief guest-writing stint and approached Ferrell and McKay to tell them how much he admired *August Blowout.*

"He's like, 'What if you guys wrote whatever you wanted to write, and I would shepherd it for you and kind of find out how to make it?'" Ferrell explained. "We were like, 'We'd do it. We'd do it in a heartbeat.' So that's when we wrote *Anchorman.*"

The concept originated with Ferrell, after he watched a TV documentary on the life of pioneering female journalist Jessica Savitch, one of the earliest women in history to solo anchor an evening newscast. Savitch died in a car crash in 1983 when she was only thirty-six years old, and even before her death her significant career achievements were often dismissed by critics, who claimed she was only promoted through the broadcast ranks because of her undeniable beauty.

It was not exactly an obvious starting point for a comedy. In fact, Savitch's life had already inspired the 1996 Robert Redford and Michelle Pfeiffer drama, *Up Close & Personal*. But what really caught Ferrell's eye in the documentary was not necessarily Savitch herself, but the casual cruelty of her on-air colleague, Philadelphia newsman Mort Crim. Recalling his relationship with Savitch in the 1970s, Crim nonchalantly declared in the film, "You have to remember, back then I was a real male chauvinist pig."

"The first time a woman comes into the newsroom, and you just have this petulant news team, that she's obviously ten times smarter than they are, and yet they're in the dominant position," Ferrell explained. "That was simply the idea, and we just went from there."

Well, maybe not *so* simply. McKay loved the idea of exploring the sexist world of 1970s local news (or maybe just the sexist world of the 1970s in general, or perhaps the sexist world of . . . the world), and of giving Ferrell a meaty role in the mold of so many of his best *SNL* characters, that of an overly cocky master of the universe who's not nearly as smart or as talented as he thinks. But the duo's initial script was not a straightforward send-up of gendered relationships in TV newsrooms.

Instead, they wrote, of all things, a parody of the 1993 Frank Marshall film *Alive*, based on the infamous true story of the survivors of a 1972 plane crash in the Andes Mountains who resorted to cannibalism to sustain themselves while awaiting rescue. The first draft of *Anchorman* followed a group of newsmen from all over the country on a flight to a big convention in Philadelphia. Ferrell's character, Ron Burgundy, "convinces the pilot that he knows how to fly the charter jet, and he immediately crash-lands it in the mountains. And it's just the story of them surviving and trying to get off the mountainside. . . . And Veronica Corningstone [Burgundy's newsroom rival] keeps saying things like,

'Guys, I know if we just head down we'll hit civilization.' And we keep telling her, 'Wrong!'"

It was another weird, horrible, and eccentric world from McKay and Ferrell. Paul Thomas Anderson took one look at it and decided maybe he didn't want to produce a comedy from two unproven *SNL* oddballs after all. He wasn't alone; the early script (titled *Action News Man*) was roundly rejected by almost every studio in Hollywood. Ferrell and McKay claimed they received fourteen nos in a single twenty-four-hour period.

Admittedly, McKay and Ferrell's approach to film pitches might have had something to do with that. Ferrell tried to convince DreamWorks to back *Action News Man* while wearing an oversized foam cowboy hat. Later, Ferrell pretended to nod off during the meeting. Sensing the boys might need a steadying hand to look over their shoulders, Ferrell and McKay's manager, Jimmy Miller, brought in another one of his clients, Judd Apatow, to take a look at their work and offer some suggestions. His advice: more story, less absurdity.

"My main job on a film like this is to see if I can inject any additional logic or humanity to the story," Apatow explained. "I would watch them shoot all day, laughing my ass off, but also thinking, 'Is there any way that this can make sense?'"

As Apatow provided constructive criticism, McKay and Ferrell whittled away their more eccentric ideas (like, say, cannibalistic TV newsmen) and beefed up the characters, homing in on the original notion of a battle of the sexes in the testosterone-drenched world of 1970s local news. McKay and Ferrell worked well with Apatow, who pushed them to take their satire of oafish men even further than they had in their initial proposal—to essentially follow Del Close's advice and make sure they were always looking for the third thought in each scene.

But even the revised *Anchorman* script received little support in Hollywood. McKay and Ferrell held a reading of the new draft for another interested production company, New Regency. By all accounts, their updated screenplay killed in the room. When the reading ended, one executive in attendance complimented McKay's work. Naturally, McKay asked if that meant the company would produce the movie.

"No, no," the producer replied. "We're never gonna make this movie. It's too crazy."

To studio executives, the only thing crazier than a period comedy about misogynistic news anchors would be giving Ferrell and McKay tens of millions of dollars to make it. "Several studios said, 'We already said no to this! Don't ever send us this again,'" McKay remembered. "They were mad! And then *Old School* hit."

Ever the canny pitchman, Ferrell used the *Old School* publicity tour to hype not only his current film but the *Anchorman* script as well. Despite strong buzz for *Old School* and his ever-increasing national profile, thanks to his gig playing President George W. Bush on *Saturday Night Live*, Ferrell claimed he still couldn't get anyone to take a chance on his passion project, insisting, "Hollywood is like: 'Yeah, we know who that guy is! He's funny! We're still nervous about him.'"

Old School's success changed that. All of a sudden, DreamWorks—the same studio that had turned down Ferrell and McKay's *Action News Man* when Ferrell told them about it in a novelty cowboy hat—was now so desperate to buy the script they got into a bidding war with Universal over the rights. After DreamWorks agreed to put up a $20 million budget, McKay and Ferrell finally had the chance to make their movie.

A few months later, Ferrell starred in a charming off-kilter comedy called *Elf* about a human baby who grows up at the North Pole alongside Santa Claus and his elves, and then returns to New York City to locate his biological parents. At one point, *Elf*'s distributor, New Line, almost got cold feet about the whole thing, concerned that Ferrell's Frat Pack fan base would not come out for a family-friendly comedy where the actor wore spandex tights while earnestly opining about the meaning of Christmas. It wasn't until the film started getting rave reviews from test-screening audiences that New Line fully backed the project.

If *Old School* was a surprise hit, *Elf*—featuring uncredited rewrites by McKay—became a shocking sensation, grossing nearly three times as much worldwide as *Old School* and becoming an instant Christmas classic. Ferrell got most of the credit for the movie's success, thanks to his inspired turn as the naive human elf Buddy, whose cheerful disposition and upbeat attitude help to restore the world's Christmas spirit. Almost a decade after he first hit the TV mainstream on *SNL*, Ferrell was finally in demand in the film business.

Even so, he and McKay did not conceive *Anchorman* as a one-man showcase. Both envisioned the movie as a true ensemble, with Ferrell's pompous Ron Burgundy surrounded by his own "News Team" of equally incompetent and boorish sycophants. McKay and Ferrell, who'd honed their skills in the ensembles of the Groundlings, Second City, and *Saturday Night Live*, wanted to create a comedy that embraced that kind of supportive, team-driven joke telling. As Ferrell put it, "I never had that feeling of, 'I've got to make everyone in the room laugh!' I can just as easily sit quietly and have no one speak to me. Some comedians say they have to go on stage three or four times a week to exercise that muscle of 'being funny.' That's not me."

The duo also wanted to find performers who shared their background with (or at least enthusiasm for) improv comedy, and who could bring their own ideas to the already funny script. Their dream cast included John C. Reilly as Ron's oafish sportscaster sidekick Champ Kind, and Ben Stiller as the station's wolfish field reporter Brian Fantana. Neither of those ideas panned out, but Ferrell's increasing star power allowed McKay and Apatow to target lesser-known actors with the comedic chops to hold their own during extended on-set improvisations. That included Second City alumnus Steve Carell as the impossibly stupid weatherman Brick Tamland, Ferrell's former *SNL* costar David

Koechner as Champ, and Paul Rudd as Fantana. Although best known at the time as Alicia Silverstone's hunky love interest in the teen movie *Clueless*, Rudd was also a hardcore comedy fan who had already appeared in a small role in one of the funniest movies of the 2000s, *Wet Hot American Summer*.

The crux of *Anchorman*'s story—inspired by Jessica Savitch and honed by McKay and Ferrell, with some pointers from Apatow—focused on the fall and subsequent rise of Ron Burgundy, the king of San Diego news as the lead anchor of top-rated KVWN Channel 4. Life for the Channel 4 News Team is an endless swirl of parties, hangouts, and lightweight broadcasts that end with Ron's signature sign-off: "You stay classy, San Diego." Everything's going great for the News Team until the arrival of the network's first on-air female talent, Veronica Corningstone (Christina Applegate), who becomes the target of Ron and his cronies' ire for breaking up their boys club. ("It is anchor*man*, not anchor lady, and that is a scientific fact!" screams Champ in one meeting.) Even as they push back against Veronica's intrusion into their workplace, the men also squabble over the right to romance their beautiful new coworker. ("She's terrible! She has beautiful eyes and her hair smells like cinnamon!" a smitten Ron stammers.)

Like many other comedies of this period, *Anchorman* is about the terror a boys club faces when its sanctity is threatened by a female intruder. Unlike some of its contemporaries, though, *Anchorman* is deeply committed to mocking its boys club's members for their fragile egos, their unearned confidence, and their absolute ignorance about the ways of love (despite their insistence on their amorous abilities). Veronica easily and brutally cuts down all of the News Team's feeble pickup attempts—at least until Ron takes her on a friendly tour of San Diego and she's astounded by his virtuosic gifts with a jazz flute, including Ron slurping up a martini through his flute, then spraying the booze into a Zippo lighter, sending a huge flame bursting out the back of the instrument.

Bits like that one were scripted. (It's generally not advised to improvise jokes centered around large quantities of fire.) But by McKay's estimation at least 25 percent of *Anchorman* consists of material that was improvised on set. As a first-time director without an entrenched idea of the proper way to make a movie, McKay developed his own approach, one that encouraged collaboration and experimentation. First, the cast would film the scripted dialogue a couple times word for word. Then they would keep the cameras rolling and let the actors try whatever they wanted—"alts," in the parlance of a McKay set.

Improvisation had been a cornerstone of American comedy for decades by the early 2000s, but for the most part it remained siloed off in the world of live performance. With a few rare exceptions, like the occasional film from *Waiting for Guffman* director Christopher Guest, Hollywood considered improv antithetical to a fiscally responsible production. "Making it up as you went along" was an easy way to waste time and, more importantly, money. As a result, comedies could be wild and gross, like *Animal House* and *There's Something About Mary*, but they were rarely permitted to be spontaneous—at least until filmmakers like Adam McKay came along.

Some of *Anchorman*'s most memorable bits emerged from alts. At one point, the entire film stopped so Ron and the News Team could work through their feelings about Veronica by singing a note-perfect a cappella rendition of the Starland Vocal Band's "Afternoon Delight." Paul Rudd threw out the idea in the middle of production, prompting a flurry of rehearsals. Likewise, an oft-quoted moment late in the film, when Ron collapses into sobs in a phone booth and wails, "I am in a glass case of emotion!" after his beloved dog, Baxter, gets kicked off the side of a bridge by a misanthropic biker (it's a long story), emerged from an improv run sparked by a single line in the script.

"I gave the brilliant note of 'Keep going, only bigger,'" McKay recalled, "which is a great note to give Will."

"Keep going, only bigger" describes the creative impulse behind all of *Anchorman*. It features a psychedelic dream sequence in lieu of a love scene between Ron and Veronica, and a violent back-alley brawl between the News Team and their rivals from San Diego's other TV stations—including Ferrell's *Old School* costars Luke Wilson and Vince Vaughn, plus Ben Stiller as a Spanish-language newsman—in which several reporters get brutally murdered. One even gets impaled by a trident hurled by the oafish Brick Tamland. ("Brick, I've been meaning to talk to you about that," Ron counsels in the rumble's aftermath. "You should find yourself a safe house or a relative close by. Lay low for a while, because you're probably wanted for murder.")

In other words, *Anchorman* did not lack in the silliness department. It was also steeped in McKay's love of confrontation, if a slightly gentler strain than the one practiced by the Upright Citizens Brigade. *Anchorman* is loaded with superficial trappings of 1970s nostalgia; Ron and the crew saunter through the film in gaudy vintage fashions, soundtracked by a playlist of golden oldies. But the movie constantly interrogates the notion that these were the "good old days," at least for anyone who wasn't a straight white guy. Ron and his buddies possess so little self-awareness they believe their own hype, unaware that perhaps reporting on Nutty the Water-Skiing Squirrel is not the most effective use of their channel's resources or their audience's time.

Even in the film's big climax, where Ron "rescues" Veronica after she falls into a pen filled with bears while reporting a story at a local zoo, Ron himself fixes nothing. His dog, Baxter, is the one who actually saves Veronica. (Baxter survived the bridge punting—it's also a long story.) Then Ron, who got fired for cursing on the air and broke up with Veronica after he accused her of swiping his spotlight, gets his job *and* Veronica back for . . . not really doing anything of note. Ron doesn't learn or grow or change or apologize. He simply fails upward, as so many Ron Burgundys in the world do. Howling in a glass case of emotion, he doesn't even stay classy while doing it.

Anchorman was an exceptional comedy about how macho mediocrity masquerades as exceptionalism. The film's reception in theaters was not necessarily exceptional, though, at least not right away. *Anchorman* earned $90 million at the box office, only a few million more than *Old School* and nowhere near what *Elf* had grossed the year prior. And some of the reviews were savage. The one in the Manhattan newspaper *amNewYork* compared *Anchorman* to a bad Jim Carrey movie and said, "It mistakes unfunny male chauvinist buffoonery for [comedy]."

Its most important impact on the world of comedy arrived later, with the release of a film that might never have happened without *Anchorman*. It all stemmed from a conversation Judd Apatow had with Steve Carell between takes on the set, when he asked if Carell had any movie ideas of his own.

CHAPTER 12

Smart-Dumb Comedy

One day you'll look back on all this and laugh. Say we were young and stupid. Couple of dumb kids running around.

—Jeremy Grey, *Wedding Crashers*

Two weeks before *Old School* opened in theaters and rejuvenated his film career, Vince Vaughn attended the Hollywood premiere of a rival movie comedy.

Shanghai Knights was a sequel to the 2000 hit *Shanghai Noon.* The franchise offered a unique blend of genres: mismatched-buddy Western comedy martial arts pictures headlined by Jackie Chan as, ahem, "Chon Wang." (Say it aloud; that helps sell the joke.) The indomitable action hero's sidekick in both films was played by Owen Wilson, whose mellow onscreen vibes played well opposite the hyperactive Hong Kong action star.

Vaughn went to the *Shanghai Knights* premiere to support its director, David Dobkin. The two had worked on Dobkin's directorial debut, 1998's *Clay Pigeons*, one of the many serial killer–centric movies Vaughn made after *Swingers*.

"We had a great connection and had been looking for years for something," says Dobkin. "He was in the foreground talking to me. He was giving me notes on the movie, which was kind of funny, little trims that he would have done. And I was watching him, and across the room I can see Owen talking to somebody. And I was looking at Vince and looking at Owen; the thing that popped in my head was Abbott and Costello. I love buddy comedy, and my agent knew I had been looking for an R-rated comedy. That's where my sensibility was. Everything I liked was R. And I turned to my agent and said, 'You know the movie I've been looking for? Let's find something for Vince and Owen.'"

Two months later, Dobkin's agent brought him something. It originated as a very simple idea from a producer named Andrew Panay. Years earlier, Panay was hanging out in Vegas when he stumbled across a wedding reception. The guests looked like they were having so much fun that Panay couldn't help himself; he snuck into the party and joined the festivities. He only did it that one time, and only for a few minutes. But it was such a great experience, he couldn't get it out of his mind. Eventually, he wondered: What if a couple buddies snuck into weddings as a hobby? It sounded like a movie.

Panay pitched the idea to a pair of screenwriters, Steve Faber and Bob Fisher, who had written a comedy script called *We're the Millers* that was getting some attention around Hollywood. Initially, Faber and Fisher weren't convinced Panay's notion had enough juice for feature-length comedy.

"We weren't sure, right off the bat, if it was going to be able to sustain a whole movie," Bob Fisher said. "We figured, obviously, one of the guys will fall in love and that'll be kind of his thing. It really came together for us, however, when we came up with the idea that the family the two women that Vince and Owen are interested in are very much like the Kennedys. . . . When we thought about that, we knew we were on the road to [the idea] becoming a cool movie."

Fisher had once spent a summer interning for a congressman in Washington, D.C., and sneaking into lobbyist events for the free food and booze. The script Faber and Fisher wrote blended their interest in the inner workings of powerful political families with Panay's wedding-crashing concept, yielding a script that Dobkin said contained "a couple of the funniest set pieces" he'd ever read. He then added several more scenes beefing up the friendship between the two leads, yielding "a coming-of-age story for thirty-five-year-old men still in their 'chasing girls mode' and hadn't dealt with love yet . . . that was very much built out of trying to find something for Vince and Owen."

Vaughn and Wilson would ultimately play Jeremy and John, two best friends who work together as divorce mediators. In their spare time, they crash weddings, both because weddings are really fun, and also because they're filled with swooning single women so besotted with their romantic surroundings that they're easily swept off their feet and into the heroes' beds by a series of false identities. (At one wedding, Vaughn pretends to be a member of the French Foreign Legion; at another, he wistfully recalls the good men they lost climbing Mount Everest.)

But then John breaks one of the cardinal rules of wedding crashing set down by the duo's often-mentioned, never-seen mentor Chazz Reinhold: He falls in love. Smitten with Claire (Rachel McAdams), the sister of the bride at a glitzy Washington, DC, wedding, John cons his way into an invite to her family's compound in Maryland, where his obvious feelings for her put him into conflict with Claire's obnoxious boyfriend (Bradley Cooper). While John and Jeremy hobnob with Claire's father, the U.S. secretary of the treasury (Christopher Walken), and John's relationship with Claire gets more serious, Jeremy contends with Claire's younger sister, Gloria (Isla Fisher), who hooks up with him at the wedding, then reveals that she was, at least until their meeting, a virgin. The now-deflowered Gloria spends the rest of the film forcing Jeremy to help her tap into all sorts of wild but previously undiscovered sexual proclivities.

Just how wild those proclivities could get, though, was a matter of debate between Dobkin, the cast, and the studio. From the very beginning, *Wedding Crashers* was conceived as a throwback to the R-rated comedies of yesteryear.

"I grew up [loving] these rated-R comedies like *Animal House* and this stuff," Vaughn said during the *Wedding Crashers* press tour in 2005. "So for me, if you're going to do an adult themed movie called *Wedding Crashers*, well, what are you going to do? You gotta get into it, and it's *fun* to get into it."

In the case of *Wedding Crashers*, a story about two unapologetic cads sleeping their way around the Washington, D.C., wedding scene, it definitely made sense to push the envelope a little. (*Wedding Crashers*' big partying montage was set to a cover of the Isley Brothers' "Shout," the same song used in *Animal House*'s big toga party scene—an homage Dobkin says was "absolutely" intentional.) Including a little nudity and several sex scenes didn't necessarily lend the film a sense of maturity—if anything, it lent the film the *opposite*—but it did allow the film to speak in the four-letter language that guys like John and Jeremy would use in real life.

That didn't mean that the studio was necessarily keen on the plan. An R rating meant that teenage boys, traditionally the core audience for raunchy comedies like *Wedding Crashers*, would be unable to buy a ticket to the movie. From a box office perspective, the film could be shooting itself in the foot if its R rating kept its target demographic away. Dobkin says the studio at one point even offered him money—"like, a lot of money, like twice as much as I made on the movie"—to cut *Wedding Crashers* down to PG-13.

"I really fought to keep [the rating] what it is, and they ultimately honored that," Dobkin recalled. "I also just think that real life is R-rated—as an adult, that's just how people really talk."

Some sequences got *so* R-rated, though, they threatened to tip the film over into NC-17 territory. In one of *Wedding Crashers*' most graphic scenes, Gloria gives Jeremy a hand job under the table during a family dinner. The initial cut included close-ups of her rubbing his crotch through his pants; those images had to be reshot after editor Mark Livolsi got a look at the initial footage, which employed a prosthetic stunt penis, and realized they would never get an R rating if they used it. A second version that, in Livolsi's words, was "a little subtler," was filmed. (If you've seen the movie, the fact that *this* was the "subtler" take might surprise you.)

All through production, *Wedding Crashers*' raunchy sexual humor, along with the central conceit of dudes lying their way into weddings (and then into some of the more attractive guests' arms) kept those in charge at the film's distributor, New Line Cinema, nervous. Dobkin recalled meetings with the studio, where they warned him that they couldn't sell the film.

"The head of marketing was like, 'They're predators. This is such a dark movie,'" recalls Dobkin. "I had a completely different interpretation. I was like, 'They *love* weddings. They love the music, the grandparents, the kids, the food. It's a good time! And the by-product is they get girls—but they get the girls by attracting them. The girls are choosing them. . . . [Jeremy and John] are creating the best weddings ever.'"

Ultimately, audiences agreed with Dobkin. While *Wedding Crashers*' sexual content might have pushed a few boundaries for a studio movie, and its premise could read on paper like a celebration of misogyny, its storyline was pure screwball comedy, with a pair of mismatched couples facing various obstacles to their love before an inevitable resolution. Jeremy and John begin the movie as unrepentant scoundrels, but they both wind up in committed relationships. Wild as some individual scenes may have been, *Wedding Crashers*' celebration of monogamy and marriage was almost old-fashioned.

It also showed the power of great casting, not just of Wilson and Vaughn as a duo, but also in picking relative unknowns like McAdams, whose star-making turn in *The Notebook* had yet to premiere when she was hired, and Cooper, who was best known at the time for a character on the TV spy series *Alias* who became so superfluous to its ongoing espionage storyline that he was eventually written out of the show.

The movie also showed the value of casting guys like Vaughn and Wilson—both skilled improvisers and working screenwriters—as the leads of a comedy. Dobkin let the pair each tailor their characters to their own voices, and to punch up their dialogue whenever they deemed necessary. Vaughn later said that when they worked with the script during rehearsals "there wasn't a scene that we didn't go through and change." ("We wanted to make sure it wasn't just about some tomcats, some frat guys," Wilson concurred.)

That included massaging the plot to push the buddy dynamics between John and Jeremy to the center of the movie. Like *Starsky & Hutch*, *Wedding Crashers*' true love story is the platonic one between the two male leads, who even undergo a classic sort of rom-com breakup during the second act after John discovers that Jeremy has fallen for Gloria. ("The secret of *Wedding Crashers* is that it's a chick flick dressed up like a guy movie," notes Dobkin.) In the original script, John was supposed to interrupt Claire's wedding to Cooper's evocatively named Sack Lodge, an homage to the famous climax of *The Graduate*. In the revised version, the climactic wedding is between Jeremy and Gloria, and John shows up not only to win back Claire but to make amends with his best bud as well.

"That's what the movie is really about. 'Wait a minute. You fell in love with someone? What about *us*?'" Dobkin explains. "It was one of those moments where I had a very personal story to tell about being young, being kind of a nerd and a loser, my group of friends was really tight, none of us had girlfriends. And then finally someone had a girlfriend—and they're dragging the girl along or they're not around anymore. And either version felt like a breakup."

Despite *Wedding Crashers*' R-rated sexual humor—or maybe because of it—a huge audience showed up to see the film in theaters. By the time *Wedding Crashers* ended its run in multiplexes, it had become the first R-rated comedy in history to gross more than $200 million at the U.S. box office. Coming closely on the heels of *Old School*, it was clear: The moviegoing audience wanted more adult comedies.

Susan Wloszczyna's *USA Today* article that dubbed Stiller, Ferrell, Wilson, and Vaughn part of Hollywood's "Frat Pack" was reported from the *Wedding Crashers* set and published back in the summer of 2004. By the time *Wedding Crashers* debuted in theaters on July 15, 2005, the rest of the media had taken the ball and run with it. In March of that same year, *The New York Times* published a 2,500-word profile of the crew it dubbed "Hollywood's Funniest Clique," citing all the same on-screen performers, but also mentioning filmmakers Adam McKay and Judd Apatow, and even agents like United Talent Agency's Nick Stevens, who represented Stiller, and talent managers like Eric Gold and Jimmy Miller, who worked with Ferrell, Vaughn, Apatow, and others.

The group, the *Times*' Sharon Waxman wrote, was "reshaping screen humor to their liking" by "coming up with their own concepts, finding screenwriters and then offering the whole package for production—script, director and cast, take it or leave it." Stiller's producer Stuart Cornfeld told the *Times* that the men not only collaborated on shared projects, they also offered support and suggestions on films they weren't directly involved in, citing an instance where Apatow had recently attended a reading of one of Stiller's scripts and offered his notes, despite the fact that Apatow wasn't technically working on the film. Cornfeld labeled their collective body of work "smart-dumb comedy."

The whole piece was bullish about this "clique" and their enormous success, but small hints of concern creep in at the margins of the article. In one paragraph, Waxman notes that the studios like making these comedies because of "their low production cost and their huge return at the box office." In the next, she reveals that those production costs weren't as low as they used to be. The more the Frat Pack's movies made money, the more its actors, writers, and directors could charge for their services.

The script for Vince Vaughn's follow-up to *Wedding Crashers*, *The Break-Up*, for example, had recently sold at auction for $2.25 million, plus another $12 million to Vaughn to star in the film and produce it. A few years earlier, that figure would cover almost the entire cost of one of these comedies. A few months after the *Times*' article, *Wedding Crashers* opened in theaters, shattered records for an R-rated comedy, and ensured that Wilson's and Vaughn's salaries would rise even higher.

One of the guys who saw *Wedding Crashers* in the summer of 2005 was Judd Apatow, who was getting ready to release his feature directorial debut later that year. Like *Wedding Crashers*, Apatow's movie was an R-rated comedy filled with provocative jokes. Apatow liked *Wedding Crashers*, but when he left the theater he only had one thought about his own movie:

"Oh my gosh, we're 100 times dirtier than that."

CHAPTER 13

Wax Philosophical

I respect women! I love women! I respect them so much that I completely stay away from them!

—Andy Stitzer, *The 40-Year-Old Virgin*

People in Hollywood talk about the lingering pain of a canceled project. For Judd Apatow, that sting was all too literal.

Apatow became so stressed-out fighting to keep *Freaks and Geeks* on the air that he wound up with a herniated disc. Surgery helped ease the physical discomfort, but the emotional hurt only worsened over time, especially after he created another critically acclaimed and low-rated show called *Undeclared*—ostensibly a spiritual sequel to *Freaks and Geeks* with a similar group of misfits struggling to survive their freshman year of college.

Undeclared may have aired on a different network (Fox instead of NBC), but the results were uncannily similar. The series was canceled after a single season of seventeen episodes, exactly one less than *Freaks and Geeks* had produced the year prior. As if that wasn't infuriating enough, the executive who had canceled *The Ben Stiller Show* nearly a decade earlier put the kibosh on *Undeclared*—right as *Time* magazine declared it one of the ten best series on television. An understandably agitated Apatow framed the article and mailed it to the exec with a Post-it note attached. It read: "I don't know if you just fucked me in the ass again or you just never took it out in 1992. Merry Christmas, Judd."

The early 2000s were filled with disappointments for Apatow. He channeled some of these frustrations with the industry (along with his anxieties about having failed his *Freaks and Geeks* cast) into a pilot about unemployed actors called *North Hollywood*. He managed to convince the network to let him cast *Freaks and Geeks* star Jason Segel, along with *Sick in the Head* alum (and future *Saturday Night Live* star) Amy Poehler, future *Mad Men* star January Jones, and future comedy megastar Kevin Hart. *North Hollywood* was produced for yet another network (ABC), but the result was the same: The pilot never went anywhere. By that point, Apatow had spent almost a decade ping-ponging back and forth between movies and TV, each time with about the same level of success—that is to say, not much.

"What I used to do," he explained, "is if a movie failed, I would go back and work on television, and if my television show got cancelled, I would go and make a movie."

So Apatow went and produced *Anchorman* for Will Ferrell and director Adam McKay. At last, something he worked on broke through the mainstream. And on *Anchorman*, Apatow met Steve Carell, whose prodigious improvisational skills impressed him so much, he suggested they collaborate on a vehicle that Carell could headline himself.

After *Anchorman* wrapped, Carell pitched Apatow an idea he really liked, based on a sketch he'd done in Second City about a group of buddies playing poker. The men begin sharing stories about their sexual exploits, each more graphic than the last—all except the ones shared by the character played by Carell, whose interjections are so bizarre it quickly becomes clear he has never had sex in his life.

"He's saying things like 'Oh you know when you feel a woman's breasts and it feels like a bag of sand?'" Carell recalled. "And all the other guys are going, 'What? What are you talking about?' 'Well, you know, kind of like a bag of sand! You know what I'm saying!' And he tries to just get by, and they finally call him out on it."

"I just thought, 'That's the greatest idea I've ever heard,'" Apatow said. "And I was really afraid to direct a movie and had not really pursued it because I didn't feel like I would do a good job. And then I heard that idea, and I said, 'Unfortunately I understand this.' It's not like I was a virgin till I was forty, but I certainly had very long spans in between sex. I'd go a decade here and there. I understood the issue."

Carell explained the scenario and reiterated to Apatow that this virgin character he had in mind was "not a weirdo," just a guy "who's my age but hasn't experienced *that*. . . . [Sex] just passed him by."

"And that's a lot of what *Freaks and Geeks* was," Apatow added, "just terror of intimacy and that people will think that you're a freak; they'll discover the thing that you're afraid might be true."

Apatow immediately took Carell's concept to Universal executive Mary Parent. Her response: "I'll buy that." Apatow and Carell had a deal to write *The 40-Year-Old Virgin*.

"We turned [the script] in on Friday," Carell said, "and they greenlit it on Monday."

For Carell, the deal meant an overnight success decades in the making. Already forty-three by the time *The 40-Year-Old Virgin* came to theaters, he'd worked as an actor for more than twenty years before his moment finally arrived. His dream all through those years was not to become a movie star; he just hoped to stay employed.

"I set the bar there for myself," Carell said. "I dreamt of being able to make a living doing something that I love, and that really does make me happy and is fun. Being a leading man . . . that's like saying I want to be an astronaut. That's not going to happen."

And yet it did, eventually, for Steven John Carell, born in 1962 in Massachusetts, the youngest of four sons to Edwin, an engineer, and Harriet, a psychiatric nurse, who recalled that she and her husband were "obsessive and uptight" raising Steve's three older brothers, and were "worn out" by the time he came along. "So we just relaxed and enjoyed him, and he entertained us."

But his parents also worked hard enough to send Carell to private school. As a result, he "felt a responsibility to make good on their investment" to such a degree that for most of his childhood he never considered a career in acting, despite a lifelong love of performing and a double major in theater and history from Denison University. It wasn't until Carell graduated from college and prepared to apply for law school that he started to second-guess things.

"I remember I sat down with my mom and dad," Carell recalled, "and I knew *they* knew my heart wasn't in it. And I remember we made a list of all the things I liked to do. Like, well, I played hockey growing up. Am I gonna be a professional hockey player? Probably not. And acting always came up. It was always like an extracurricular something that I always did, I always had fun doing. So that was a reoccurring theme. So they said, 'You know what? Just do that. At least give it a shot.'"

So he did. He moved to Chicago, partly because he was intimidated by New York and Los Angeles and assumed he'd get lost in the shuffle on either coast. He also loved Chicago's theater scene, in particular Second City, famed for its decades of sketch and improv alumni who had gone on to perform on *Saturday Night Live* and in movies. The Second City touring company had swung through Denison while Carell was there. For a guy who'd never dreamed bigger than becoming a working actor, the life of a Second City member traveling the world and performing at colleges sounded like a pretty sweet job.

Carell claims he wasn't a natural at improv; he found it "scary and frustrating" at first and spent his whole first semester "yelling at other people . . . mostly out of fear." Eventually, he got comfortable, and then he got good—so good that he was promoted to Second City's main company and taught in its school. He told students to look at improv as "a prolonged game of chess. There's an opening gambit with your pawn in a complex game I have with one character, and lots of side games with other characters." By the mid-'90s, Carell was one of Second City's grand masters—but he was already in his thirties with little else of note on his resume besides a couple of fast-food commercials. An agent warned him: "If it doesn't happen for you soon it's not going to happen."

And then it happened. Carell landed an audition for *The Dana Carvey Show*, the *Saturday Night Live* cast member and master impressionist's attempt to branch out into prime time. Series co-creator Robert Smigel said they couldn't believe their good fortune that a guy as talented as Carell had gone under the radar so long and fell into their laps.

"Out of everybody who auditioned," he said, "it was just like, '*That* guy's gonna be on the show.'"

In a strange twist, Carell got cast alongside his understudy from Second City, another improv wizard named Stephen Colbert. Already comfortable working together, the pair developed some ingenious sketches on *The Dana Carvey Show*, including a hilariously simple one with the extremely descriptive title "Waiters Who Are Nauseated by Food." Colbert based the sketch on something he used to do with his coworkers as a waiter back in Chicago. He looked directly into the camera and attempted to read off a list of specials, but kept getting derailed trying to describe "creamy fish chowder with chunks of potato, corn, and scallops" because, well, he's a waiter who is nauseated by food.

With its incredible cast, and a writing staff that included Smigel, future *30 Rock* showrunner Robert Carlock, and future Academy Award–winning screenwriter Charlie Kaufman, *The Dana Carvey Show* looked like a surefire hit. But the show's anarchic comedic style—the very first sketch of the very first episode included Carvey as President Clinton stripped to the waist while infants and puppies suckled from six doglike teats surgically implanted into his torso—made for a poor fit with its lead-in, the family-friendly sitcom *Home Improvement*. ABC canceled *The Dana Carvey Show* after only eight episodes.

Carell could have been bitter about his big break turning into a big flop, but with characteristic humbleness, he said that his only takeaways from the experience were "gratefulness" and the confidence that he could hang on a network television show. "To this day," Carell said in the documentary *Too Funny to Fail: The Life & Death of The Dana Carvey Show*, "I point to Robert [Smigel] and to Dana [Carvey] as the main factors for what happened with the rest of my career. They absolutely put me on the map."

Stephen Colbert deserves some credit, too. Because in 1997, he was the one who landed a job as a correspondent on the political comedy series *The Daily Show*. And when a few years later, producers asked if he could recommend anyone else as a potential correspondent, Colbert pointed to his former castmate at Second City and *The Dana Carvey Show*. When the producers asked Colbert what they might know Carell from, it was "Waiters Who Are Nauseated by Food" that got their attention and landed Carell *The Daily Show*—over the advice of his agents, who warned him he shouldn't take the job on a low-rated cable series.

Then *The Daily Show* exploded in popularity during its coverage of the 2000 presidential election. Carell and Colbert, often playing off each other in collaborative segments (though never, alas, as News Reporters Nauseated by Food), both became audience favorites. Carell's *Daily Show* schtick as a pompous broadcaster led to more gigs, including a crucial supporting turn as a TV news blowhard in 2003's *Bruce Almighty*. In Carell's big scene, Jim Carrey's Bruce, who has been imbued with all of God's powers, uses his divine gifts to compel Carell's Evan Baxter to read the wrong copy off the teleprompter, and then boast in a pompous anchorman voice about his "tiny little nipples," audibly fart a couple times, and spew torrents of wild gibberish.

It was a tour de force performance, one that starts very small—Carell manages to communicate the fact that he's not in control of his mouth (or his bowels) with several tiny deer-in-the-headlights glances—and ends about as big as humanly possible, with Carell wailing at the top of his lungs. With his slicked newsman hair and crisp suit, he

Judd Apatow and Ben Stiller at the 1993 Primetime Emmy Awards, celebrating their win for Outstanding Writing in a Variety or Music Program nine months after Fox pulled *The Ben Stiller Show* from the air.

National Lampoon cofounder and *National Lampoon's Animal House* cowriter Doug Kenney, John Belushi, and *Animal House* cowriter Chris Miller, on the set of *Animal House*. Kenney and Miller also played Delta House members Stork and Hardbar in the film.

Ben Stiller at the precise moment he became a massive comedy star in *There's Something About Mary*.

Stiller (right) with Owen Wilson,
both so hot right now as they star in Stiller's *Zoolander*.

Above: The stars of *Old School*: From left, Will Ferrell, Luke Wilson, and Vince Vaughn.

Left: Will Ferrell (and some convincingly mortified background extras) as he prepares to go streaking in *Old School*.

Below: Director Todd Phillips (left) works on a *Starsky & Hutch* scene with stars Owen Wilson and Ben Stiller.

John C. Reilly and Will Ferrell surrounded by (and clothed in) product placement in a scene from *Talladega Nights: The Ballad of Ricky Bobby.*

Above: Will Ferrell and Adam McKay staying classy on the set of *Anchorman: The Legend of Ron Burgundy.*

Below: Reilly, McKay, and Ferrell welcome you to the set of *Step Brothers.*

Owen Wilson and Vince Vaughn filming the scene from *Wedding Crashers* that inspired the name "Frat Pack."

Judd Apatow (right) directs Steve Carell on the set of *The 40-Year-Old Virgin*.

Above: Sacha Baron Cohen (right) as his Kazakh alter ego Borat Sagdiyev in a scene from *Borat: Cultural Learnings of America for Make Benefit Glorious Nation of Kazakhstan.*

Below: The real Seth Rogen (far left) and Evan Goldberg (far right) with their fictional alter egos from *Superbad*, played by Jonah Hill (center left) and Michael Cera (center right).

Todd Phillips (center right) with the "Wolfpack"—Ed Helms, Bradley Cooper, and Zach Galifianakis—on the set of *The Hangover Part II*, which grossed a staggering $586.7 million worldwide.

Director Paul Feig (left) and star and cowriter Kristen Wiig sharing a laugh on the set of *Bridesmaids*.

Vince Vaughn and Owen Wilson attempting to recreate the magic of *Wedding Crashers* eight years later, on the set of *The Internship*.

Judd Apatow and Ben Stiller, thirty years after their first chance meeting, at a 2022 screening of Stiller's Apple TV+ series *Severance*.

looked every bit the mild-mannered broadcaster—which made his sudden bursts of uncontrollable madness even funnier.

It was the first time most moviegoers discovered that no one alive is funnier while yelling on camera than Steve Carell. He doesn't even need a joke—in fact, sometimes he's funnier *without* a joke. Just let Steve Carell shout. He'll make people laugh. One of his most memorable *Dana Carvey Show* sketches was something called "Germans Who Say Nice Things." The whole joke is Carell and Dana Carvey bellowing innocuous sentences like "IT VAS A PLEASURE BABYSITTING KEVIN!" in over-the-top Teutonic accents. In *Bruce Almighty*, Carell was so funny screaming nonsense that he did the impossible: He stole a Jim Carrey movie from Jim Carrey. Soon after, Carell played idiotic TV weatherman Brick Tamland in *Anchorman*, where he got one of the biggest laughs in the film simply by howling, "LOUD NOISES!" in costar Fred Willard's face.

The 40-Year-Old Virgin gave Carell several opportunities to show off his gift for shrieking, most famously in the set piece where his character, virginal Andy Stitzer, agrees to get his chest waxed as part of a misguided attempt to become more appealing to women. Apatow and Carell had envisioned the scene as their answer to rom-com makeover montages where a supposedly ugly caterpillar takes off their glasses, blows out their hair, and metamorphoses into a beautiful butterfly. In *The 40-Year-Old Virgin* the caterpillar gets brutally, hilariously waxed. Committed actor that he is, Carell insisted they wax him for real and film his genuine reaction to the sticky agony.

So Apatow set up five cameras, hired an actress with waxing experience, and, well, let 'er rip. They only got one shot at it—you can't *un*-wax someone's chest, after all—and so they kept rolling as the actress playing the aesthetician yanked out chunks of Carell's body hair, all while he shouted nonsense like "NOOOOOO KELLY CLARKSON!" If you look closely, you'll see drops of blood accumulating in the waxed areas. (Even though they cast an actress who claimed to have waxing experience, Apatow now suspects she exaggerated her resume "because she clearly didn't know how to do it, and we almost ripped [Steve's] nipples off during the shoot.")

The waxing scene became an iconic comedy set piece, but Apatow and Carell envisioned *The 40-Year-Old Virgin* as more than an over-the-top laugh fest. They conceived virginal Andy Stitzer not as a punch line but as an authentic, imperfect person. Apatow could relate to Andy's fear of humiliation and his endless array of bad dates. Like Apatow, the guy who turned to stand-up comedy to help him understand a world that didn't make sense, Andy is a searcher looking for answers to life's big questions. ("I don't think I've ever written anything more personal than that," Apatow said in 2014.)

Certain scenes (like, say, the one where a woman waxes random areas of Steve Carell's body) were clearly heightened. But most of *The 40-Year-Old Virgin* was downright mundane. Andy works in the stockroom of "SmartTech," a Circuit City–esque electronics retailer, and a large portion of the movie is set in and around the store as Andy and the other employees assist customers, complain about the nonstop soundtrack of Michael McDonald songs, and discuss their jobs and lives. When Andy's not at work, he collects vintage toys he keeps in their original packaging—an obvious metaphor for the virgin's pristine, untouched condition.

The 40-Year-Old Virgin's outer packaging was a sex-obsessed comedy about a horny guy who really wants to get laid. But that surface belied a surprisingly sensitive portrait of a lonely and in some ways tragic figure. Andy's first sexual encounter at the movie's climax (sorry) is not treated as a big goof but an emotionally cathartic moment, a delicate balance of tones inspired by one of Apatow's favorite movies, *Fast Times at Ridgemont High*, the Cameron Crowe–written, Amy Heckerling–directed portrait of teen life in the 1980s.

"It pulls off a couple of things at the same time," Apatow explained. "One is it has this really hilarious broad humor with Sean Penn as Spicoli. But Jennifer Jason Leigh gets pregnant and has an abortion in it and it's played straight. . . . That has always been one of the main models: Can I have this feel real but still wax Steve Carell? Can I have you care about him, but when I wax him does the reality level not go out the window?"

Like *Fast Times*, *The 40-Year-Old Virgin* is also an ensemble piece with a great cast, including Carell's *Anchorman* costar Paul Rudd as Andy's SmartTech colleague (and pornography fanatic) David. Apatow loved Rudd's chemistry with actor Romany Malco in an improvised movie called *The Château*, so he joined the SmartTech crew as their coworker Jay. Their boss at the shop was played by Second City alum Jane Lynch. Apatow's wife, Leslie Mann, played one of Andy's potential romantic partners, a woman who is so drunk she nearly kills them both driving home from a bar. (She also pukes on Andy in the process—a, ahem, gag that Mann felt so strongly about she made her own fake vomit from yogurt and granola.)

Carell's first choice for Andy's love interest, the kind divorcée and hot grandmother Trish, was Catherine Keener—who was not necessarily a comedian, but who could bring a real sense of weight to Trish and Andy's relationship, which goes through a tumultuous series of ups and downs, partly because Andy keeps his virginity a secret from her for as long as he possibly can.

Many members of *The 40-Year-Old Virgin* cast, including Carell himself, were enormously talented comics who had never been given the right outlet onscreen to show the full range of their gifts. Just as he had when he helped assemble a cast of unknowns for *Freaks and Geeks* who would later become huge stars, Apatow had a great eye for untapped potential.

"One of Judd's very special qualities is he really pushed a lot of people," says Rodney Rothman, who collaborated with Apatow on *Undeclared* and films like *Forgetting Sarah Marshall* and *Year One.* "Behind the scenes there was a tremendous amount of creative freedom given to people who were chomping at the bit to do interesting things. From the vantage point of twenty years later, that was really unusual. Judd was not a micromanager. He was more of a mentor figure. He made space for these people to do this stuff and he seemed to genuinely enjoy when people connected." *The 40-Year-Old Virgin* producer Clayton Townsend compares Apatow to "a master cook who finds an ingredient that's obscure and different and puts it into a dish and makes it distinct to his style."

No ingredient in *The 40-Year-Old Virgin*'s supporting cast was more important than *Freaks and Geeks* alum Seth Rogen, who was one of Apatow's first hires on the film as Andy's filthy coworker Cal, and as Apatow's coproducer and unofficial sounding board. "Seth was invaluable coming to the set every day when he wasn't performing and just pitching jokes to everybody," Apatow noted. "I waited a long time to direct because I wanted to have a situation I felt comfortable in and felt I could express myself, and I wanted to work with people I understood what they do comedically. I was also scared to death of doing that job and never being allowed to do it again."

If Apatow was anxious about his feature directorial debut, he hid it well. Townsend says Apatow "didn't seem like a first-timer at all" on set, thanks to his experience writing, producing, and occasionally directing a decade's worth of television prior to *The 40-Year-Old Virgin*. Still, his nerves were understandable, especially when Universal shut down production on *The 40-Year-Old Virgin* after just two days of shooting. The studio took one look at the early dailies and were horrified by endless footage of Carell riding a bicycle and walking down the street looking at posters of scantily clad women. Apatow and Carell were both summoned to an emergency meeting at the Universal lot.

"In the end, it had to do with a haircut. They thought Steve was too creepy-looking," remembers Townsend.

Executives peppered the duo with questions: "What *is* this movie? He looks like a serial killer! Is he going to kill someone?" They explained that what they were seeing were establishing shots and material that was going to be used in montages. In context, it *would* be funny. (They did concede that out of context Carell did look kind of creepy.) One haircut later, Universal let production resume, but Carell became convinced Universal had no faith in *Virgin* and was going to bury the film.

Despite the rocky start, Apatow and Carell made a great team. Using the same techniques he'd learned from Ben Stiller on *The Ben Stiller Show*—and more recently used by Adam McKay on *Anchorman*—Apatow gave Carell and the rest of the cast the freedom to invent on set, not only to beef up *Virgin*'s humor, but also to enrich the story and the characters' relationships.

"At the end of the day, maybe it's 20 percent that gets on the screen," Apatow explained. "I like the actors to know that if they ever think of anything during any take, they can change it. What happens is then the other actor is a little more in the moment because they don't know what's coming at them. It might be the script, but it might not be the script. So everyone pays attention differently and the acting level comes way up. Some great things that we've done are only because we did improvisations."

For example, an entire scene in the film grew out of a riff that only happened because of a rainstorm. A twenty-one-year-old actor named Jonah Hill had impressed Apatow in his audition for the movie, landing a tiny role in a scene set in Trish's store, where she sells people's stuff on eBay. (Even the store was a sort of improvisation; while scouting locations in Encino, they found a real "We Sell Your Stuff on eBay" store and wrote it into the movie.) While Andy tries to ask Trish out on a first date, Hill's nameless customer wanders over with a pair of sparkly platform boots with goldfish inside the soles. But Trish won't sell them to him; she doesn't sell *anything* in the store, she only sells stuff on eBay. That prompts an increasingly tense exchange as the befuddled Hill repeatedly tries to purchase the "wonderful" boots.

"On the day we shot that," Apatow recalled, "it rained and so we had like three free hours. And as a goof, I said, 'Let's let Jonah improvise with Catherine.'" The scene went so well that he added it to a test screening of the film.

"I said, 'Let's chuck in like ninety seconds of Jonah being mean to Catherine Keener,' just to see if people like him," Apatow continued. "Not that we thought that we would put it in the movie. And it just got such giant laughs we thought, 'Well, maybe for no reason the movie can stop its story cold to just let Jonah Hill go nuts.' And people liked it." Those couple hours of improv on a rainy day launched Hill's career.

Initially, Apatow's improv-driven style did not endear him to his crew. After a two-hour riffing session between Rudd and Rogen, Apatow remembers "the crew seemed really annoyed." Rogen bumped into some of those same crew members after shooting had wrapped; he chuckles on *The 40-Year-Old Virgin* DVD commentary that they "seemed shocked the movie cut together. . . . I literally don't think they thought it would cut together into what you would call 'a movie.'"

Ironically, the scene that annoyed the crew so much became one of the most famous in the entire film, with Rudd's and Rogen's characters smoking from a bong and playing the ultraviolent video game *Mortal Kombat* while they trade a series of back-and-forth homophobic insults like "Do you know how I know you're gay? You like the movie *Maid in Manhattan*," and "You know how I know *you're* gay? I saw you make a spinach dip in a loaf of sourdough bread once."

The sequence got enormous reactions in test screenings, but the degree to which the scene is mocking the homophobia of straight men or using that scenario as a pretext to land a few cheap laughs at gay viewers' expense remains a matter of some debate, even among those who made it. Asked about the sequence in 2025 during *The 40-Year-Old Virgin*'s twentieth-anniversary rerelease, Apatow said that while "it's hard to know if we would do it again," they had created that exchange "with a very positive spirit" and that in his opinion "all of the comments were meant as compliments." (Rogen, on the other hand, told an interviewer in 2019 that he came to regret the scene after people began to tell him "it's not fun to be in the theater when people are laughing at that, knowing what they're probably actually laughing at.")

"So much of this stuff is in the delivery of it," says Alonso Duralde, film critic and author of *Hollywood Pride: A Celebration of LGBTQ+ Representation and Perseverance in Film*. "I never came away from that scene thinking, 'These guys hate queer people and so they're trying to drag each other down by tarring them with that horrible accusation.' To me, it felt like two straight dudes who live in a world where they understand the existence of queer people and are amused and chill about it, ultimately, and can goof on each other in a way that friends goof on each other by calling out habits or likes and dislikes or whatever. I know it's a thin line and it's very much how you look at it, but as a queer viewer, the year that movie came out I thought it was funny. And I still do."

For much of *The 40-Year-Old Virgin*'s development, Apatow and Carell struggled with how best to end their story. Apatow's mentor Garry Shandling insisted that the key to the entire film was that when Andy finally does have sex it needs to be better than everyone else's sex, because Andy had waited all that time to find true love. But *how* do you communicate that someone's having incredible, mind-blowing sex without just having the characters say all of that?

Finally, one day, Carell threw out, "Maybe afterwards I just sing a song?"

The surreal finale, with Carell and the entire supporting cast performing "Aquarius / Let the Sunshine In" from the Broadway musical *Hair*, became the jubilant capper for *The 40-Year-Old Virgin*, and sent audiences out on a high. Budgeted in the neighborhood of $25 million, *The 40-Year-Old Virgin* grossed $109.4 million in the U.S. and more than

$177 million worldwide—huge numbers for a comedy of any kind, much less one based on an unused improv idea from a first-time director and first-time leading man and cowriter. It catapulted Steve Carell onto the Hollywood A-list and helped propel his new TV show, the American adaptation of the BBC sitcom *The Office*, from a struggling mid-season replacement to one of the fastest-growing series on all of television.

It also gave Apatow his first hit as a director—one that established him as a major voice in the world of comedy who could deftly combine lowbrow humor with genuine warmth and heart. Anyone who had seen *Freaks and Geeks* and *Undeclared* had known for years he could do that. But very few people watched those shows. On a practical level, after a decade-plus scraping by making cult favorites, he finally had a huge, unqualified smash.

"Everything changes when people think you *can* have a success," Apatow said in 2015, "because for the first half of my career nothing was a financial success. So it's hard to tell people your next one will be a hit when none of them have been a hit. So that was probably the turning point."

The executives so quick to cancel his shows were suddenly desperate to green-light whatever Apatow wanted to do next. And any promises he made in 2005 that his next project would be a hit were absolutely correct.

CHAPTER 14

If You Ain't First, You're Last

Hi. I'm Ricky Bobby. If you don't chew Big Red, then fuck you.

—Ricky Bobby, *Talladega Nights: The Ballad of Ricky Bobby*

Anchorman's subtitle was prophetic.

The film grossed $85 million in the U.S. and a couple million more overseas—enough to ensure a solid profit. But it was only the twenty-ninth highest-grossing film of 2004, behind titles like the animated kids movie *Shark Tale*, the bloated historical epic *Troy*, and the live-action *Scooby-Doo* sequel *Monsters Unleashed*. Thanks to its debut in theaters on the heels of the gargantuan *Spider-Man 2*, *Anchorman* never topped the weekend box office chart a single time during its theatrical run.

But then, as its title foretold, the legend of Ron Burgundy began to spread. Adam McKay said the movie's slow-creeping success didn't become apparent to him until 2005, when he saw people dressing like Ron and the rest of the Channel 4 News Team for Halloween. Then he started noticing how often he heard people quoting the film. He got wind of fans hosting whole *Anchorman* festivals. Like Channel 4 reporter Brian Fantana's odoriferous cologne Sex Panther, *Anchorman* lingered in the air. Once it wormed its way into people's heads, they couldn't seem to shake it.

By that point, though, McKay and Will Ferrell had already moved on to their next project. Before *Anchorman* even opened in theaters, they began developing a follow-up informed by their interminable struggle to find someone willing to bankroll their concept about sexist newsmen.

"*Anchorman* was too abstract for studios to get their heads around. In the process, we started half joking, half not—we said we should just pick an idea that's really accessible. What's the biggest, fattest, funniest undeniable idea you could ever pick?" said Ferrell. They eventually decided a broad comedy set in the world of NASCAR was the half-joking-half-not slam dunk they were looking for.

The project picked up speed a few months later when Ferrell brought McKay a name for their racing movie's hero—Ricky Bobby—along with a distinctive voice that blended a little of Ron Burgundy's unearned machismo with a fair amount of Ferrell's dim-witted nepo baby impression of President George W. Bush from *Saturday Night Live.*

"The second he started doing it, I was like 'Oh, we're going to be shooting race cars,'" McKay said. Sure enough, when Sony wanted the *Anchorman* team's next idea, McKay and Ferrell sold them *Talladega Nights: The Ballad of Ricky Bobby.*

After a series of short prologues that reveal his hard-luck origins—Ricky's father, Reese (Gary Cole), abandoned him as a baby and only visited him once during his entire childhood, when he imparted him with the words that become Ricky's credo: "If you ain't first, you're last!"—the film follows Ricky's meteoric rise from pit-crew member to elite NASCAR driver. Soon he's the king of his own stock car kingdom: ensconced in a mansion with his "red-hot smoking wife" Carley (Leslie Bibb) and his two "beautiful, handsome, striking sons, Walker and Texas Ranger" (Houston Tumlin and Grayson Russell).

While it's a safe bet the oblivious, self-centered Ricky Bobby never watched the local news, he and Ron Burgundy were very much cut from the same cloth: arrogant blowhards with all the confidence in the world in their own abilities, at least until someone comes along with the temerity to challenge them for their position. The characters' stories follow similar trajectories as well: Ferrell's cocksure hero basks in his glory, then is stunned and dethroned by a new rival, only to regroup and regain his mojo just in time for the closing credits.

Many of McKay and Ferrell's *Anchorman* collaborators returned for *Talladega Nights*, including producer Judd Apatow, editor Brent White, and composer Alex Wurman. A few members of *Anchorman*'s ensemble reappeared in the film as well, like David Koechner, who played News Team member Champ Kind and one of the members of Ricky Bobby's pit crew. But *Talladega Nights* also added many new stars to McKay/Ferrell's comic cosmology, including John C. Reilly as Ricky's best friend and teammate Cal Naughton Jr.

While Reilly's career to that point had largely been defined by character work in auteurist movies like Paul Thomas Anderson's *Boogie Nights*, Ferrell and McKay knew he had untapped comedic chops, thanks to his contributions to one of their early table reads of the *Anchorman* script. (Reilly had also played a small role in Tom Cruise's NASCAR drama *Days of Thunder*, which, if nothing else, made for very funny stunt casting.) When they started developing *Talladega*, they only had one person in mind to play Cal.

"They had asked me to do *Anchorman*, but I was working on another movie, and I couldn't do it," Reilly remembered. "I was crushed by that, because I knew that that movie was gonna be amazing, and sure enough, it's like this classic now. When they called, I said, 'Well that's great, I've played the best friend a lot, and of course I want to work with you guys and I would love to, but if I'm gonna be the best friend again, it has to be the ultimate best friend.' And they're like, 'Yeah, whatever you want, if you have any ideas,' and from that very first phone call when they called me, they started soliciting my ideas."

"There are tons of technically dramatic actors who are wickedly funny," McKay said. "John C. Reilly's one of those guys. . . . We had to get on the phone and kind of talk him into doing *Talladega*. And then when we hit that set, we were just blown away. The guy can improvise, everything's grounded, he's wicked smart. He shows up when it's not his scene to throw out ideas 'cause he knows I like to collaborate like that. He's a monster." Reilly didn't share Ferrell's and McKay's background in improv, but when he'd studied acting at the Theatre School at DePaul University he had learned many of the same techniques taught at places like Second City and the Groundlings.

"A lot of the rules that you operate by are the same, so I didn't feel like a fish out of water,'" Reilly recalled. "It felt like 'Yeah, this is what those fun days in acting class felt like, like getting to riff.'"

The riffs arrive early and often in *Talladega Nights*, thanks to the same "alts" technique (shoot the script as written, then invite the actors to improvise based on suggestions from McKay and other members of the cast and crew) that yielded so much comedic gold on *Anchorman*. Unlike other directors who paid lip service to the notion of creative partnership, McKay and Ferrell really wanted Reilly and the rest of the actors to contribute their own ideas.

Some entire *Talladega Nights* scenes were improvised. After Ricky experiences a terrible crash at Charlotte Motor Speedway, Cal visits him in the hospital. With Ricky lying unconscious in his hospital bed, Cal confesses a secret he's wanted to tell him for years: While Ricky was away one summer at community college, Cal did a spread for *Playgirl* magazine.

"I mean *spread*, man, I pulled my butt apart and stuff," he adds. "I was totally nude. It was weird. I mean, you probably didn't hear about it because I went under the name of 'Mike Honcho.'" Reilly improvised the entire speech on the day—and Ferrell found the whole scenario so hilarious that you can see him "hanging on for dear life" trying not to laugh during his close-ups.

Despite the fun the actors (and audiences) were having, critics' reviews were mixed. The overwhelming amount of real-world products featured in the movie rattled some viewers. Cal's NASCAR fire suit is emblazoned with the Old Spice logo, while Ricky's promotes Wonder Bread, the perfect symbolic foodstuff for the film's hero, who is practically the dictionary definition of the adjective "white-bread," and who subsists entirely on a diet of highly processed corporate foods. The faux TV broadcast of *Talladega Nights*' climactic race even gets interrupted (mid-crash!) by a full-blown commercial for Applebee's Cajun Steak & Shrimp.

All of this earned a fair amount of hand-wringing from cultural critics in 2006. (*The New York Times*'s review of *Talladega Nights* claimed the film "may break new records for product placements per frame.") But unlike typical Hollywood product placement, in which brands pay for screen time in blockbusters, *Talladega Nights* received no money from any of the corporations that appeared in the movie; Sony wouldn't allow it.

"I don't know where that integrity came from," McKay quipped, although a *Hollywood Reporter* feature on the film and its corporate tie-ins implied a less virtuous explanation: While Sony did follow a policy never to ask for "integration fees" for product placement, they would instead cut deals for "backend promotions" with companies to create ads that doubled as de facto movie trailers.

The whole world of NASCAR and its rampant sponsorships became the perfect venue for McKay to mock not only Hollywood's addiction to product placement, but also the egregious commercialization of modern-American life in general. "Real products are disgusting when you see them pop up in movies," McKay explained. "And that's all NASCAR is, is just products everywhere. And it's a little gross. It makes you a little vomitous. So I kept saying, 'I gotta get real products.'"

Many brands, like Applebee's, gladly agreed to serve as the butt of McKay's jokes, despite the fact that the *Talladega Nights* scene set in the restaurant concludes with Reese Bobby screaming, "Applebee's has rats! I found a whole rat in my Cobb salad!" ("I think the audience is sophisticated enough to see this is a Will Ferrell parody and that it's all over-the-top and in good fun," said an Applebee's executive of the film's decision to link the chain's eateries with rodent infestation.)

In *Talladega Nights*, NASCAR becomes a microcosm of all of 2000s America. Ricky Bobby's nemesis throughout the film, for instance, is an effete gay Frenchman, the living embodiment of multiple hot-button issues in the country at the time, including the growing debate over the legalization of same-sex marriage and France's opposition to the U.S.-led invasion of Iraq, an international insult deemed so egregious by some segments of the American populace that many venues (including several restaurants that served the U.S. Congress) temporarily renamed French fries "freedom fries."

To play the French driver, McKay and Ferrell turned to a rising star in the world of comedy they met at the weekly pickup basketball game held every Sunday for twenty-five years at Garry Shandling's house.

Sacha Baron Cohen wasn't French; he was raised in London and educated at Cambridge. But he had studied clowning in France with the legendary practitioner of the form, Philippe Gaulier. When Baron Cohen needed to come up with an accent to play Ricky's French racing adversary, Jean Girard, Baron Cohen simply imitated his old teacher.

Outlandish foreign accents were something of a specialty for Baron Cohen. His taste for broad comic characters dated back to a childhood spent watching Peter Sellers and Monty Python, two inspirations who would fuel his own interest in lacerating satire and absurdist pranks. (He mainly went to Cambridge to join the Cambridge Footlights, the comedy troupe where most of Python first met.) By the time he was nine, Baron Cohen was writing and performing comedy sketches for his Jewish youth group; within a few years, he was playing senior living facilities dressed like a Hasidic Jew and crooning parody songs of his own creation like "Schvitzing." ("And it would go down terribly," Baron Cohen said. "These old-age homes would hate it.")

Where most comedians would do whatever they could to stave off such a negative reaction, Baron Cohen came to relish an audience's contempt. When he wasn't doing comedy, Baron Cohen was also an aficionado of early hip-hop culture, and he became fascinated with one particular white hip-hop DJ on BBC Radio named Tim Westwood, who adopted the persona of a street-tough gangsta. Using Westwood as his model, Baron Cohen created a character named MC Jocelyn Cheadle-Hume, an upper-class white guy masquerading as a wannabe rapper, who he played in short films that aired on an obscure satellite TV station in the mid-1990s.

During the filming of one such short, Baron Cohen stumbled into the discovery that rocketed him to comedy immortality. Dressed as MC Jocelyn Cheadle-Hume, Baron Cohen encountered a bunch of skateboarders; he spontaneously began interacting with them in character, but the kids remained oblivious to the deception. In the middle of all this, a tour bus pulled up to the curb near where the impromptu comedy sketch was unfolding. Baron Cohen grabbed his tiny crew, jumped aboard, and, in Baron Cohen's words, "commandeered the bus."

"I took the microphone and I was like, 'Yo, check it out. I is here, and this is me bus. Booyakasha!'" Baron Cohen stayed in character as he kept wandering London, from a pub to an office tower, while his cameraman documented the chaos. It was a lightning-bolt moment.

"We were walking over the Waterloo Bridge, back to the London Weekend Television studio, and the adrenaline was pumping and we were just so excited," Baron Cohen said, "because here was this new form of comedy that we discovered. Probably it existed, and other people had done it, but we'd never discovered it before—this idea of taking a comic character into a real situation."

Baron Cohen kept evolving and refining his hip-hop character, who was eventually renamed Ali G by a producer at Channel 4. And he kept adding other characters to his repertoire. One began life as a clueless journalist from the tiny Eastern European nation of Moldova who was supposedly visiting England to learn and report on Western customs. That alias worked until the day Baron Cohen did a segment on etiquette and wound up at an official state dinner seated next to the actual ambassador of Moldova. Thinking fast, Baron Cohen accused the real Moldovan ambassador of being a spy and had him ejected from the event.

After that, the reporter became Kazakhstani, and was rechristened Borat Sagdiyev, an identity that allowed Baron Cohen access to all sorts of notable public figures, who gladly consented to an interview they believed would air exclusively on Kazakh TV. It wasn't until the interviewee had agreed to chat and signed an airtight release form that Baron Cohen would appear as Borat, complete with his cartoonish accent and rumpled tan suit. (To heighten his air of authenticity, Baron Cohen never cleaned Borat's only set of clothes, reasoning that if Borat really existed, he would probably smell awful.) A stint on *The 11 O'Clock Show* on the UK's Channel 4 led to a spin-off series for Ali G, Borat, and a third Baron Cohen character named Brüno, a flamboyantly gay fashionista. After the show began airing in the U.S. on HBO, Baron Cohen became a cult hero on the other side of the Atlantic.

Although the series was named *Da Ali G Show* after Baron Cohen's first and most famous character in the UK—and despite the fact that Ali G managed to wrangle interviews with the likes of former Speaker of the House Newt Gingrich, former Secretary of State and Secretary of the Treasury James Baker, and future U.S. president Donald Trump—the comedian sensed that Borat had the potential to break out beyond the confines of the confrontational sketch comedy series. 20th Century Fox agreed and gave Baron Cohen $18 million to create a feature film around the fake reporter.

To call the production that followed troubled would be an understatement. The film, officially titled *Borat: Cultural Learnings of America for Make Benefit Glorious Nation of Kazakhstan*, was supposed to be directed by *Old School* and *Starsky & Hutch*'s Todd Phillips, but he dropped out over "creative differences" with Baron Cohen after just eleven days of filming, including a shoot in Virginia where Borat managed to perform a fake Kazakh national anthem to the tune of "The Star-Spangled Banner," with lyrics like "Kazakhstan number one exporter of potassium / All other countries have inferior potassium." The rodeo attendees were not amused.

Baron Cohen broke his foot playing basketball at Garry Shandling's house, and production had to shut down for several months, giving the crew time to regroup and recruit *Seinfeld* producer Larry Charles to replace Phillips. Baron Cohen and Charles adjusted their storyline, which sent Borat on a cross-country journey in a beat-up ice cream truck to find *Baywatch* star Pamela Anderson and make her his bride. They added the character of Borat's ineffectual producer Azamat Bagatov (Ken Davitian), who wound up taking part in one of *Borat*'s more memorable sequences, when the pair get into a heated wrestling match while completely nude. The fight spills out of their hotel room and into a mortgage brokers' convention—which was a reshoot after their first attempt to elicit a horrified reaction at the sight of two flabby naked men roughhousing at an engineering conference in Dallas generated no reaction whatsoever. ("They ran into the lecture, the lecturer gazed up, all the attendees gazed up, and they all just went back to what they were doing," remembered *Borat* writer Dan Mazer.)

Baron Cohen and Davitian could have run afoul of public nudity laws if they had pulled that stunt in the wrong spot, and throughout the shoot, the *Borat* crew struggled to stay a step or two ahead of the police. The FBI wound up receiving so many complaints about a terrorist in an ice cream truck that they actually started keeping a file on the film and eventually visited the production. Before they could question Baron Cohen, he disappeared.

Baron Cohen was so deep in character that even when the police *did* manage to track him down, he answered their questions as Borat. In the end, Sacha Baron Cohen estimated 150 lawsuits arose from various incidents during the filming of *Borat*—and that's before the actual nation of Kazakhstan threatened the movie after they got wind of the way they were depicted as a quasi-feudal society rife with prostitutes, incest, and anti-Semitism. After the country banned *Borat*, Baron Cohen released an "official" video response as Borat, in which he announced he "fully supported my government's decision to sue this Jew."

Baron Cohen claimed surprise over Kazakhstan's fiery response because he "always had faith in the audience that they would realize that this was a fictitious country . . . the reason we chose Kazakhstan was because it was a country that no one had heard anything about, so we could essentially play on stereotypes they might have about this ex-Soviet backwater." In his mind, the purpose of *Borat* was not to make fun of Kazakhstan; it was to make fun of Americans that might think someone as ignorant as Borat could actually exist.

"Borat essentially works as a tool . . . by himself being anti-Semitic, he lets people lower their guard and expose their own prejudice," Baron Cohen explained. And not just anti-Semitism, but all other sorts of biases. In one eye-opening sequence, Borat attends a formal dinner party at the well-appointed home of a Southern family, where he can practice the tips he's received from an etiquette coach. The hosts of the party remain relatively polite throughout the evening, even as Borat insults several of the women in attendance and feigns ignorance about the proper use of indoor plumbing, going so far as to shit into a plastic bag and present it to the hostess. But they draw the line when Borat invites an African American woman to join the party; suddenly Borat is ordered to leave and the sheriff is called to come and arrest them both.

If the joke in *Borat* was on America, though, America didn't seem to mind. Whatever Fox had to pay to settle all those lawsuits, it was worth it. After their initial $18 million investment, plus a few million more to reshoot a new ending after the original one—in which Borat interrupts Pamela Anderson's dogs' wedding on a Jet Ski—was deemed unsatisfactory, *Borat* became a pop culture phenomenon. It grossed $128 million in the United States alone, and another $134 million around the world (minus Kazakhstan). The film even earned an Academy Award nomination for Best Adapted Screenplay.

While Larry Charles edited the four hundred hours of raw footage down to eighty-five minutes for *Borat*'s theatrical release, Baron Cohen joined McKay and Ferrell to film his role in *Talladega Nights*. Like Borat, gay French driver Jean Girard is an outsider in the United States whose preposterous behavior exposes all of America's deepest prejudices. In his very first scene, he breaks Ricky Bobby's arm after Ricky refuses to say that he loves crepes, even after Ricky recognizes crepes as the "really thin pancakes" he loves with sugar and lemon juice. Shortly thereafter, Ricky learns that his own racing team hired Jean as its new driver—and that Jean is married to a man. A mortified Ricky Bobby immediately passes out as he moans, "The room's startin' to spin real fast . . . 'cause of . . . 'cause of all the gayness."

Although *Talladega Nights*' rednecks were all fictional creations, the film still let Baron Cohen flex his confrontational comedy muscles. As they did with Reilly, McKay and Ferrell welcomed Baron Cohen's suggestions for his character, including his big idea for the film's finale: After Ricky Bobby wins the final race, Baron Cohen wanted Jean and Ricky to kiss, and for Jean to say, "You taste . . . of America."

Baron Cohen presented the idea to McKay, who was initially uncertain.

"Why don't we just try it and see?" Baron Cohen said. "What do we lose? It would take like forty-five seconds."

Ferrell was game, and so in the spirit of alts and collaboration, they tried a passionate embrace between Jean and Ricky—in front of a thousand NASCAR fans working as background extras, who began loudly booing the stars. Baron Cohen was delighted, and then even more pleased when the same-sex embrace made it into the final cut.

Thanks in part to the film's surprisingly intense racing footage (filmed by cinematographer Oliver Wood, who'd previously shot the car chases in *The Bourne Identity*), *Talladega Nights* wound up costing Sony roughly three times what DreamWorks paid for *Anchorman*. But *Talladega Nights* also wound up nearly doubling *Anchorman*'s already solid total at the box office; all told, the movie grossed $162 million worldwide—not bad for a NASCAR comedy that poked fun at the sport's out-of-control commercialism and its fans' (and drivers') diets, and ended with a triumphant kiss between two men.

McKay managed to make *Talladega Nights* into a film that appealed to NASCAR fans and comedy nerds alike. He later confirmed that was exactly what he intended—to make a modern equivalent of *Patton*, the Oscar-winning biopic that was equally popular with people who admired Patton as with those who hated him. The point was not to attack NASCAR fans or Southern moviegoers, but to "just be looking at what's going on and having fun with it."

"My thinking is that you do these comedies," McKay explained. "If people are laughing and engaging with it no matter what their beliefs are, at least something is being transmitted. . . . If you're laughing at something, you know there's some truth behind it. You don't laugh at stuff that's bullshit."

Most people saw *Talladega Nights* as a big colorful comedy. McKay saw it as a political movie. Ridiculous set pieces like the one where Ricky stabbed himself in the leg to prove he can't walk—and then John C. Reilly and Michael Clarke Duncan, as Ricky Bobby's loyal crew chief, trying to dislodge the first knife by stabbing him in the same leg with *another* knife—served as a stock car–shaped Trojan horse to help him present all of his ideas about capitalism run amok and the country's senseless fear of the Other to an audience that might have refused to watch a documentary that expressed those exact same sentiments.

With two hits under their belt, and plenty of other ideas in development, McKay and Ferrell decided to form a production company. Struggling to name their partnership, Ferrell turned to a pseudonym stored on his Blackberry. Why not use their company as a tribute to a fake person they made up? Gary Sanchez Productions was born.

"And then only like four months later did I realize most people thought it was a 'Dirty Sanchez' reference," McKay added. "Which I *hate*."

CHAPTER 15

Revenge of the Nerds

Marriage is like an unfunny, tense version of* Everybody Loves Raymond, *but it doesn't last twenty-two minutes. It lasts forever.

—Pete, *Knocked Up*

French New Wave auteur Jean-Luc Godard famously (or perhaps apocryphally) said the only way to criticize a movie is to make another movie.

I'm not sure he had in mind a film filled with hand-drawn images of throbbing, veiny penises, but nevertheless the spirit of Godard's words led to the creation of one of the twenty-first century's great comedies.

It was conceived by two longtime friends who met in bar mitzvah class in Vancouver. They bonded over their shared love of movies and began producing their own lo-fi spoofs of their favorites, including *Spaceballs*—which was already a spoof of *Star Wars*. When they weren't making films, they were watching them; they were a constant presence at their local video store, where they repeatedly took advantage of a "seven movies for seven days for seven dollars" deal.

They were never too discriminating with their choices; when you are paying seven bucks for seven movies, there's no need to get picky. But one day the friends saw something so putrid that they were roused to action. (They claim to no longer remember what the movie was.) The pair knew nothing about screenwriting, but they believed they could create something better than the swill they had just watched. So when the film ended, they went upstairs to the one room in the house with a computer and began writing.

That was how Seth Rogen and Evan Goldberg started *Superbad*. Rogen was fourteen years old; Goldberg was only thirteen.

It took eleven more years for the film to finally arrive in theaters, after countless rewrites and innumerable pitches. According to Goldberg, the first draft they wrote was "awful." (In their defense, they were barely teenagers at the time.) But while their *Superbad* script got better over the nearly dozen years they worked on it, it never strayed too far from the concept they first hatched up as kids: a pair of teenagers on the verge of high school graduation try to get laid by scoring some booze for a friend's house party.

"Some of the jokes in the fucking original draft of *Superbad* that we literally wrote when we were thirteen years old are in the movie still, and are some of the funnier jokes in the movie, which is incredibly disconcerting in a lot of ways," Rogen admitted.

Fourteen is pretty young to write a coarse sex comedy, but like his future mentor Judd Apatow, Seth Aaron Rogen already knew he what he wanted to do by the time he got to high school, and didn't see any point in waiting until he was older to get started. The son of a nonprofit worker dad and social worker mom, who had met on a kibbutz in Israel, Rogen's drive stemmed from his recognition at an early age that one of the few things he could control about his life was how hard he worked at it.

"I remember I did karate as a kid, at the Jewish Community Center, and when I started I was the worst in the class," Rogen recalled. "I was the worst of 25 Jewish kids who were afraid of getting picked on. And then just because everyone else quit, three years later I was at the top of the class, and there were 25 Jewish kids who were worse than me. And that was always tangible: Just by not stopping I became the best one. It wasn't this, like, ferocious leap. I just kept going, and slowly [other] people stopped. Because a lot of people will stop."

At age twelve, Rogen told his parents he wanted to try stand-up, so they enrolled him in a local workshop on comedy where he could learn the basics. The workshop's teacher counseled Rogen that "fun isn't funny. Comedy is pain," and warned him that when he was crafting jokes, he shouldn't think, "What's funny to me?" Instead, he should ask, "What bothers me? What frustrates me? What do I wish I could I change? What can I just not fucking stand?!"

Rogen took those words to heart—not only as a budding stand-up, but as an aspiring screenwriter. He and Goldberg channeled their hormonal frustrations into *Superbad*, making it the rare movie about teenage virgins that was written (at least in the beginning) by actual teenage virgins. Write what you know, they say—or, in the case of *Superbad*, write what you don't know because you've never had it but you think about it constantly. That was how they came to pen a script about two horny kids named Seth and Evan. They even wrote a part based on their other best friend, another dorky kid named Fogell.

"We were younger than the characters were when we first started writing it. It really tapped into a very visceral sense that we were never going to get laid, it was just never going to fucking happen. That was all we talked about, all we thought about, and it seemed like it was impossible," Rogen recalled.

For a long time, turning *Superbad* into a real movie seemed impossible as well. Even worse, Rogen began to sense he wasn't going to graduate high school. So he rededicated himself to his budding career in comedy. He landed an agent, who started sending him on auditions. The second one Rogen ever went on was for a TV pilot called *Freaks and Geeks*.

Paul Feig's original concept for *Freaks and Geeks* had grown out of his own painful, anxiety-ridden high school years, and from a lifetime of watching films and shows about high school that bore zero resemblance to his own experiences. But because Feig was far more of a geek than a burnout (in Feig's Michigan high school, they were known as freaks), the half of the pilot's script about stoners didn't sing with the same level of authenticity as the half about nerds who get bullied because they're bad at dodgeball and love quoting *Caddyshack*. So as Feig and Judd Apatow set out to build the high school TV show of their dreams, featuring authentic unknown talents culled from all over North America, they worried less about fitting the specific characters they'd envisioned and more about finding gifted performers who could be nurtured into stars. That's how they found and fell in love with Rogen, a sixteen-year-old kid from Vancouver with zero acting experience.

"We went to a few different cities and did open calls. I think Vancouver was the first place we went," Feig remembers. "I was like, 'Throw open the doors! We're gonna see everybody!' Then we get there and there's, like, five hundred kids. I'm like, 'Okay, we can't do this!'"

Out of the five hundred kids, Feig and Apatow instead auditioned the handful who had agents and were pursuing acting professionally. Fortunately, Rogen happened to be in that handful.

"When I audition people, I'll just write a speech," Feig says. "If you're hearing lines from the movie, you're not getting enough. So we had this whole monologue about growing pot in a cave, and how if a cop showed up you could blow up the cave and it would hide all this stuff. It was ridiculous. But [Rogen] started reading it in his way. It's burned into my brain: Judd and I were sitting around a table and the minute he started reading, we were going, 'Oh my god, this guy is hilarious.'"

Sure enough, Rogen got the role. His Ken Miller spends a lot of *Freaks and Geeks*' early episodes in the margins of the stories, delivering sardonic quips in Rogen's singular voice and sputtering car engine laugh. As Rogen grew more comfortable on camera, Feig and Apatow started pushing Ken into the spotlight. In the penultimate episode of the first season, "The Little Things," Ken discovers that his girlfriend was born with ambiguous genitalia, leading him to question his own sexuality. In Rogen's big scene, he pours his heart out to the other freaks, played by James Franco and Jason Segel, shifting effortlessly between dry jokes and heartfelt soul-searching.

"I remember watching it and just thinking, 'Oh, Seth's a movie star,'" Apatow said."

Hollywood disagreed. NBC canceled *Freaks and Geeks* before Rogen's showcase episode even aired. Apatow was devastated, and determined to keep working with as much of the *Freaks and Geeks* team as he could. He created a show set in college called *Undeclared*, hoping to populate it with all his favorite actors and behind-the-scenes talents from the previous series, to prove the powers that be screwed up by canceling them—a sort of revenge of the nerds against the shortsighted decision-makers at NBC.

But if NBC was hard to deal with on *Freaks and Geeks*, Fox was nearly impossible to appease on *Undeclared*. Apatow wanted *Freaks and Geeks* costar Jason Segel to play the show's lead. Fox said no. Then he tried to convince them to make Seth Rogen the star. They vetoed that idea "in about eight seconds." (In Rogen's recollection, the executives "literally laughed" at the suggestion.) Apatow acquiesced and cast Rogen in a supporting role with Segel playing a recurring guest—and Fox *still* canceled *Undeclared* after one season.

Although Rogen's *Undeclared* character—Vancouver transplant Ron Garner—was once again more of a comedy sidekick than a central protagonist, *Undeclared* was another important experience for Rogen. From the start of *Freaks and Geeks*, Feig and Apatow encouraged any of their young actors to ask questions and spend time shadowing the crew when they weren't actively involved in scenes on camera. By the time they shot *Undeclared*, Apatow had read and liked the script for *Superbad*, so he made Rogen a member of the writing staff. Rogen ultimately wound up as a credited writer on five of *Undeclared*'s seventeen episodes. He was only nineteen years old.

"Seth was incredibly funny," says *Undeclared* producer and writer Rodney Rothman. "From an early point he wasn't just writing incredible scripts, he was writing them really fast. Like overnight, he would write a script and come in and it would be amazing."

Still, in 2001 no one in Hollywood wanted to produce a sex-and-profanity-filled R-rated high school movie from the funny guy on two failed Judd Apatow shows. After *Undeclared* went off the air, Apatow kept the duo busy by paying Goldberg to spend a summer off from college in Los Angeles writing with Rogen. Apatow ordered the pair to come up with one hundred ideas for movies. They delivered fifty.

"We never made any of them," Goldberg said. "And then [Apatow] was like, 'These are awesome, but you should instead write a movie about a pothead who's a process server who gets hunted by his own dealer.' And we said, 'That's stupid, and that will end our career before it ever happens.'" Apatow kept coaxing, suggesting that they channel their love of '90s action movies into their own stoner version of one. Eventually, they decided to give it a shot. After six weeks locked in a room subsisting on a diet of pasta, cheese, and hot dogs, they had a script. They called it *Pineapple Express*.

But even after Apatow agreed to produce one of their scripts, Hollywood remained totally uninterested. The team knew they were in real trouble after they brought in an additional producer to try to help their chances, and then a few months later, that producer became the head of Paramount Pictures. Apatow was elated—"We're going to get our green light now! Our producer is the head of the studio!" he thought—until they went for an official meeting about the film.

"I can't do this," their former partner declared. "See how many dick jokes there are in this thing?"

Rogen could have neutered his dick jokes and tried to make a PG-13 movie. But he was adamant that *Superbad* should reflect real kids' high school experience—and his own high school experience was filled with booze and dick jokes.

Sticking to his guns was a risky move; after *Undeclared* went off the air, Rogen spent several years almost totally unemployed. The few jobs he got were often facilitated by Apatow, his comedy guardian angel, who recommended Rogen and Goldberg for the staff of *Da Ali G Show* after Sacha Baron Cohen came to Apatow looking for writers. But that was an exception; mostly Rogen watched as his friends kept getting work and he kept struggling. At a certain point, he all but gave up on acting as a potential career. ("I auditioned for tons and tons of things that Seann William Scott now stars in and I just felt like I was beat; 'Fuck! There's a guy kind of like me but who's handsome *and* funny!'")

Rogen's fortunes only turned around when Apatow's did—thanks to the popularity of *Anchorman*. He was actually in Apatow's office when they got the call that Universal was going to make *The 40-Year-Old Virgin*. Apatow was so elated at the news, Rogen figured he'd say yes to just about anything—so he immediately asked to be cast in the movie, which is how he wound up playing Steve Carell's coworker Cal. Apatow also made him a coproducer on *Virgin* with a remit as a kind of jack-of-all-trades at Apatow's side, pitching alts and helping with rewrites. In fact, while the very concept of a forty-year-old virgin would seemingly lend itself to a comedy loaded with sex talk (if not sex acts), the movie might have been much tamer if not for Rogen.

"I was like, 'They should be swearing casually all the time,'" Rogen said. "That was my biggest creative contribution to the movie; I was like, 'We should be smoking weed casually and swearing all the time' . . . that was always my thing. I was like, 'This is gonna be an R-rated movie, we should fucking go for it.'"

Rogen convinced Apatow to go with that approach, but Steve Carell was a harder sell. Rogen later revealed Carell was so concerned about a heavily R-rated *Virgin* that Rogen was tasked with writing a PG-13–rated version of the movie's script to see if it would still play well without all the profanity and drug use. (Rogen later claimed he did it "just so [Carell] could see how lame it was.") Apatow also asked Rogen to generate a list of things that Steve Carell could scream while getting waxed. Not wanting to leave anything to chance because they were waxing Carell's chest for real, Apatow needed a batch of funny lines at the ready. At Apatow's behest, Rogen made two lists: one full of profane exclamations and ones that were family-friendly.

"I remember the dirty list was easy and the clean list was hard," Rogen recalled. "I couldn't think of anything. And *American Idol* was on, and it was the year Kelly Clarkson was on, and I wrote, 'Kelly Clarkson!' I wrote it as just something to fill the page so Judd wouldn't yell at me. But it turned into a line that people still remember."

Carell's wariness was understandable; not too many movies introduce a character by having him describe a trip to Tijuana to watch a show where a woman had sex with a horse, as *The 40-Year-Old Virgin* does for Rogen's Cal. ("It is not as cool as it sounds like it's gonna be!" Cal reveals.) Ironically, though, Carell's discomfort worked for the movie, where his sheltered sweetness perfectly contrasted Rogen's unbridled lust. If Carell was legitimately uncomfortable with *Virgin*'s raunchy gags, that only served the movie because Andy himself is supposed to be ill at ease with his coworkers and their vulgar appetites.

Rogen never lost faith that his instincts were correct; two weeks before the movie opened in theaters, he, Apatow, Carell, and a group of *Virgin* cast members recorded a commentary track for the movie. When the subject of the film's box office prospects came up, Rogen bullishly declared, "I think it's gonna be a huge hit, I'm just gonna say it right now." Not only was Rogen right, all his dirtiest jokes about bestiality and masturbating while high on Excedrin PM drew huge laughs from audiences. And after *Anchorman* and *Virgin* hit back-to-back, Rogen finally had an opportunity to get one of his scripts made. But his initial ideas were all very ambitious.

He first tried pitching Apatow a concept for a massive $100 million sci-fi movie. Apatow pointed out that Rogen didn't need all those accoutrements to make a successful film. "You're funny just sitting in the stock room in *40-Year-Old Virgin*—you barely move and you're funny," Apatow said. "You could be funny in any normal situation—like you could get a girl pregnant."

On August 7, 2005—two weeks before *The 40-Year-Old Virgin* debuted in theaters—Apatow pounded out an email to himself with the subject line "Pregnancy." Its bullet points included:

- *A couple gets pregnant on the first date.*
- *Older sister of the woman has kids and represents its difficulties and complications.*
- *Going through this helps her adjust her life in a positive way. She doesn't like Seth. Maybe Seth admits she is right at some point.*

Rogen might have been a bachelor, but as the father of two, Apatow had tons of personal experiences he could draw upon for a story about the way pregnancy impacts a relationship. As he fleshed out the barebones concept, he kept making the story even more personal than *The 40-Year-Old Virgin*, largely eschewing big broad comic set pieces in favor of more honest and painful scenarios.

Apatow's script, eventually dubbed *Knocked Up*, tackled the subjects of parenthood and marriage from two distinct perspectives. In Rogen's storyline, a slacker named Ben spends his days getting high in a dumpy house with his equally stoned roommates, until a chance encounter with an on-air E! News reporter named Alison leads to a one-night stand and an unexpected pregnancy. Meanwhile, Alison lives with her brother-in-law, Pete (Paul Rudd); her sister, Debbie; and their two kids—played by Apatow's own family: wife, Leslie Mann, and daughters, Maude and Iris.

Apatow originally wanted actress Anne Hathaway for the role of Alison, until she objected to his plan to insert footage from a real birth into *Knocked Up*'s climax. Instead, he pivoted to *Grey's Anatomy* star Katherine Heigl, who had less experience in comedies but who, in his estimation, "was the only woman who could keep up with Seth." For his part, Rogen felt Heigl was "the only woman you could buy, maybe, would sleep with me, maybe, if her blood alcohol content was truly at a lethal limit." ("All the other women literally treated you the way Alison treats you in the movie," Apatow replied.)

While Apatow related to a lot of the material in *The 40-Year-Old Virgin*, many scenes in *Knocked Up* came straight from his own life. "Every time my wife and I went through childbirth, terrible things would happen," he explained. "I thought, 'I've got to write about this because it's so awful that I must get something from it.'" He and Mann chose a gynecologist who guaranteed they would be there for their birth, and then was inexplicably out of town on the big day, leading to a frenzied last-minute search for a replacement, who wound up being someone the couple had previously rejected, a story that went into the film's third act. So did an incident where Alison tries to have sex with Ben during her third trimester and he resists because he's worried he's going to poke the baby with his penis.

He also drew inspiration from stories other members of the cast told him. Paul Rudd mentioned that his wife hated the fact that he refused to read any of her baby books. "People have been doing this for thousands of years! Cavemen didn't have *What to Expect When You're Expecting*!" he shot back. In *Knocked Up*, Ben repeats Rudd's complaint to Alison almost verbatim.

Arguments between both Ben and Alison and Pete and Debbie were inspired by Apatow's own relationship with Mann. One of the first scenes filmed between Rudd and Mann involved a fight between the couple; their performances got so intense that Rudd left the set that night genuinely rattled, worrying that he'd actually made his costar angry.

"Somehow it got back [to her]," Rudd said, laughing. "And the next day Leslie came over to me and goes, 'I heard you think that I'm mad at you.' I said, 'I hope not, because I didn't want to upset you.'"

"Of course not," Mann replied. "I don't hate you, my god. I hate Judd!"

A lot of the Ben character prior to his meeting with Alison was based on Rogen's own life; like the actor, Ben is a Vancouver transplant who spends a lot of his time out of work getting high with his buddies. In a further autobiographical touch, all of Ben's roommates were played by Rogen's real-life friends. And all of them—Jay Baruchel, Jonah Hill, Jason Segel, and Martin Starr—used their real first names in the film. Even some of the set dressings in their grimy L.A. house were authentic; the couch and coffee table belonged to Rogen's writing partner, Evan Goldberg.

Ben and his roommates functioned much like the SmartTech crew from *The 40-Year-Old Virgin*—only, *Knocked Up* subbed in the vulgar Ben for the naive Andy at the center of the story. *Knocked Up*'s sweetness instead comes from Apatow's kids, appearing intermittently as, essentially, themselves—a choice Apatow made to counteract the unconvincing child actors he saw in most films. Surrounded by their real family both in front of and behind the camera, Apatow reasoned, his kids would just act like themselves.

To capture them at their most authentic, he placed multiple cameras around the set, then let the kids dictate the improvised conversation. (He also didn't feed them prior to shooting, then plopped them down in front of big plates of food so they'd be too interested in their meals to be self-conscious about the cameras.) Once Apatow's daughters found material they connected with, the group would then configure the rest of the scene around them to match—like Maude explaining her theory of where babies come from as a process where a stork drops it down and then "a hole goes in your body and there's blood everywhere, coming out of your head and then you push your belly button and then your butt falls off and then you hold your butt and you have to dig and you find the little baby." ("That's exactly right," a bewildered Mann replies.) The adult members of the cast did their fair share of improvisation throughout the film as well, including Rogen's reaction to Alison telling Ben she was pregnant—"Fuck off!"—a line Apatow said he "never would have thought to write."

Knocked Up didn't sugarcoat much of anything, right down to the big delivery scene at the end, which included multiple shots of a real birth, a choice Apatow said had less to do with shock value than truth telling. ("The truth of a birth is a baby comes out of there! For a man, a lot of the experience is having to see that," he said.) All the characters come off as flawed, complicated, and deeply human. They don't always do the right thing—in fact, they often screw up, like when Rudd's Pete lies to Mann's Debbie about what he's doing when he goes out and then gets caught participating in a fantasy baseball draft—but they're always doing the best they can under difficult circumstances.

That warts-and-all depiction of relationships, coupled with the movie's constant laughs, helped make *Knocked Up* an even bigger hit than *The 40-Year-Old Virgin*; it would end up earning almost $220 million in theaters for Universal. A few years after back-to-back canceled sitcoms, a few years after losing part after part to Seann William Scott, Seth Rogen was the star of one of the biggest comedies in years—and the poster for the movie was a giant close-up of his face with the tagline "What if this guy got you pregnant?"

"*40-Year-Old Virgin* did really well," Rogen said, "and I think people started to see that dirty sensibility would play." After *Talladega Nights*, produced by Apatow, opened in the summer of 2006 and became another massive hit, the head of Sony, Amy Pascal, let it be known she'd make anything that came from his crew.

Rogen and Evan Goldberg still had their script for *Superbad* sitting around; before *Knocked Up* blew the doors off multiplexes around the country, *Superbad* already had its long-awaited green light. Apatow and Rogen quickly nailed down their director, Greg Mottola, a veteran indie filmmaker who had worked on *Undeclared*. Mottola had attended a table read of the *Superbad* script in the early 2000s and instantly loved it.

"I thought, *Wow. This is one of the funniest things I've ever heard*. It has an authenticity to it that you don't often get with big teen comedies. I was also aware of the fact that teen comedies had kind of slowly morphed into PG-13, soft, brightly lit, palatable comedies," said Mottola. Afterward he approached Goldberg and Rogen and said if they ever got the project off the ground, he'd love to be considered. They never forgot, and when Sony bought the script, they hired him.

Unfortunately, so much time had elapsed since Rogen and Goldberg had first dreamed of making *Superbad* that Rogen was now too old to take the role he wrote for himself. (After you've played a man who's impregnated Katherine Heigl on a first date, you may not be the ideal fit for a high school kid who can't get laid.) The solution to their problem came from an unlikely source.

One day during preproduction on *The 40-Year-Old Virgin*, Rogen was watching *The Life Aquatic with Steve Zissou* at an L.A. movie theater when he felt a tap on his shoulder. It was a curly-haired kid in glasses. "You don't know me, but I'm auditioning for this role in a movie that you're a producer on next week," he said.

It was Jonah Hill; the role he was auditioning for was the kid trying to buy knee-high boots from Catherine Keener in *The 40-Year-Old Virgin*. Rogen had worked on rewrites for that scene just a few weeks before. Sure enough, Hill showed up for the audition, and, in Rogen's words, was "leagues funnier" than everyone else. Hill got the part, and then was so funny improvising with Carell and Keener that they cast him as one of Ben's maladjusted roommates in *Knocked Up*.

But even though Hill proved to be a repeat scene-stealer, when he came to Rogen pleading for the opportunity to audition for *Superbad*, Rogen resisted. Hill was just twenty months younger than Rogen, and with a dirtier sense of humor, if that was even possible. (In one *Knocked Up* scene, he berates Jay Baruchel for shaving his body hair over the toilet, screaming, "Last time I went to the bathroom, Jay, I took a shit and my shit looked like a fuckin' stuffed animal!") But Rogen, Goldberg, and Apatow kept auditioning potential Seths, and after upward of 150 candidates, none of them matched what they had in mind.

"Jonah was like, 'I should play Seth. I should play Seth. I should play Seth.' And we said no like 100 times," remembered Mottola. 'You are too old looking.' And he said, 'No, you're too old looking. I'm not! I can do this with makeup and hair.'"

Finally, they relented. One day during a break on *Knocked Up*, Rogen pulled Hill into his trailer and recorded him reading a Seth scene from the script. "It was just so funny," Rogen said, "we were like, 'Oh, we were wrong, he can totally do this very well.'" They showed the tape to Pascal and she agreed. Jonah Hill was the new Seth.

The team had almost as much trouble finding someone to play Goldberg and Rogen's dork of a best buddy Fogell, who in *Superbad* scores a fake ID with the mononym "McLovin." Casting director Allison Jones combed through Los Angeles high schools, putting up flyers seeking "an 18-year-old who looks 13 who's a loser who thinks he's awesome." One day, a couple of kids at West Hills High School in Santee, California, approached their friend Christopher Mintz-Plasse with the piece of paper and a message: "This is you!"

Mintz-Plasse had never acted in anything outside of a couple high school plays before. After a series of auditions in which his unflappable confidence and his willingness to roast his costars annoyed Jonah Hill so much he told Mottola, Apatow, and Rogen, "Fuck that guy, don't cast that guy," they decided that Hill's irritation was exactly the dynamic they wanted between Seth and McLovin.

Searching for an Evan to round out their lead trio, they met with Michael Cera on the advice of *Undeclared* and *Knocked Up* star Jay Baruchel, who had worked with Cera on the indie comedy *Fanboys*. A baby-faced Canadian who had first broken out playing Jason Bateman's son on the cult TV comedy *Arrested Development*, Cera was nothing like the real Evan Goldberg, and not much like the character Rogen and Goldberg envisioned, either.

"In the script, [the dynamic between Seth and Evan] was kind of like 'a straight man and a funny guy.' But [Cera] made the straight man just as funny as the funny guy, which was like something that I've really grown to marvel at over the years," Rogen said.

By all accounts, they had an easier time finding the objects of the fictional Evan and Seth's affection. Martha MacIsaac was cast as Becca, Evan's crush. For Seth's potential love interest Jules, they cast a young actress named Emma Stone, who had done some television work but never appeared in a movie before. Stone had a natural comfort on camera, and she had an easy chemistry with Hill. But she looked a little like MacIsaac, and the two shared similar brown hairstyles. Apatow suggested Stone could color hers for the role to differentiate the two characters.

"So we dyed her hair red, which I think she had never done before," Apatow said. "And since then, she has cursed me because now people love her with red hair and she's had to live with that for a lot of her adult life."

Rogen didn't get to play Seth, and they didn't make the movie in Canada, where the script originally took place. Otherwise, quite astonishingly, the two lifelong friends got to make the movie they envisioned as young teens—only better, because the years under Apatow's guidance had helped them turn *Superbad* into more than a collection of McLovin jokes.

"What Judd has taught me more than anything is to start with a very simple emotional story and I just know from my own experience working on rewriting other comedies that almost no comedies begin with that," Rogen explained. "Honestly the jokes kind of come last. A lot of the time is spent on the emotions of the story and making sure the scenes feel real and relatable and are grounded in truth and experiences of us or people we know, and then we kind of just hope that if you get a bunch of funny people on set then funny shit'll happen also."

Indeed, for a movie with so many jokes about underage drinking and menstrual bloodstains, *Superbad* is ultimately a genuinely touching story about a friendship. Seth and Evan, like the real Rogen and Goldberg, are inseparable pals—but their impending journeys to different colleges is about to push them apart, and possibly for good. Unlike so many other films about high school virgins looking to score, only the mighty McLovin actually gets laid. Despite their overwhelming drive to have sex for the first time, neither Seth nor Evan beds their intended targets; instead, the buddies sleep together (non-sexually) and reaffirm their bond before they head off to different schools.

Whether viewers connected more to that theme or to the jokes about terrible fake ID names, *Superbad* became the most improbable hit from the Apatow collective to date. Against a budget around $20 million, *Superbad* earned $174 million worldwide, further cementing Apatow as Hollywood's premiere comedy producer of the moment, and establishing Rogen and Goldberg as potential superstar screenwriters. Rogen's unshakable faith that people wanted an edgy high school movie had been proven right.

Looking back on the *Superbad* experience, Apatow would say he was most proud of the fact that when Seth first showed him the script in the year 2000, he never forced Rogen and Goldberg to bow to the demands of people who thought a tamer movie would be a less risky proposition.

"I always knew it was funny," Apatow explained. "And Seth always believed that if you made this kind of movie that was really edgy and real to his experience that people would go crazy for it. And I always believed him, so when we started showing the movie and the audience would just explode I was just happy that I didn't chuck it in a drawer and assume Seth was wrong."

But success as enormous as *Knocked Up* and *Superbad* back-to-back in the summer of 2007 must be fed with more movies. The question was not if they should make another movie, but what that movie should be. During a panel at the New Yorker Festival, film critic David Denby marveled at the duo's recent hits and noted, "You guys have done amazing things for the adolescent male and young men. Could you do the same thing for women? Can you imagine a girl trio or quartet or a female protagonist of one of your movies?"

The answer to that question was already on the way.

CHAPTER 16

Action!

When I was a little boy, I always wanted to be a dinosaur. I wanted to be a Tyrannosaurus rex more than anything in the world. I made my arms short and I roamed the backyard. I chased the neighborhood cats and I growled and I roared. Everybody knew me and was afraid of me. And one day my dad said, "Bobby, you are seventeen, it's time to throw childish things aside," and I said, "Okay, Pop." But he didn't really say that. He said, "Stop being a fucking dinosaur and get a job."

—Dr. Robert Doback, *Step Brothers*

On paper, *Drillbit Taylor* had a blockbuster pedigree. It was produced by Judd Apatow, cowritten by Seth Rogen, based on a concept by legendary director John Hughes, and starred Owen Wilson as a homeless man who takes a job as a bodyguard to a couple of bullied high school kids—but it underperformed in theaters, making it the rare film from Apatow in this period that didn't become an instant smash.

Its failure could be attributed to several factors, from its odd title to its PG-13–rated content, which landed it in the no-man's-land between a typical Apatowian filth fest and Hughes's child-focused comedies like

Uncle Buck or *Home Alone.* In 2008, though, the most commonly cited reason for *Drillbit Taylor*'s disappointing performance was the fact that Wilson did zero interviews to promote it.

At the time, Wilson's publicists blamed his absence from the *Drillbit* press tour on his busy schedule. But on March 28, 2008, the *Los Angeles Times* wrote that Paramount made the "intentional choice" not to involve Wilson because they were "worried that rather than let Wilson plug the movie . . . his interviewers would steer the conversation toward the 39-year-old actor's hospitalization last summer following an apparent suicide attempt."

On August 26, 2007, police were called to Wilson's home in Santa Monica. In the days that followed, tabloids swirled with speculation about Wilson's mental state, and breathlessly reported on the actor's "dark history of depression," his apparent suicide attempt, and his recovery at Cedars-Sinai Medical Center in Los Angeles. Despite the enormous amount of attention on him, Wilson never publicly discussed the incident, and only released a brief statement afterward: "I respectfully ask that the media allow me to receive care and heal in private during this difficult time."

Wilson's subsequent recovery resulted in some big changes on several comedies in 2008. Prior to the incident, he was scheduled to reunite with Ben Stiller for his first effort as writer/director/star since 2001's *Zoolander.* The new film would combine Stiller's gift for inspired pop culture mimicry with his fascination with vain but brittle men. It would mock both Hollywood war epics and the insecure actors who populated them. Stiller called the film *Tropic Thunder.*

The idea for the movie came to him decades earlier, when he witnessed firsthand the complexities of a war movie's production while playing a small role in Steven Spielberg's *Empire of the Sun.* The late 1980s were dominated by a slew of films set in and around the Vietnam War, like *Full Metal Jacket*, *Hamburger Hill*, and *Platoon* (which Stiller auditioned for and didn't get). Performers in those movies were expected to attend "actor boot camp," where Vietnam veterans would teach hunky twentysomethings how to act like real soldiers.

"It seemed like there was a time when all actors were going away to fake boot camp and talking about these incredible experiences that they had and how it really changed their lives, and there was something there that seemed funny to me," Stiller recalled. "Maybe it was because I wasn't getting parts in those movies, but I was like, 'Oh, wow. You're going off and getting all of that. What about people who actually go to war?'"

At first, Stiller envisioned a movie "about actors who went and did the boot camp and made a movie and came back and felt like nobody cared, like the actual Vietnam veterans." Realizing he was coming perilously close to mocking real vets, Stiller tabled the idea—until he sensed it could work if instead of looking at a movie's aftermath, he focused on overly serious (and overly pampered) actors in the midst of an exhausting blockbuster production.

By the mid-2000s, Stiller had recruited writer/actor Justin Theroux and writer Etan Cohen to flesh out the concept into a full script. Stiller's dream casting for the role of the central character, an A-list action star named Tugg Speedman hungry for recognition as a legitimate actor, was A-list action star Tom Cruise. Stiller had playfully impersonated Cruise as far back as *The Ben Stiller Show*, and the two had become friendly after Stiller appeared with Cruise as his stunt double "Tom Crooze" in a comedy sketch on the 2000 MTV Movie Awards.

Stiller sent the *Tropic Thunder* script to Cruise—who responded less to Tugg Speedman than to a deficiency he found in the storyline. In *Tropic Thunder*'s early drafts, the movie was set entirely in Vietnam during the filming of an out-of-control movie. Tugg and the other actors got lost in the jungles of Southeast Asia, where they ran afoul of a twelve-year-old drug kingpin.

"I think you need another villain other than just the 12-year-old," Cruise told Stiller. "What about some greedy pig studio executive who really represents the gross part of Hollywood?"

"His idea to show the studio head actually fixed a problem we had for a long time," Stiller explained. "We never cut back to the real world for any of the previous drafts. All the Grossman scenes totally fixed the plot holes."

"Grossman" as in Les Grossman, an overweight, abusive, borderline psychotic, and altogether appropriately named studio mogul. As Stiller and the writing team continued fleshing out that character, they added more Hollywood satire—back in Los Angeles, Grossman threatens to cancel the film unless its director (British comedy star Steve Coogan) can get his gormless cast back in line. Like any good director of a 2000s-era comedy, Coogan's character realizes he can extract more authentic performances from his actors if they improvise. So he deposits Tugg and the rest of the cast in the middle of the jungle and tells them that hidden cameras will record their every move on their march back to civilization—right before he steps on a mine and blows himself up, which the oblivious Tugg attributes to a special effect.

With Cruise tied up in a series of massive productions of the sort that would make Tugg Speedman weep with envy, Stiller eventually realized he (or maybe Tom Crooze) would need to play *Tropic Thunder*'s lead instead. Then Cruise called Stiller back. He couldn't stop thinking about the movie. But by that point, the wheels were already in motion for Stiller to play Tugg.

"What else is open?" Cruise asked.

"Well, we haven't cast the Les Grossman role yet," Stiller replied.

Cruise said he'd do it on two conditions: He wanted to have fat hands, and he wanted the character to dance.

"Sometimes with a character you just get an instinct on what you want to do," Cruise recalled in 2019. "I remember for about a couple of months [Stiller] kept saying, 'Maybe we don't do the makeup and maybe you just look like yourself.' I said, 'No! Ben, I *really* need fat hands. And I'm gonna dance.'"

Stiller and the production designed the makeup—not just prosthetic hands, but a large jiggly belly and a bald cap with a hellacious comb-over—and did a camera test. Cruise showed up and started gyrating. Stiller took the test, filled with Cruise's wild movements, and added in some hip-hop music. The results were explosively funny. Tom Cruise would get his fat hands and dancing.

Even by the standards of the Frat Pack era of Hollywood, when comedy stars routinely crossed over into each others' projects, *Tropic Thunder*'s cast was absurdly loaded. Besides Stiller and Cruise, the film featured up-and-comer Danny McBride ("one of the most uniquely funny guys to come around since Owen Wilson and Vince Vaughn," according to Stiller) as the film-within-a-film's overeager pyrotechnics expert, Jack Black as a heroin-addicted comedian, Nick Nolte as the grizzled Vietnam vet who wrote the book that inspired his film, *Saturday Night Live* star Bill Hader as Les Grossman's right-hand man at the studio, *Undeclared* alum Jay Baruchel as the youngest member of the film's ensemble, and Matthew McConaughey as Tugg's loyal agent, Rick—the role originally intended for Owen Wilson—who goes to nonsensical lengths to ensure Tugg receives the TiVo promised to him in his contract.

But by far the most important and most potentially fraught role in *Tropic Thunder* was that of Australian actor Kirk Lazarus, a five-time Oscar winner who takes his job so seriously, he claims not to break character until he's recorded each film's DVD commentary. To that end, Lazarus undergoes an experimental "pigmentation alteration" surgery to more convincingly portray the part of African American Sergeant Lincoln Osiris in the fictional *Tropic Thunder.* Which meant whoever played the role of Lazarus would essentially be doing it in blackface—a repulsively racist trope dating back to live theater and early silent cinema.

The actor Stiller asked to take up that challenge was then in the midst of a remarkable career resurgence. Once one of the most acclaimed young actors of his generation, Robert Downey Jr.'s personal and professional lives bottomed out in the late 1990s and early 2000s as a result of rampant drug and alcohol use. At one point, Downey's substance abuse got so bad that it wasn't a matter of whether directors wanted to hire him or not; directors *couldn't* cast him in movies because no one would insure any project he became attached to.

After years in various prisons and rehab facilities, Downey got sober and began working again, gradually dipping his toe in major Hollywood films like *Kiss Kiss Bang Bang* and *Zodiac.* Stiller met Downey and quickly realized he was one of the few actors who might be able to pull off the tightrope walk that was Kirk Lazarus. ("It had to be a guy who [you] would actually believe is this incredible award-winning actor and also be really funny and also be able to do that character because he's in character for the whole movie," Stiller said.)

Downey's reaction to the role: "This is the stupidest idea I've ever heard."

"I know. Isn't it great?" Stiller replied.

Downey was understandably apprehensive. But he also thought, "in the right context, it could be entertaining." Then again, he admitted, "it could be disastrous." Downey agreed to play the part.

After first conceiving the project on a Steven Spielberg set, Stiller got the $90 million he needed to convincingly mimic a massive Hollywood war film from Spielberg's own DreamWorks Pictures. Despite its origin as a vehicle for Stiller to poke fun at actors who sincerely compared their sacrifices to those of actual combat veterans, *Tropic Thunder* was not exactly the smoothest production of the filmmaker's career. Largely shot on location in Hawaii over a period of thirteen weeks, the cast and crew battled constant rainstorms, bug bites, illnesses, and injuries. Robert Downey Jr. took to jokingly referring to the film as "Ben Stiller's Comedy Death Camp." Not a cheap Comedy Death Camp, either; *Tropic Thunder* reportedly wound up going $15 million over budget.

It also garnered a fair amount of controversy, not only for Downey's use of blackface, but also for the movie's repeated use of the word "retard"—not necessarily to describe people with intellectual disabilities but as part of the movie's broader satire of self-important actors, specifically those who portray people with intellectual disabilities in a shameless attempt to impress Oscar voters. In *Tropic Thunder*, Tugg Speedman, who built his career in soulless action sequels, makes a bid for artistic credibility with a movie titled *Simple Jack*, an inspirational drama about a mentally challenged young man. Tugg's plan to impress the Academy failed, Lazarus (in character as Lincoln Osiris) explains, because he went "full retard," something an actor should never do in their quest for awards for critical hosannas.

The joke was clearly aimed at Stiller's colleagues in the world of filmmaking, and perhaps even himself. But that didn't necessarily negate *Tropic Thunder*'s repeated use of the antiquated and offensive term, and the movie ultimately drew some protests from disability activists. In defending the movie, Stiller insisted that "in the context of the film I think it's really clear, they were making fun of the actors and actors who try to use serious subjects to win awards."

Between its edgy, relatively niche subject matter (movies about Hollywood have historically never been massive moneymakers) and nearly nine-figure budget, *Tropic Thunder* was a risky project for DreamWorks. But the film got great reviews—and, in yet another irony, a movie that openly mocked navel-gazing actors wound up earning Downey an Oscar nomination for Best Supporting Actor. *Tropic Thunder* ultimately earned $195.7 million worldwide, despite the fact that it opened in theaters just one week after a similarly scaled action comedy produced by Stiller's old collaborator, Judd Apatow: *Pineapple Express*.

* * *

Apatow's big action movie could be traced back to another A-list actor: Brad Pitt. Unlike *Tropic Thunder*, which mocked Hollywood's self-absorbed stars and their puffed-up Oscar-baiting productions, Apatow's project celebrated over-the-top action—starting with *True Romance*, where Pitt played a laid-back stoner named Floyd.

"He's so funny in a two-minute scene," Apatow explained, "that the kernel of the idea was 'What if there was a movie that was all about *that* guy? And: How come there's no good action in Cheech and Chong movies?'"

"Judd originally had the idea for a weed-action-comedy and he kind of handed it off to me and Evan [Goldberg]," said Seth Rogen. "And we thought if it could really function in all those terms: As a weed film and as an action film and as a comedy and it had a story to it that you actually cared about, that'd be a movie I'd want to go see! That's really where we started."

Rogen had written the initial drafts of the script that became *Pineapple Express* during the lean years between *Undeclared* and *The 40-Year-Old Virgin*, when Goldberg would occasionally come down from Canada to visit him, and the pair would collaborate on whatever short-term assignment Apatow had for them at the time. Rogen and Goldberg always liked the idea of a weed-action-movie, but whenever they explained it to others, they were often met with confusion—or worse.

"People thought we were really crazy for making that movie," Rogen said. "I remember people would just be like, 'That sounds stupid.' And we were like, 'Yeah we're trying to make the *not* stupid version of it.'" When Apatow got on a hot streak with *Anchorman*, *Talladega Nights*, and *The 40-Year-Old Virgin*, Sony decided to take a chance on *Pineapple Express* as well.

Rogen and Goldberg's script followed a process server named Dale Denton, who witnesses a drug-related murder and then goes on the run with his bumbling dealer, Saul. Given Rogen's own amiable pothead persona, he and Goldberg always intended that he would play the dealer, while they would pursue a more traditional leading man to play the process server. But when they met with Rogen's old *Freaks and Geeks* costar James Franco for that role, Franco—who had been the first member of the *Freaks and Geeks* cast to really break out in other projects when he costarred in Sam Raimi's *Spider-Man* as Peter Parker's friend Harry Osborn—expressed more interest in Rogen's part; that of the perpetually stoned Saul.

"We were like, 'You know what? That is probably more interesting.'" Rogen said.

It was Danny McBride, cast as Saul's supplier, Red, who suggested they consider his old friend from the University of North Carolina School of the Arts, David Gordon Green, as a potential director. Although Green's features to that point drifted into more dramatic territory, McBride knew he had a wicked sense of humor and had made several comedy shorts back in film school. Apatow and Rogen screened them and liked what they saw. They also liked the results when they had previously paired their outrageous comedy style with a filmmaker who was good with actors, like Greg Mottola on *Superbad*.

"Instead of hiring the people who do these big, like, *Wedding Crashers*, let's hire someone who does independent movies with emotional stories that we really like," Rogen said in 2019. "Because we really knew that the most important thing was the emotional stories." After meeting with Green a single time for forty-five minutes, they hired him to direct *Pineapple Express*.

Green delivered exactly what they asked for. *Pineapple Express*, like the weed its characters love to smoke, is a true hybrid: equally hilarious and exciting. Some scenes seamlessly meld the two modes, as when the paranoid Dale and Saul attempt to make a swift getaway from a police officer (who, in an amusing twist, was about to help them) by stealing the cop's car. That leads to a wild chase that becomes even more chaotic when Saul gets his foot lodged in the car's dirty windshield while attempting to kick it out. Embracing its inevitable R rating given its level of drug use and profanity, the film is also surprisingly violent, with many of the major characters getting whacked in comically excessive ways. (One dirty cop is shot, then has an exploding, flaming car dropped on them for good measure.)

Like *Superbad* before it, *Pineapple Express* is about a male friendship in crisis—one that's far more central to the story than the protagonist's nominal love interest (a high school student, played by Amber Heard). Instead, Dale is squarely focused on his budding rapport with Saul, who he previously was embarrassed to associate with, but comes to see as a loyal friend. True to Apatow and Rogen's plan, Green emphasizes the bond between the two men, and later with McBride's Red, who initially betrays the duo, only to come to their rescue after a change of heart. The film's final scene, which was entirely improvised by Rogen, Franco, and McBride, consists of nearly four straight minutes of the three men celebrating their survival and mutual appreciation of one another in a diner.

Pineapple Express continued the Apatow-Rogen hot streak at the box office. Against a budget of just $25 million it earned more than $100 million worldwide. And it wasn't the only R-rated Apatow production in theaters in the late summer of 2008, either. When *Pineapple Express* debuted in multiplexes on August 6, it was competing for screens and ticket sales with Apatow's third collaboration with director Adam McKay and star Will Ferrell.

Step Brothers grew out of McKay, Ferrell, and John C. Reilly's successful collaboration on *Talladega Nights*. Before that movie was even edited, the trio began discussing how to work together on another project, this time with Reilly involved from the earliest stages.

"We sat down and we had dinner and we pitched a bunch of different ideas," Ferrell said. "And it was really Adam who later said, 'What about two grown men, one lives with his mother and the other lives with his father. They get married and they're forced to live together under the same roof. And we'll figure it out later, but for whatever reasons they're allowed to live there.' And we immediately without any sort of thinking or any explanation or exploration of male adolescence, we just thought it struck us as such a funny premise to create a comedy."

"I do remember saying to Will and John, 'I just picture you guys in bunk beds,'" McKay recalled. "And I was like, 'Is there a way to have that?'" With little more than those bare bones of a concept—and with Ferrell and McKay coming off back-to-back hits—Sony gave them a green light. The trio brainstormed the deeply strange story from there, drawing a surprising amount from their own childhoods. Ferrell had bunk beds in his room growing up, built by his father—but poorly, so they were just the slightest bit unstable. Ferrell remembered carefully climbing up every night and thinking to himself, amid the creaking, "Bunk beds aren't what they're cracked up to be." Reilly contributed a tale from his own relationship with one of his brothers, who played drums and was fanatical about people touching his kit, which, naturally, only made Reilly more tempted to mess with it.

Ferrell's previous McKay heroes had been emotionally immature men, but he and Reilly's characters in *Step Brothers*, Brennan Huff and Dale Doback, took the notion of a "man-child" to the absolute extreme. Brennan and Dale were full-blown children in the bodies of middle-aged adults. Where Ron Burgundy might have acted like a horny teenager around Veronica Corningstone, Brennan was more like a second grader who happened to resemble a beloved *SNL* performer. After the battle over Dale's drum kit reaches a fever pitch, Brennan unfurls his testicles (actually an extremely lifelike prosthetic that Ferrell claimed cost $10,000 to make) and rubs them all over the cymbals and snares.

McKay and company never did quite figure out how or why Brennan and Dale's development became so arrested; an early draft included a sequence where their newlywed parents took them for psychological testing that turned up no obvious roots of their psychoses. But they shoved every last idea they had into *Step Brothers*, whose first draft eventually ballooned to 180 pages. Conventional wisdom typically goes that one page of screenplay equates to one minute of screen time—meaning *Step Brothers* was initially envisioned as a three-hour opus of anarchic infantilism.

The movie did not necessarily shrink once they got on set, either. Assembling an eclectic and enormously talented group of actors, comedians, and improvisers, they continued to utilize the collaborative process that McKay honed on *Anchorman* and *Talladega Nights*: performing scenes as written, then encouraging everyone involved on and off camera to pitch alts that might improve and expand upon the script. On *Step Brothers*, it might have worked too well. When McKay got into the editing room, he found that his first rough cut ran five full hours.

"There was so much footage," McKay said. "It was brutal. It was, like, a lot of stuff. So you just go and you start testing it. You put it up in front of audiences. You get a sense of where it's kind of feeling right, where the story's kind of working. Even though the story is pretty minimal, pretty simple in this film, always that's what takes precedence. There's certain jokes that just fall out when they don't work for the arc of the movie."

Even after McKay hacked *Step Brothers* down to a manageable ninety-eight minutes, there were times where that arc gave way to flights of total nonsense. After Brennan and Dale mend fences over the testicular drum kit incident, they begin to collaborate on all sorts of oddball projects. They launch their own company named Prestige Worldwide, and create a music video called "Boats 'N Hoes," the lyrics of which are largely summarized by its title. After their antics gradually drive a wedge between their parents (played by Richard Jenkins and Mary Steenburgen) and the couple decide to divorce, Brennan and

Dale attempt a belated move toward responsible adulthood, which leads to Brennan overseeing an all-important event for a helicopter-leasing company called the Catalina Wine Mixer. There, Dale and Brennan reunite and save the day by performing a shockingly earnest (and inexplicably Spanish-language) rendition of Andrea Bocelli's "Con te partirò."

McKay summed up *Step Brothers*' appeal in 2010 when he said, "All of our movies are a joke that we're even making them as movies. That's part of the inherent joke of them is they gave us this equipment and let us do this." Even as you watch *Step Brothers*, you can't believe the thing actually exists.

Although it was not initially as well received by critics as *Talladega Nights*—film critic Roger Ebert alleged that "in its own tiny way, it lowers the civility of our civilization"—McKay and Ferrell's fan base turned out once again. With $128 million in worldwide grosses, *Step Brothers* became the pair's third hit in a row. And it came at a time when the market was absolutely saturated with comedies. By the end of the summer of 2008, moviegoers had their choice between *Tropic Thunder*, *Pineapple Express*, and *Step Brothers*—plus Anna Faris in the very funny *Playboy* playmate parody *The House Bunny*, the musical comedy *Mamma Mia!*, the Ice Cube sports comedy *The Longshots*, and *The Rocker*, starring Steve Carell's *The Office* costar Rainn Wilson and Ferrell's *Anchorman* costar Christina Applegate.

And that was just during the summer. The release calendar in 2008 also included Jack Black in the quirky indie video store comedy *Be Kind Rewind*, *Freaks and Geeks* costar Jason Segel baring his soul and his genitals in the Apatow-produced *Forgetting Sarah Marshall*, Steve Carell in an update of the old spy spoof *Get Smart*, Adam Sandler in the Judd Apatow cowritten *You Don't Mess with the Zohan*, Seth Rogen in Kevin Smith's *Zack and Miri Make a Porno*, and Vince Vaughn in a holiday movie called *Four Christmases*.

Most of these projects were hits; some were huge blockbusters. (Did you know *You Don't Mess with the Zohan* grossed more than $200 million worldwide? You really don't mess with that guy!) But it ultimately didn't matter. Despite the enormous amount of creative energy flowing from these intertwined comedic filmmakers, the cinema of 2008 was defined by another genre.

Superhero films had been on the rise since the early 2000s, when Fox made their first movie based on Marvel Comics' long-running *X-Men* franchise, and Sony released *Spider-Man*. Hollywood took notice of both projects' enormous popularity and began cranking out more and more comic book adaptations.

In 2008, after decades licensing their characters to other studios, Marvel got into the moviemaking business itself. Their first project right out of the gate—*Iron Man*, starring *Tropic Thunder*'s Robert Downey Jr.—became a surprise smash, eclipsing all industry expectations and grossing more than half a billion dollars. In July, one week before *Step Brothers* teabagged its way into theaters, Christoper Nolan's Batman sequel *The Dark Knight* became one of the biggest movies in history.

Nolan's previous film, 2005's *Batman Begins*, had done well, earning $375.4 million. *The Dark Night* became a full-blown pop culture phenomenon. By the time it ended its theatrical run the following winter, it had earned over $1 billion, more than double *Tropic Thunder*, *Pineapple Express*, and *Step Brothers* combined. When Ben Stiller quipped on the *Tropic Thunder* DVD commentary, "It's Spider-Man and Iron Man!" at Tobey Maguire's cameo during one of the film's fake movie trailers (for an arthouse drama about gay monks called *Satan's Alley*) it was more than a joke. It was an unwitting acknowledgment that the whole Hollywood ecosystem—and the 2000s comedy boom—had reached a tipping point.

CHAPTER 17

Where No Man Has Gone Before

Look, as a friend, I'm gonna tell you something: You're not funny. I mean, you look funny, but you're not funny.

—Chuck, *Funny People*

A few days before New Year's Eve 2008, MTV debuted a reality show about a group of eight "regular guys" fighting for the right to join reality TV hunk Brody Jenner's entourage. In naming Jenner's show, MTV seized upon a word that had grown increasingly popular through the early 2000s: *Bromance.*

Jenner's series got canceled after a single season, but the fact that MTV made a show called *Bromance* at all speaks to just how that term—first used by skaters in the 1990s—had exploded into the public consciousness by the end of the twenty-first century's first decade, thanks in large part to the movies described in this book: dude-forward comedies about the misadventures of (and intimate friendships between) quippy heterosexual guys.

Bromances were everywhere in 2009, including massive blockbuster reboots of *Sherlock Holmes* and *Star Trek*, along with the biggest comedy of the year. It came from Todd Phillips, whose *Old School* was one of the films that helped launch the bromance trend. In 2007, Phillips needed a project to get his career back on track. He'd just had his first real box office flop: 2006's *School for Scoundrels*, a failure he later blamed on its distributor-imposed PG-13 rating. ("I go, 'Bob, I don't do that. I don't speak in PG-13. I'm an R-rated human being,'" Phillips said of his debate over the project's rating with Miramax chief Bob Weinstein. "He goes, 'It's gotta be PG-13.' So that's what we did, and it hurt the movie.")

Searching for something in his preferred milieu, Phillips fell in love with a script by Jon Lucas and Scott Moore about a Las Vegas bachelor party that goes horribly wrong. The writers cooked up the screenplay after they heard a story about a Hollywood producer who went missing at his bachelor party. They turned that thread into a comic mystery where the groomsmen wake up after a depraved night with no memory of what they did—or, more importantly, where they left the groom. The script was almost titled *What Happens in Vegas*, but the rights to that name, inspired by the famous Las Vegas ad campaign, were hard to pin down. So instead, the project became known as *The Hangover.*

"I don't want to get too specific, but something about the premise just spoke to me," Phillips told *Variety* in 2007, when they reported that Warner Bros. had spent $2 million to acquire the rights to Lucas and Moore's script for him to direct. Phillips and screenwriter Jeremy Garelick rewrote the material to add all sorts of additional complications, brainstorming the craziest things the groomsmen could find after they wake up from their drugged stupor, including a Bengal tiger owned by Mike Tyson, after Phillips recalled reading that the real Tyson once owned one.

Phillips approached several big-name stars to appear in the film, including Paul Rudd and Jack Black, but they turned him down. Instead, he started to look at lesser-known actors, hoping to replicate the same formula for success he'd found with *Old School* when he helped Vince Vaughn reinvent himself as a comic leading man and proved Will Ferrell was more than a sketch player on *Saturday Night Live.*

The first actor cast was Ed Helms, a costar on *The Office*, chosen to play the henpecked dentist Stu. To play the crew's cocky ringleader Phil, Phillips picked Bradley Cooper, who had previously appeared as Vaughn's slimy nemesis in *Wedding Crashers*. Cooper had also starred in several TV series, including an adaptation of chef and TV host Anthony Bourdain's memoir *Kitchen Confidential*, but he'd never headlined a comedy before; Phillips responded to the confidence he projected onscreen. ("There's this swagger that he seems to have that I think was important for his character . . . so we kind of built it around that.")

For the final third of the so-called "Wolfpack," the eccentric Alan, Phillips considered everyone from Jonah Hill to Thomas Haden Church before thinking of Zach Galifianakis, a favorite stand-up of Phillips's who, like Cooper and Helms, was still searching for his big-screen break. Galifianakis was in Canada at the time, and he had to fly himself down to Los Angeles for the audition. He told himself, *This is going to be a waste of money because I'm not good at auditions*, but he managed to land the part.

Or at least he had the part if Warner Bros. would agree to fund the film at all. With zero A-list stars involved, Warner Bros. was hesitant to back the project.

"I presented a number for the budget, and they did not want to make that version of the movie with this group of guys," Phillips later recalled. "I said, 'Tell me the number that I can just go and make a movie, and we'll see you at the premiere.'" To get the budget under $35 million, Phillips gave up his $6.5 million directing fee in exchange for a stake of the movie.

That was a canny choice by Phillips, and not just because of what it ultimately did for his bank account. Keeping the budget low not only allowed him to cast his preferred performers; it enabled him to push the envelope comedically with very little argument from the studio. When Phil, Stu, and Alan awaken from their forgotten rampage through Las Vegas they not only discover a tiger in their hotel suite bathroom, they also find a baby—who they later leave inside a hot car in the middle of a hot Las Vegas afternoon. (They do crack the windows for the kid.) Galifianakis also has the baby mime masturbation at one point, something he initially did between takes to the baby's inanimate stand-in as a goof, but which Phillips found so amusing he then had to ask permission from the child's father to re-create the moment on camera. When he asked the dad, he replied, "[My wife is] going to be gone for a half-hour. Can you do it in the next half-hour?" They could, and they did.

At times, the production was nearly as wild as the characters' onscreen exploits. After they filmed a scene where costar Ken Jeong leapt out of the trunk of a car completely naked in full view of the Mandalay Bay casino, the police showed up threatening to shut the film down. For the scene where (fictional) cops use the Wolfpack as guinea pigs in a taser demonstration, Phillips tried to talk the actors into letting him tase them for real. ("Then the Warner Brothers lawyers stepped in, thank God," said Galifianakis.)

The Hangover's final scene takes place at a wedding, but the marriage it establishes is largely beside the point. The bride, played by Sasha Barrese, only appears as an occasional voice on a phone. The only other significant female character is a stripper played by Heather Graham, who marries Stu during the trio's lost night of drugs and booze. Like *Old School*, *The Hangover* featured a central trio of men—each film contains an arrogant alpha, a lovelorn nebbish, and an unpredictable wild card—and sent them careening through a series of wild exploits, a core dynamic Phillips once again attributed to his ongoing fascination since childhood with the awkwardness of men's friendships.

Where most other bromances accentuated touchy-feely moments between the leads, *The Hangover*, in keeping with Phillips's taste for the dark side of human behavior, focused instead on a series of kidnappings, beatings, car crashes, roofies, tiger maulings, and tasings. (At least they weren't real tasings.) The jokes often veered into outright cruelty; Jeong's character repeatedly calls Galifianakis's Alan fat, a drug dealer mockingly calls the Wolfpack "retarded," and Phil's outgoing voicemail message includes an admonishment not to text him because texting is "gay."

The Hangover may not have had a cast with a lot of marquee appeal, and it might have contained pervasive callousness and occasional bursts of homophobia, but that original hook by Jon Lucas and Scott Moore—a comedy that unfolds like a detective story with a bunch of hungover bros trying to piece together what happened during a wild night in Vegas they can't remember—was an undeniably brilliant concept. And Phillips and his cast exploited it to the hilt. While Warner Bros. expected the movie to gross in the neighborhood of $20 million its opening weekend, which already would have been a solid debut for a movie that only cost $35 million to produce, *The Hangover* wound up opening to $45 million, along the way to earning more than $469 million in theaters worldwide. It became the tenth-biggest film of the year worldwide—earning more money in theaters than expensive franchise films like *G.I. Joe: The Rise of Cobra*, *X-Men Origins: Wolverine*, and *Terminator Salvation*. According to *The Hollywood Reporter*, the film earned so much money that the piece of the backend profits that Phillips accepted in lieu of a typical salary eventually netted him $70 million.

Bromances were so pervasive in 2009 that Judd Apatow even put a joke about them in his movie that summer—when a talent manager tells a hotshot movie star played by Adam Sandler, "You can't swing a dead cat without hitting an offer for you. You ready for this? Paul Rudd wants to do a bromance with you!" (Rudd himself starred in yet another 2009 bromance, *I Love You, Man*.)

That bit of meta humor came in *Funny People*, which Apatow stitched together from several different concepts that he had been contemplating for a while. For years, he'd wanted to make a movie about his first and biggest passion, stand-up comedy. He'd also tinkered for a long time with the idea of a relationship between a mentor and a protégé, another important facet of his early career, but he struggled to find a compelling hook for a story because all of his mentors were so supportive when he was starting out, and a bunch of nice people who lift each other up does not exactly make for scintillating drama. Apatow also wanted to collaborate with Adam Sandler, an old friend and former roommate from their early years working the L.A. comedy scene.

The last piece of the puzzle that brought all those disparate elements together, unfortunately, was death. Now in his early forties, Apatow had begun to lose people close to him, including his mother, who passed away in the spring of 2008 after a battle with ovarian cancer. Apatow watched as his mom went through the ups and downs of new treatments, each with their own incremental improvements and setbacks—and, he said, he noticed "she seemed much more at peace" when she thought she was going to die because "a lot of her daily concerns disappeared."

"I have to assume that if she'd gotten a new treatment and had another year of life, she would've gone back to being neurotic about the same stuff she was always neurotic about," he said. "It's hard to hold on to any peace you find. That's what I was trying to talk about with *Funny People*."

Apatow blended together all those disparate elements to create a story about two comedians at opposite ends of the Hollywood spectrum: George Simmons (Sandler), a former stand-up turned mega movie star, and Ira Wright (Seth Rogen), a struggling comic at the start of his career. Despite his wealth, fame, a gorgeous mansion overlooking the Pacific Ocean, and easy access to casual sex with countless women, George is miserable—and that's before he gets diagnosed with an aggressive form of leukemia. Given an experimental drug with an 8 percent chance of curing his condition, he resigns himself to his fate and starts doing rambling stand-up sets at clubs around Los Angeles—where he bumps into Ira performing at an open mic night.

Ira impresses George enough that he hires him to write some jokes and lets him tag along to some private corporate gigs. Later, George receives stunning news: His experimental treatment actually worked. He will live, and perhaps for a very long time.

His second chance inspires him to reconnect with his lost love, a woman named Laura he dated and cheated on in his youth, played (of course) by Apatow's wife, Leslie Mann. Laura, a former actress, moved out of L.A., married a traveling salesman (Eric Bana), and had two kids, played (of course) by Apatow and Mann's daughters, Maude and Iris. George drags Ira along on a visit to Laura's family in Northern California, where he tries to convince her to leave her husband, while Ira tries to convince George to abandon his quest to win her back. "Why does everyone else get to be happy?" George asks him, to which Ira responds, "It seems like your happiness might come at the cost of destroying this family!"

Given that Apatow was taken under the wing of numerous older comics in his youth, and that the Ira character, like Apatow, is a product of divorce and a young transplant to the L.A. comedy scene, a viewer might want to read *Funny People* as a semi-autobiographical story about Apatow's own early years as a struggling stand-up—except Apatow claims all of his mentors were kind, while George is selfish in the extreme. And while Apatow, unlike George, had been married with kids for years by the time he made *Funny People*, he could also relate to the isolating nature of fame and success George experiences in the movie—meaning the film is probably best understood as a story about two Apatow avatars, young and old, past and present, in conversation with one another.

While *Funny People* could be described as Apatow's third bromance in a row, he largely rejected that descriptor. "I look at it like Marx Brothers movies, [which were] comedies about these weird male friendships," he explained. "There's a grand tradition—*Stripes*, *Animal House*—about the weird ways guys interact with each other because they're idiots. They're fun to watch."

But *Funny People*, despite its title, willfully explored a different sort of comic territory than Apatow's earlier films. It was about comedians dealing with unfunny subjects; illness, death, personal rejection, marital strife. Its stand-up comedy milieu—including numerous scenes where Sandler, Rogen, and other members of the cast performed their own jokes in front of real comedy club audiences—was the spoonful of sugar Apatow used to make a serious film look more like another of his risqué romps. If *Funny People*, which clocked in at 146 minutes in its theatrical cut, was about two construction workers from different generations grappling with those same issues, it might not qualify as a comedy at all.

That—combined with all the competition in 2009 from other bromances—could explain why *Funny People* was Apatow's first stumble at the box office as a director. Even critics, who had largely praised his two previous movies, were more muted in their enthusiasm for *Funny People*. And, *The Hangover* notwithstanding, most of 2009's top-grossing titles were once again big-budget spectacles and sequels like *Transformers: Revenge of the Fallen*, *Harry Potter and the Half-Blood Prince*, and *The Twilight Saga: New Moon*. It was another harbinger of things to come, one hinted at by George's toast during the Thanksgiving dinner he spends with Ira in *Funny People*: "It's good to be young. It kind of sucks being old, so just enjoy this. Enjoy time. Time slips away. I promise you."

CHAPTER 18

God's Great Miracles

"I just feel, like, I'm excited, and I feel relaxed, and I'm ready to paaaaar-taaaay!"

—Annie Walker, *Bridesmaids*

The 2000 edition of the U.S. Comedy Arts Festival in Aspen, Colorado featured the first public performance anywhere of *The Simpsons* scripts by the series' voice cast and a career tribute to beloved comedy team Mike Nichols and Elaine May. But all anyone remembered about the festival was a stray remark by legendary seventy-three-year-old comic and filmmaker Jerry Lewis.

Lewis was feted with his own career retrospective in Aspen, hosted by Martin Short and attended by one thousand festivalgoers. During the Q&A portion of the event, someone in the audience asked Lewis what female comics he admired.

"I don't like *any* female comedians," he shot back.

When Short suggested Lewis must have admired someone like Lucille Ball, Lewis said no, then doubled down: "A woman doing comedy doesn't offend me, but sets me back a bit. I, as a viewer, have trouble with it. I think of her as a producing machine that brings babies in the world."

The blowback was swift. Lewis got so much negative publicity that within days he felt compelled to make an apology—although his apology insisted his comments were "misinterpreted" *and* reasserted that "when women, doing comedy, do routines written for them by drill sergeants, I take objection. Their filth makes me and many ashamed to be in our business, and to me women doing anything, especially comedy, are looked upon by me as one of God's great miracles—they can make a baby." (As apologies go, this is not a particularly strong one.)

Most corners of the comedy world loudly rejected Lewis's statements as ludicrously out of touch; attitudes that belonged to an earlier, less enlightened era. But movie comedies starring and especially created by women during the period in which Lewis made his infamous pronouncement were so few and far between, it's hard not to wonder whether some in power in Hollywood tacitly agreed with him.

Certainly the movies covered in previous chapters of this book contain roles for women, some fairly substantial, a few absolutely essential. But it's also true that women were never the central focus of any of these comedies. Even in a film like *There's Something About Mary*—which made actress Cameron Diaz a major star—the title character exists to be pursued by the various male characters, and Diaz herself is mostly resigned to the role of object of desire and observer of (or, in the case of the infamous "hair gel" scene, the wearer of) the jokes.

In the years after *There's Something About Mary*, Diaz largely shifted her focus to dramas like *Any Given Sunday* and *Vanilla Sky* and big blockbusters like the film adaptation of *Charlie's Angels*. But right as the Frat Pack era took off in the early 2000s, Diaz headlined a rare example of an R-rated comedy presented from a female perspective. In 2002's *The Sweetest Thing*, she plays Christina, a single woman who enjoys frequenting San Francisco nightclubs with her best friends, Courtney (*Anchorman*'s Christina Applegate) and Jane (Selma Blair). On one of their evenings out, Christina meets a nice guy named Peter (Thomas Jane), who is supposedly attending a bachelor party with his brother

(Jason Bateman). Christina and Peter hit it off, so she and Courtney travel to the wedding to crash it (three years before *Wedding Crashers*). As it turns out, Peter wasn't simply attending the bachelor party; he was its guest of honor, and the wedding Christina and Courtney are headed to is, in fact, his.

Those basic story beats could belong to almost any romantic comedy of any era; what makes *The Sweetest Thing* unusual and marks it as a product of this period of movie comedies are the ribald set pieces that punctuate the narrative. Screenwriter Nancy Pimental, who also worked on the adult animated series *South Park* and once described her sense of humor as "like a 12-year-old boy," filled her script with outrageously explicit moments to rival any of the biggest movies of this era, including Blair getting a man's penis stuck in her throat while giving a blowjob, a calamity that requires assistance from EMTs to resolve. (Absurd as it sounds, Pimental claimed in a 2018 interview she based that scene on an incident that happened to a friend of hers who was dating a "super punk guy" who "did get his piercing caught behind her tonsils.")

Director Roger Kumble also filmed an entire musical sequence where Diaz, Applegate, Blair, and a chorus of extras sang a tribute to penises to the tune of Right Said Fred's "I'm Too Sexy." But the entire number wound up getting excised from the final cut, a move indicative of executives' broader concerns about a film about and for women that was filled with so much explicit humor. "We were going to push way more boundaries, and they got scared," Applegate said. "They got really freaked out about it and they were like, 'Oh, women shouldn't be talking like this,' and they toned it down? We couldn't say cock and things like that. And then the penis song went away."

The drastic trims are apparent in *The Sweetest Thing*'s final form, which ran only eighty-five minutes and races at breakneck speed from one gross-out moment to the next. The film got miserable reviews and wound up earning only $24.7 million in U.S. theaters, a fraction of *There's Something About Mary*'s total from 1998.

Inevitably, given its poor box office performance, *The Sweetest Thing* became the exception in an era when movie comedies rarely made space for their female stars to shine. Instead, the primary role they typically played was bewildered straight woman and love interest, witnessing and occasionally scolding the men's actions—like Christine Taylor, who played opposite her real-life husband, Ben Stiller, in his movies *Zoolander* and *Dodgeball: A True Underdog Story*, or Amy Smart, chasing after the heroes of *Road Trip* and playing a crucial police witness in *Starsky & Hutch*, or Ellen Pompeo, who maintains a safe distance from the middle-aged frat house shenanigans in *Old School* even as she flirts with Luke Wilson's character.

Amid these films' generally spotty track record with female characters, there were occasional bright spots. Christina Applegate gave as good as she got in *Anchorman*, returning Ron Burgundy's sexist jabs as the ambitious Veronica Corningstone. And *Wedding Crashers* became a breakout movie for Isla Fisher by casting her as a character who appears at first to be another undemanding conquest for Vince Vaughn and his barrage of pickup lines, only to reveal her own wild side. Still a relative unknown in America at the time she was cast, audiences got to discover Fisher's committed comedic intensity right along with Vaughn's character.

In Judd Apatow's films, no performer was more reliable or more fearless than his wife, Leslie Mann. They met when she auditioned for *The Cable Guy*; at their first encounter, Apatow supposedly turned to Ben Stiller and said, "That's so weird that the future Mrs. Apatow just walked in the door." The two married in 1997 and Mann remained a fixture in almost every Apatow project from that point forward.

As Apatow's subsequent films grew more autobiographical, he cast Mann and his daughters as a loosely fictionalized version of his own family in scenes that became a space to examine his own life and marriage—scenes that were all the more interesting because Mann's characters in films like *Knocked Up* and *Funny People* rarely seem satisfied with domestic life. When Mann's Debbie discovers *Knocked Up*'s Apatow stand-in (played by Paul Rudd) has been lying to her in order to spend time going to the movies alone, she tells him, "You just think because you don't yell that you're not mean. But *this* is *mean*!" Apatow later called the exchange "one of the scenes I'm most proud of and ashamed of at the same time" because it was "a little too accurate" to his actual marriage.

But Apatow's unflinching approach to relationships, coupled with storylines that often depicted male characters as fun-loving goofballs and his female characters as nagging scolds, started attracting criticism—including from one of Apatow's stars. Less than a year after *Knocked Up* opened in theaters to massive grosses and positive audience response, its female lead, Katherine Heigl, publicly criticized the film, calling it "a little sexist."

"It paints the women as shrews, as humorless and uptight, and it paints the men as lovable, goofy, fun-loving guys," she added. "It exaggerated the characters, and I had a hard time with it, on some days. I'm playing such a bitch; why is she being such a killjoy? Why is this how you're portraying women? Ninety-eight percent of the time it was an amazing experience, but it was hard for me to love the movie."

Amplified by Heigl's comments, the arguments that Apatow's work was somehow misogynistic followed him for years. But Apatow said in a 2017 interview that he "never felt any of those criticisms were accurate," having cut his teeth writing jokes for Roseanne Barr, and helping guide *Freaks and Geeks*, whose Lindsay Weir was one of the most complex female characters in broadcast television history. "I never felt like the idea that I wasn't interested in women or was portraying them negatively warranted much reflection," he added.

Elsewhere he claimed the issue was largely based on how his films looked in comparison with traditional comedies where, he said, "women are presented as trophies. So if you show a real woman who's not necessarily pleasant every moment, there are certain people who say you're being mean. 'You're making women look like shrews.' Well, why wouldn't she be mad right now? She's in a tough situation with a guy who's not ready. Wouldn't you be pissed off some of the time? It's kind of an accurate tone. When you show immature guys, you might be showing misogynistic behavior, but that doesn't mean the movie is misogynistic. You're mocking immaturity."

When Apatow's first several movies all focused on immature men, he'd insist "it would be weird if the first movie I wrote was all about the issues of a woman, because I'm a young idiot." In fact, he *did* want to produce movies from a woman's point of view. He was just self-aware enough not to write them himself.

"People thought we weren't doing female-focused projects," Apatow said. "We were; the scripts just weren't good yet."

Bridesmaids, the film that changed a lot of that perception, grew from seeds that were planted years earlier.

While he was casting *Knocked Up*, Apatow brought in one of *Saturday Night Live*'s newest stars to audition for a tiny role as one of Katherine Heigl's bosses at the E! channel. The part was so small Apatow didn't even bother with a script at the audition; he simply had Kristen Wiig improvise a bunch of different personalities she could bring to the role. Apatow loved the version where Wiig played it passive-aggressive, and he asked her to do it in the movie.

"She was so funny, we couldn't even believe how funny she was," Apatow recalled. "She didn't even have any lines. I just said, why don't you be the other executive and just chime in. And she was on fire." Apatow was shocked when he tested *Knocked Up* and Wiig got huge laughs from the very first words out of her mouth. Just as he had when Steve Carell impressed him with his wicked improvisations on *Anchorman*, Apatow asked Wiig if she had any ideas for movies of her own. ("That's kind of my M.O.," said Apatow. "Someone's really funny—you got any movie ideas?")

Like Carell before her, Wiig made an improbable movie star. Raised in upstate New York and Pennsylvania by a father in the boat business and a mom who worked in a variety of places, including a jewelry store, Kristen Carroll Wiig grew up fascinated by show business and terrified of public speaking. She studied art at the University of Arizona, and figured she'd probably wind up as a teacher somewhere until she had to take an Acting 101 course to complete a requirement for her major.

She did well enough that the professor encouraged her to think seriously about pursuing acting as a career, something she had never done before. Working a job she hated in a plastic surgeon's office one day, she suddenly had an epiphany.

"I went in the bathroom and I looked in the mirror and I was like, 'Okay, what do you want to do?'" Wiig recalled. "And it just came out: I want to move to L.A. and I want to try acting."

That's what she did—even though she had never been to Los Angeles before, and she had no idea how to get into the business. Before she could reconsider (and without telling her parents she was dropping out of school) Wiig packed up her things and moved west. She started studying acting and working a variety of jobs; at one, a friend turned to her and said, "Have you ever heard of the Groundlings? I went to a show last night and I thought of you." Wiig had never seen improv comedy in her life. But on her friend's recommendation she went and had a second epiphany.

"I go and see a show," she said. "And it was like the opposite of Arizona. It was like when you know you're in the right place. I was like, 'Oh, I was supposed to find this theater.'"

Wiig immediately started studying at the Groundlings' school; after a few years she made it into the troupe's main company. Not long after that, her manager sent a tape of Wiig's sketches and characters to *Saturday Night Live*; after several auditions, she joined the cast in the fall of 2005. When Apatow asked Wiig for movie ideas a few years later, she turned to Annie Mumolo, a friend and frequent collaborator from the Groundlings. Mumolo had recently gone through a period where she had served as a bridesmaid seven times in two years. Her friends were all settling down, getting married to guys who made a lot of money while she was barely scraping by. That seemed like the good starting point for a film about female friendships.

"My friend's engagement party was at this beautiful country club," Mumolo said. "My car had both rearview mirrors duct-taped on. I came home with this crazy party favor and the door to my apartment was swollen shut, so I had to crawl through the space between my window frame and air conditioner. I just remember sitting there thinking that this was the great divide between where I was headed and where my friend was headed. Our lives had suddenly become very different."

They pitched the idea of a bridesmaid movie to Apatow, who responded to the concept immediately. But the night after their meeting, Wiig and Mumolo had second thoughts—and stumbled upon a second idea they liked even better than the first.

"We were like, 'Oh, we should probably do that other idea,'" Mumolo recalled. "So we called him and told him and then he was like, 'No, oh yeah, no, I already sold the other one.'"

Mumolo and Wiig had written plenty of comedy sketches, but had zero experience with film scripts. They bought Syd Field's famous book on screenwriting and got to work. Their *Bridesmaids* screenplay followed a woman named Annie (Wiig) reeling from a bad breakup and the closure of her beloved bakery business. When her best friend Lillian (Wiig's *SNL* colleague Maya Rudolph) gets engaged, and Lillian asks Annie to serve as her maid of honor, Annie should be thrilled. But all she feels is jealousy—not only of Lillian but also of Lillian's new friendship with the snooty Helen (Rose Byrne). Despite her best intentions, Annie screws up one wedding-related event after another from the bachelorette party to the bridal shower, until she becomes so fixated on competing with Helen for Lillian's approval and appreciation that she begins to endanger their lifelong bond.

With skills honed churning out large amounts of material at the Groundlings and *SNL*, Wiig and Mumolo cranked out a first draft in six days. "We turned it in, we were like, 'We're done!' And [Apatow] was like, 'What?'" Wiig later said, laughing.

Instead, that was only the beginning of a four-year process of drafts, revisions, and readings. With each new version, Apatow pushed the duo to amplify the tension and heighten the stakes between Annie and Lillian. They held their first table reading for the script in 2007. *Bridesmaids* didn't open in theaters until the spring of 2011.

One of the members of Apatow's brain trust who attended that first reading was *Freaks and Geeks* creator Paul Feig. In the years after the show was canceled, Feig had shifted into directing television and several features, and he had recently cast Wiig in a small role in his Christmas comedy *Unaccompanied Minors.* Apatow knew Feig was looking for more female-driven projects—because, according to Feig, he's always related more to women than men, especially in comedies.

"When I was coming up," Feig says, "all comedies were kind of descendants of *Animal House*—which I love. It's a brilliant movie, one of my favorite comedies of all time. But then it gets watered down and becomes a formula; a bunch of slobs, and they're all trying to get laid. I just don't find it entertaining. And they always just treat the women as second-class citizens and objects. And all my friends growing up were either nerdy dudes or girls. I was close to my mom. I would watch old movies with my mom and see Katharine Hepburn and Rosalind Russell, these strong female characters. Then I'm watching these other comedies, and all the women's roles are terrible! They're props, basically, for guys to make fun of, be annoyed by."

Bridesmaids was filled with funny women. Just as Apatow had surrounded Seth Rogen with his real best friends in *Knocked Up* to enhance the on-set chemistry, Feig populated *Bridesmaids*' cast with actresses Wiig had worked with before, including Groundlings alums Wendi McLendon-Covey as the miserable married bridesmaid Rita, and Melissa McCarthy as Lillian's fiancé's aggressive sister, Megan. There were funny women in every scene; Ellie Kemper as an innocent newlywed bridesmaid, Rebel Wilson as Annie's strange roommate Brynn, and Jill Clayburgh as Annie's mother, who loves to paint portraits of celebrities like Wynonna Judd.

Feig was a great choice to direct Mumolo and Wiig's script because so much of their concept was built around the growing tension between Annie and Lillian, and the cringe-inducing laughs sparked by Annie's repeated screwups—Feig's favorite sort of humor, and a staple of *Freaks and Geeks.*

"I like people being very uncomfortable, because I've been made to feel so uncomfortable throughout my life," Feig says, laughing. "And I'm so guarded about not making other people feel uncomfortable in real life that I think it's therapeutic for me. I'm gonna make you feel really uncomfortable. It's like making a horror movie. You can sit there safely and we can do terrible things on the screen, and you're fine. It's cringey because it hits close to home."

No scene in *Bridesmaids* generates more discomfort than its famous set piece at a high-end dress shop. Before Lillian's wedding party goes shopping, Annie takes the group out to lunch at a dubious Brazilian steakhouse; by the time they arrive at the store, everyone but Helen (the only one in the group wise enough to avoid eating any tainted meat) is in the throes of violent food poisoning. Kemper pukes on McLendon-Covey while she is *also* puking into a toilet, as McCarthy shits into a nearby sink and screams, "Look away!" Trying on her wedding dress in another corner of the shop, Lillian gets struck by such an intense urge to take a dump that she runs outside into traffic whimpering, "It's happening! It's happening! It happened. . . . It happened," as she pops a squat in the middle of a bustling city street.

The dress shop scene was a showstopper—but it was one of the few sequences in *Bridemaids* that wasn't in Wiig or Mumolo's script. They had originally conceived a shopping sequence where Annie tried on a dress she liked so much she drifted off into a fantasy that resembled a parody of a perfume ad, complete with men (including a cameoing Christian Bale) chasing her through a forest.

Everyone agreed the sequence as written could have been funny, but Apatow believed they needed something bigger and bolder, a moment that would give Annie the chance to make a really big mistake that placed her at odds with Helen and Lillian—like, say, inadvertently causing the entire bridal party to shit and puke all over a bougie dress shop. (Did I mention the whole place is covered in white carpets?)

When Apatow pitched that concept, Wiig later admitted, she and Mumolo "didn't love the idea" and resisted it. They didn't want to see their characters vomiting on each other and crapping everywhere; that didn't fit their vision for the movie at all. But Apatow insisted they at least try it; he promised if the scene didn't work, they wouldn't use it. After Mumolo and Wiig wrote their version of what Apatow wanted, they realized it did contain a lot of potential for the sort of character-based comedy they liked. Annie is so desperate not to concede that the restaurant she picked made the whole bridal party sick, for example, that she refuses to reveal her own food poisoning. That leads to an uproariously squirmy beat where Annie tells a suspicious Helen that she's still hungry, and then reluctantly accepts a Jordan almond to prove it. As Wiig queasily crunches down on the candy, her face grows paler and sweatier.

"[That's why] I love Judd so much," Wiig said in 2017, "he taps into that part of me that can be like, 'Well, we're gonna write this' and then 'Here's the plan.' And *he's* like, 'Let's see what else we can do' and 'Let's play' and 'Let's throw that away for a second' and 'Let's try this.' And he inspired me to think that way."

That approach suffused the entire production of *Bridesmaids*. Mumolo once described the production's unorthodox filming process thusly: "We would have our shooting script, which we would always shoot. And then we would shoot several other versions of our favorite stuff from other drafts if we had the opportunity. And then we would improvise off the script sometimes. And then also the days before, we would prepare for the upcoming scenes by writing other new stuff. And so it was a fluid sort of process of us constantly writing and feeding dialogue and feeding scene ideas and feeding areas and feeding lines to people after we shot the written stuff."

The result was a comedic meritocracy where every imaginable idea was tried and the best one went into the movie, thanks to a production nimble enough to adapt when they needed to change something at the last minute. When Wiig and Mumolo first envisioned *Bridesmaids* in the mid-2000s, for example, *The Hangover* was still years away, so one of the big set pieces in their script—a disastrous bachelorette party in Las Vegas—felt fresh. (The scene they wrote would have involved Annie trying to keep up with the well-heeled Helen and quickly exhausting her limited finances, followed by an uncomfortable encounter with some extremely sweaty male strippers.)

By the time *Bridesmaids* began filming in 2010, though, *The Hangover* had exploded into the public consciousness and become synonymous in audiences' minds with wild Las Vegas exploits. A lot of potential viewers were already going to compare the two raunchy R-rated comedies anyway; setting a chunk of the movie in Vegas would only exacerbate the issue. So weeks before production officially got underway, Apatow announced that the entire Vegas sequence had to go.

Scrambling for a story solution, Feig hit on an idea: What if the bridal party *tried* to go to Vegas, but never arrived, because something goes horribly wrong on their flight? "Annie was like, 'Oh, I know how to write that,'" Feig recalled. Soon, she and Wiig had supplied sixteen new pages.

The new concept, enhanced by copious on-set improvisations, involved Annie medicating her fear of air travel with a combination of alcohol and sedatives provided by Helen, which eventually gets her so stoned that she winds up arrested by an air marshal, forcing an emergency landing. The plane, just like the film itself, never made it to Nevada. "I remember sitting there [reading], laughing so hard. . . . I was like, this is way funnier than anything we would've done in Vegas," Feig said.

But even without the wild bachelorette party, as *Bridesmaids'* release date in the spring of 2011 drew closer, the media began framing the film as an intentional response to *The Hangover.* There were some obvious parallels, including wedding backdrops and a fair amount of suggestive humor. When it came time to promote the movie, Wiig and Mumolo were called upon to explain whether they had planned *Bridesmaids* as some sort of response to that film—or any of the guy-heavy comedies of the previous decade and their bro-heavy vibes.

"We never approached it that way," Wiig insisted in 2017. "We wanted to write something that we thought was a funny story and that had a lot of places for women, 'cause we know a lot of funny women and hadn't really been seeing a lot of that. And so that's really what it was. I mean Annie and I, it's very simple: We just sit down and write stuff that makes us laugh. And there's usually no deeper meaning."

Still, Hollywood saw *Bridesmaids'* release as some sort of bellwether for female-driven movies. Paul Feig says that in the months leading up to the premiere, he began to feel like the entire future of women in comedy was resting on his shoulders.

"I had a few women writer friends who were excited going out and trying to pitch their female-led comedies, and they would be told, 'We just gotta wait and see how *Bridesmaids* does first,'" Feig says. "It was a sobering moment."

Up until the last minute, things did not look promising. Feig says all he heard about the film's early marketing was "Oh, this looks terrible, clearly all the funniest jokes are in the trailer." The studio's experts who predict each film's weekend box office projected it would make $13 million in its first three days in theaters—which would have spelled disaster for *Bridesmaids* and any chance of another comedy like it for years to come.

On the day *Bridesmaids* opened in theaters, though, Feig kept getting calls from the studio adjusting their predictions in real time. First $13 million became $15 million—better, but still not fabulous. Then more messages came in; $15 million was still too low, it was looking more like $18 million. Then $18 million became $19, then $22, then $24—and then a final total of $26.2 million. *Bridesmaids* never topped the box office charts—in a further sign of changing times in Hollywood, yet another superhero movie, Marvel's *Thor*, claimed the top spot in theaters that weekend in May—but it played well all through the summer. It ultimately earned more than $288 million worldwide. As of this writing, it remains the highest-grossing title Judd Apatow ever produced.

It's not hard to see why; *Bridesmaids* is one of the funniest Hollywood comedies of the twenty-first century. Unlike so many studio films produced to open on a specific release date, yielding movies that are not so much "good" as "good enough to come out when their distributor demands," *Bridesmaids* marinated for years as Wiig, Mumolo, Apatow, and Feig refined their work over and over. And Apatow's instructions to push the emotions and heighten the drama around the gross-out gags yielded one of modern movies' most trenchant studies of female friendships, and how fraught they can become when people move into different phases of their lives.

Bridesmaids was also the rare R-rated comedy to earn some accolades from the notoriously comedy-averse Academy Awards. In the spring of 2012, *Bridesmaids* received two Oscar nominations—one for Melissa McCarthy for her whirling dervish of a supporting turn, and one for Wiig and Mumolo for their insightful and hilarious screenplay. The movie wound up losing in both categories at the Oscars, but it did earn several other prizes, including one for Best Comedy at the Critics Choice Awards. Accepting his trophy at the show, Judd Apatow got onstage and said, "Jerry Lewis once said that he didn't think that women were funny. I'd like to say, with all respect, fuck you."

CHAPTER 19

This Is the End

Strap it in, boys. 'Cause it ain't pretty out there. And you two are dinosaurs.

—Sammy Roscoe, *The Internship*

In the field of psychology, an "extinction burst" refers to a sudden increase in a behavior after it stops producing the desired outcome. Any parent who's sleep-trained a baby has witnessed an extinction burst firsthand. For months, when your child cried in the middle of the night, you reinforced that behavior by rewarding it; you dragged your exhausted carcass out of bed to pick them up, feed them, and soothe them.

When you start sleep training, you teach the baby to soothe itself. Said baby typically does not pick up this lesson on the first try, which might lead to a night with *more* crying—so much crying, in fact, that you come to believe your daughter has been possessed by some sort of "Night Demon" and requires an exorcism. Assuming you don't give in and pick the baby up again—and thus reinforce the undesired behavior—that excessive, almost demonic level of crying, enough to wake neighbors and small animals, will eventually recede and go extinct. (This is just a hypothetical example, not based on any specific child or night from hell. I would never call my daughter a "Night Demon." Never.)

The extinction burst for this generation of movie comedies came in 2013. Nearly every major figure who participated in their rise released a new project, but everywhere they looked, there were signs that audiences' tastes had evolved and this type of movie was on the verge of a steep decline. 2011 saw the release of several comedy hits, including *Bridesmaids* and Todd Phillips's massive sequel to *The Hangover.* But there were also major flops as well, like *The Dilemma*, about a man played by Vince Vaughn who discovers his best friend's wife is cheating on him and then has to decide whether or not to tell him. The film performed so poorly with audiences that its director, Ron Howard, later called it the only title in his entire career he considered a disappointment.

It didn't help *The Dilemma* that it opened in theaters against major competition from Seth Rogen and Evan Goldberg. Hot off the success of movies like *Superbad* and *Pineapple Express*, and with superhero movies exploding in popularity thanks to *Iron Man* and *The Dark Knight*, Sony pitched the duo a movie based on *The Green Hornet*, a radio program about a masked vigilante that debuted in the 1930s. By the 2010s, the Green Hornet was mostly remembered for his short-lived 1960s TV show, which made Bruce Lee a star as the Hornet's sidekick, Kato. But that was enough for Sony to offer Rogen and Goldberg the chance to make a $70 million action comedy out of the property. They leapt at the chance—and wound up spending three years on what Goldberg called "the hardest job we ever had."

"We fell into the trap," Rogen explained in 2013. "When you start doing well, you inherently gravitate towards the notion—we did anyway—of doing the biggest thing that you can. You think, like, 'What are we working towards?' And then you start to think, 'Well, these superhero movies are popular, they make all sorts of different ones. This is kind of like the Holy Grail of what movies are right now.

This is like the biggest game in town.' So I think we got excited about the prospect of having that opportunity that we [were] completely naive as to exactly how much of what makes us good would be basically stifled and evaporated," he said. "It's a PG-13 movie, and just most of what makes us funny is not that type of thing."

Superbad had cost less than $20 million—cheap enough "that the studios always had bigger fish to fry," per Rogen. *The Green Hornet* ultimately cost the company around six times that much.

"What I didn't appreciate," he added, "was that now *we* were the bigger fish and we would get all the attention that was being absorbed by other movies on our earlier movies. I remember telling people, 'They don't fuck with us, it's great,' and then we were sitting in a meeting where [the executives] were like, 'All right, notes. Page one,' and I was like, 'Page *one*?! What the fuck?' I was like, 'I've written two movies for you guys over the last few years, I thought we were cool. What are we doing here?'"

Directed by Michel Gondry, a brilliant filmmaker of heartfelt arthouse indies like *Eternal Sunshine of the Spotless Mind* also making the transition from small-scale fare to big-budget action, *The Green Hornet* wound up doing reasonably well at the box office, grossing over $227 million worldwide. But it got some of the harshest reviews of Rogen's career—the *New York Post* called the film "deadly"—and it garnered a reputation as an expensive mess; proof that trying to shove the square peg of raunchy bro humor into the round hole of the big-budget superhero movies may not work.

Technically the comedic extinction burst of 2013 started in the final weeks of 2012, when Judd Apatow released *This Is 40*, a "sort-of sequel" to *Knocked Up* about that movie's fictionalized version of Apatow's family played by Paul Rudd, Leslie Mann, and Maude and Iris Apatow. (Given her remarks about how she did not enjoy the way *Knocked Up* depicted her as a "shrew" and a "bitch," it may not surprise you to learn Katherine Heigl did not return.)

In a sense *This Is 40* was also a return to the middle-aged malaise of Apatow's first film, which also put the number "40" front and center in its title. (As if courting comparisons between the two, they also end with the same climax: The male lead gets into a bicycle accident, sparking an emotional reconciliation for the story's central couple.) But *The 40-Year-Old Virgin* also had a big marketable hook at its center—a man in his forties who's never had sex contemplates getting laid for the first time—while *This Is 40* is a rambling, episodic examination of a marriage. Rudd's Pete and Mann's Debbie deal with the physical discomforts of aging (mammograms, prostate exams), money woes, and constantly squabbling kids. (I wonder if Apatow ever called his daughter the Night Demon?) The film wanders through their lives, following some threads and discarding others. It could be described as a mess. But then, most people's forties are messy.

"One person said, 'There wasn't enough story,'" Apatow told *GQ* the week of *This Is 40*'s release. "But that's the whole point of the movie . . . it's not about a gigantic incident happening. It's about the normal ebb and flow of your family life and your relationship—the little moments of connecting or not connecting. And not understanding why."

Apatow's stand-in, played by Rudd, owns his own record label, which he uses to promote artists like Graham Parker who have a lot to say, but struggle to find commercial success for their deeply personal artistic expression—about as good a metaphor as you're going to find for a director trying to convince audiences to support autobiographical comedies in the mid-2010s. *This Is 40* grossed $90 million worldwide, more than *Funny People*, but not by much, and certainly nowhere near the level of *The 40-Year-Old Virgin* or *Knocked Up*.

It also grossed far less than 2013's biggest comedy sequel, *The Hangover Part III*, which continued the exploits of the Wolfpack after two remarkably successful films. *The Hangover Part II* replicated the first movie's structure, with the same trio of screwups played by Bradley Cooper, Ed Helms, and Zach Galifianakis suffering another lost night, this time in Bangkok, then retracing their steps to find another missing member of another wedding party. The third film finally abandoned that structure and instead forced the men to reckon with the repercussions of their depraved actions in the first film, when a gangster (John Goodman) holds the Wolfpack's friend Doug (Justin Bartha) hostage and demands they locate Ken Jeong's Leslie Chow, who has stolen his money.

Phillips once said *The Hangover* movies "always start with darkness." But *The Hangover Part III* starts with darkness and only gets darker from there. Galifianakis's Alan accidentally decapitates a giraffe, an incident that gives his father (Jeffrey Tambor) a fatal heart attack. At the father's funeral, Alan delivers the eulogy and declares, "I'll always remember the last words he said to me. 'I'm proud of you Alan. Never change.' Well, I heard you loud and clear, Daddy. I will never change. *Never ever*!" (In fact, in his final moments Alan's father had begged him to get his life back together, and to go back on his medication.)

That air of defiance feels very appropriate for Todd Phillips, who kept pushing *The Hangover* movies into bleaker territory with each subsequent installment. By *Part III*, the series played far more like an outlandish crime story than a traditional comedy. It also occasionally acknowledged, at least in a meta way, that the concept had run out of gas, as when Helms's Stu declared in one scene, "Someone needs to burn this place to the ground. I told myself I would never come back." After two extraordinarily successful films that launched all of its stars' big-screen careers, *The Hangover Part III* almost seemed to resent its own existence. The only hangover this time was entirely metaphorical; like their characters, the actors appear to be trapped in an unending nightmare, held hostage by a franchise that gave them everything and now demanded payback.

As sour and nasty as *The Hangover Part III* got, it did also acknowledge the fact that times were changing. As the comedians who wrote, directed, and starred in so many of these movies got older, the man-child characters at their centers needed to grow up as well. When Alan says he will never change, what he really means is he will never accept responsibility for his actions (like, say, murdering a zoo animal), or staid adulthood more generally.

But by *The Hangover Part III*, Alan *does* mature in his own quirky way. He begins a relationship with a woman he meets in Las Vegas (played by a cameoing Melissa McCarthy) and formally resigns his membership in the Wolfpack. He might not completely put away childish things, but he's definitely thinking about it.

The Hangover Part III made $362 million worldwide, an incredible total by the standards of almost any comedy series—except *The Hangover*, whose previous two films had averaged over half a billion dollars in ticket sales. (It also cost over $100 million to make, a far cry from the original's $35 million budget.) Audiences were growing weary of the gimmick, too; they gave the original *Hangover* an A via the moviegoing polling company CinemaScore. The second film scored an A–; *The Hangover Part III* earned a B. If nothing else, the third *Hangover* proved how difficult it is to make a good sequel to a truly original idea.

That fact also hung over *The Internship*, released a few weeks after *The Hangover Part III* in June of 2013. For years, DreamWorks had developed a potential sequel to *Old School* that would have sent Vince Vaughn's, Will Ferrell's, and Luke Wilson's middle-aged frat boys to spring break. But the actors involved never loved the concept, and their schedules were so busy that the project never came together. Similarly, a sequel to *Wedding Crashers* appeared to be impossible; it's hard to tell another story about the antics of a pair of reprobates after they settle down in committed relationships.

So Vaughn mashed concepts from both of his previous hits together and conceived the story of *The Internship*, which worked as a kind of spiritual successor to those earlier movies, as well as a reunion between Vaughn and *Wedding Crashers* star Owen Wilson. Once again, they play a pair of work buddies, Billy (Vaughn) and Nick (Wilson), whose lives flame out in spectacular fashion, this time after they lose their jobs as watch salesmen. As in *Old School*, they respond to their simultaneous midlife crises by surrounding themselves with college kids—in this case, by landing exclusive internships at the tech giant Google. As in both earlier movies, Vaughn and Wilson's nonconformist ideas put them in conflict with the unbending rules of a stuffy establishment, represented here by Google's disapproving mid-level executives, and other interns with the temerity to be actual college students with degrees in computer science and engineering.

Proud Luddites, neither Billy nor Nick own a webcam, so they apply for their Google internship using a computer in the children's section of their local library, where the tiny desks and chairs make them look like two overgrown children, a perfect visual symbol of the immaturity running through so many of the comedies of this era. But like *The Hangover Part III*, *The Internship* also nods at the fact that Vaughn and Wilson, now in their early forties, were getting a bit long in the tooth to play reckless sensualists. Their main concern isn't getting laid without any sort of emotional attachment; it's finding a stable career path through a world that's suddenly shifting under their feet.

Vaughn stumbled on the idea for *The Internship* when he watched a TV show about Google's corporate culture; they provide free food to employees and emphasize team building through leisure activities. He and Wilson met with executives from the tech giant to convince them to sign off on their concept. But gaining the company's approval to use their name and logo onscreen in a $58 million Hollywood comedy meant giving Google what Reuters described as "creative control over how the film portrayed its products." That arrangement meant in lieu of any sort of satire of bizarre workplace behavior or the corporatization of the internet, *The Internship* had to celebrate everything "Googley"—a word spoken aloud in the movie countless times.

So when the men first arrive at Google headquarters in Mountain View, California, Vaughn enthusiastically gushes, "The place is amazing! They got nap pods! They got massage rooms! They got a volleyball court! They got the whole nine! It's ranked as the greatest place to work at in America!" Forget the pointed capitalist critique of *Talladega Nights*; *The Internship* felt less like product placement in a movie than movie placement in a product, and moviegoers seemed to sense that, too. *The Internship* wound up earning less than $45 million in U.S. theaters.

By that point, there was a vaguely ominous feeling in the air about the state of these comedies, one heightened further by the next big one just a week later. Judd Apatow had produced all of Seth Rogen and Evan Goldberg's early work, but when they wanted to make a comedy about their friend's experiences with cancer around the same time that Apatow was already developing the similarly themed *Funny People*, they decided to strike out on their own. The cancer comedy, *50/50*, became the first release from Goldberg and Rogen's production company, Point Grey, named after the school where the men first met.

Their next effort was 2013's *This Is the End*. Based on a short film they had made a few years earlier, it stars Rogen and nearly all of the other onscreen graduates of Apatow University, including James Franco, Jay Baruchel, Jonah Hill, and Jason Segel, all playing fictionalized versions of themselves. In the film, the biblical apocalypse begins in the middle of a drug-filled party at Franco's house. Most of the partygoers die in gruesome ways—a coked-out Michael Cera is impaled by a falling streetlight, Jason Segel slips into a sinkhole to hell—while the few survivors (including Rogen, Franco, Baruchel, Hill, and Craig Robinson) barricade themselves in Franco's mansion to ride out the chaos.

Although nominally a comedy about the apocalypse, Rogen and Goldberg's *This Is the End* was ultimately another exploration of friendship after *Superbad* and *Pineapple Express*. The film begins with Baruchel's Jay arriving in L.A. to spend time with Rogen's Seth after a period where the two formerly close buddies had drifted apart. Once they arrive at the party, a kind of platonic love triangle plays out, with Rogen caught between his old pal Jay and his new buddy James Franco.

At the end of *This Is the End*, the subtext that Seth might be holding his friend back from moving on with his life becomes the actual text of the story, as Jay earns his way into heaven with good deeds and is sucked into the afterlife by a godly beam of light. But then Seth tries to hitch a ride into the Great Beyond with him, and must literally let his friend go, willingly sacrificing himself to save Jay—a selfless act that earns him his own ticket to the divine. After Seth and Jay arrive in heaven together, they celebrate their eternal reward by dancing with the Backstreet Boys (also playing themselves) to their hit song "Everybody (Backstreet's Back)."

This Is the End wound up making even less money in theaters than *The Green Hornet*. But it's also hilariously funny; the film's prolonged second act is an improviser's paradise, as the cast riffs on all the different conflicts that could arise from being trapped with a bunch of petty, pampered celebrities in the End Times—especially after Danny McBride shows up, severely hungover and having slept through the apocalypse, and immediately wastes all their remaining food and bottled water on a gluttonous breakfast and a footbath. Still, by casting himself and his buddies as themselves, Rogen seemed to acknowledge with *This Is the End* that a phase of his career—and perhaps an entire era of comedy—was coming to a close.

After all, this crew of comedians rose to popularity playing stoners and dorks at the fringes of polite society. A few years later, that identity no longer fit. Rogen, Franco, and the rest were now major stars at the epicenter of American culture, not to mention grown men who couldn't convincingly play slacker kids anymore. In one of the most heated exchanges before their heavenly reconciliation, Jay accuses Seth of selling out, and Seth tells Jay he needs to stop acting like he's still eighteen years old. The message was clear: It was time to start growing up.

Adam McKay and Will Ferrell had been interested in making a sequel to their popular tale of San Diego's handsomest and stupidest newsman for years, and had proposed the idea several times to Paramount Pictures, which rejected all of their pitches—in part because in the years since the original *Anchorman* premiered in 2004, most of its cast, including Paul Rudd and Steve Carell, had become major stars, and now commanded major star salaries. After everyone involved "cut their price substantially," per Adam McKay, Paramount finally announced the film in the spring of 2012.

The sequel built off the first *Anchorman*'s ending, where Ferrell's Ron Burgundy and Christina Applegate's Veronica Corningstone left San Diego for New York City to anchor a national news broadcast. As *Anchorman 2* begins in the late 1970s, Veronica is promoted and Ron is fired, setting off a series of personal and professional disasters for the mustachioed newsman. Separated from Veronica, fired from a crummy job hosting shows at SeaWorld, and contemplating suicide, he receives a lifeline from a company that wants him to be the face of a new twenty-four-hour-a-day news network. Ron's response to their offer: "That is without a doubt the dumbest thing I've ever heard! You mean news going twenty-four hours around the clock? A channel that's never off? No offense, but you are a stupid asshole."

While Ron Burgundy's business acumen might leave something to be desired, it's fairly clear that Adam McKay doesn't think a twenty-four-hour news channel is a great idea, either. Oh sure, it might make money. But buried beneath *Anchorman 2*'s mountain of absurd jokes—there's a whole running gag about Ron Burgundy raising (and bottle-feeding!) an injured baby shark—lies a fairly pointed critique of the cable news industry and its deleterious impact on the United States.

After Ron reassembles his team and goes to work for "GNN" (owned by an eccentric Australian billionaire clearly meant to resemble Rupert Murdoch), he realizes he can only succeed by telling people what they want to hear (i.e., crass sensationalism and blind patriotism) instead of what they need to hear, namely "boring" fact-based reporting. His plan works, of course, and Ron's broadcasts about how much America "kicks butt" garner huge ratings. ("It's total crap, but they can't stop watching it!" a character pointedly exclaims during one of Ron's more egregious ratings-chasing stunts.)

Most sequels suffer from a debilitating sense of sameness, but in Adam McKay's movies, familiarity breeds quotation rather than contempt. When *Anchorman 2* repeats gags or motifs from the original movie, it doesn't feel like a rehash so much as a reunion with old friends. At 119 minutes, it's also almost a half hour longer than the original *Anchorman*, and jammed with callbacks to the first film (Rudd's Brian Fontana now has a cabinet full of intimacy aids instead of wacky colognes) and several new characters, like Kristen Wiig's Chani Lastnamé, a love interest for Steve Carell's brick-headed weatherman who is somehow even more moronic than he is.

But overstuffed as it may be, *Anchorman 2* also takes unexpected risks, with McKay and Ferrell pushing their jokes into more absurd territory than ever before—as in the sequel's update of the first film's cameo-laden anchor fight. As one new surprise guest after another appears—including Jim Carrey, Marion Cotillard, Tina Fey and Amy Poehler, Sacha Baron Cohen, and Will Smith—the gags keep moving further from anything like our recognizable reality, until Steve Carell blows up a New York City skyscraper (along with Kanye West!) with a laser gun from the future while the Ghost of Stonewall Jackson (played by John C. Reilly) watches.

Anchorman 2 rode a massive wave of promotion into theaters, with Ron Burgundy–themed ice cream on grocery store shelves and Ferrell appearing as Ron in a series of cross-promotional ads for Dodge trucks.

Still, while the sequel outperformed the first *Anchorman*, it never topped the weekend box office, debuting in second place behind the middle chapter of a trilogy of films based on J. R. R. Tolkien's novel *The Hobbit.* By all accounts, Ron Burgundy's return to movie theaters was successful. It was also the twenty-third-biggest movie of 2013 in the U.S. It made more money than *This Is 40*, *The Hangover Part III*, and especially *The Internship*, but it lagged far behind franchise films like *The Hunger Games: Catching Fire*, *Iron Man 3*, *Man of Steel*, *Fast & Furious 6*, *Star Trek into Darkness*, and *Thor: The Dark World.*

Even when the Frat Pack filmmakers tried to adapt to the modern world of Hollywood mega-blockbusters with lavish spectacles and sequels, they struggled to measure up. More and more their over-the-top comedies looked like relics; the last members of an ancient species from some bygone epoch now headed for extinction.

EPILOGUE

No Laughing Matter

They don't even make movies like that anymore. It's all superheroes and fighter pilots. You want art, you watch TV.

—June Fleisher, *The Studio*

The most consequential movie comedy of the 2010s involved Seth Rogen shoving a missile up his ass.

To be clear, that scene is not what made *The Interview* consequential. (Impressive? Certainly. Consequential? No.) It grew out of Rogen and Evan Goldberg's fascination with North Korea and its mercurial leader, Kim Jong Un, who is roughly Rogen and Goldberg's age and supposedly loves American films and basketball.

"Knowing everything we do about celebrities—how vain they are, how easily manipulated and impressed they are, how much they like OTHER famous people—we realized: If an American celebrity came to North Korea and met Kim Jong Un in person, they'd probably be shocked to find themselves really liking the guy," Rogen wrote in his memoir, *Yearbook*.

So Rogen and Goldberg conceived a comedy where Kim Jong Un invites his favorite talk show host, Dave Skylark, to North Korea for an exclusive interview. The CIA seizes upon Skylark's trip as an opportunity to assassinate Kim. Skylark agrees to participate—until he spends time with Kim and comes to like and sympathize with him, which makes him second-guess the plan. (By this point, Skylark has lost the poison intended for Kim; the U.S. government sends a second batch via a drone strike, which is how Rogen, playing Skylark's producer, Aaron, winds up hiding a missile up his butt.) Eventually, Skylark realizes that all of Kim's hospitality during their trip was a facade designed to manipulate Skylark's affections and turn his interview into North Korean propaganda. Teaming up with a member of Kim's government who is fed up with his brutal regime, Skylark and Aaron manage to kill Kim and escape from North Korea.

Given the long-simmering tensions between the two countries, you might assume that it would be difficult to convince a multinational conglomerate to produce a movie about a CIA-sanctioned hit on a real world leader. You would be mistaken. According to Rogen, after he submitted the first draft of *The Interview*, Sony Pictures chairwoman Amy Pascal told him, "If you can get James Franco in this movie, we'll make it." And not only did Sony not mind the assassination plot, they actually asked Rogen and Goldberg to remove the fake dictator they had invented for their first draft of *The Interview* and replace him with the real Kim, a choice they compared to the famous celebrities who played themselves in Rogen and Goldberg's *This Is the End*. Except this time instead of depicting Michael Cera as a strung-out dirtbag, they'd brutally kill Kim Jong Un.

Production of *The Interview* went smoothly, and the movie scored well in early test screenings. Then the shit hit the fan. After Sony released the first trailer for *The Interview*, North Korea sent a formal letter to the United Nations in which they called the film "undisguised sponsoring of terrorism as well as an act of war." North Korea vowed retaliation if Sony released it. Suddenly, the company went from lobbying Rogen and Goldberg to use Kim Jong Un in the film to scrubbing the word "Sony" from *The Interview*'s credits and asking Rogen and

Goldberg to change the movie's ending so Kim (played by actor Randall Park) didn't die—and if that wasn't possible, to at least tone down his violent onscreen death in a massive helicopter crash a wee bit.

After much back-and-forth, all parties compromised on a slightly less graphic demise. But in late November, Sony's computer networks were hacked by a group calling itself the "Guardians of Peace," who proceeded to leak embarrassing company emails to the internet and threatened further attacks—including violence at movie theaters that screened *The Interview*—if Sony didn't pull the film. That's exactly what they did, canceling the movie's release on December 17, eight days before it was scheduled to open in multiplexes around the country, and two days before President Barack Obama weighed in on the controversy.

In his year-end press conference, President Obama said Sony made a mistake in capitulating to the hackers' demands, adding, "We cannot have a society in which some dictator someplace can start imposing censorship here in the United States. Because if somebody is able to intimidate folks out of releasing a satirical movie, imagine what they start doing when they see a documentary that they don't like, or news reports that they don't like." Within hours of Obama's remarks, Sony reversed course again and began looking into ways to release the film safely. They ultimately decided to make the movie available digitally on Google's online store, and screen it in several hundred independent theaters around the country.

If only *The Interview* itself was as compelling as the story surrounding it. While the film certainly has its share of highlights—did I mention Seth Rogen shoves a missile up his butt?—it doesn't quite possess the level of satirical sophistication its subject matter demands. For all of Rogen and Goldberg's interest in North Korea, *The Interview* was ultimately another variation of the same story of male friendship under fire they had told and retold since *Superbad*. In fact, *The Interview*'s plot outline is nearly identical to *This Is the End*: Two best buddies drift apart after a third man comes between them. (Admittedly, making the third man in this bromance North Korean dictator Kim Jong Un does mix up the formula slightly.)

Rogen later revealed that in the weeks following *The Interview* debacle he was terrified that the controversy surrounding the film would follow him "like a stain forever." But he soon realized "how fucking fast people forget shit and move on." Despite his international incident in November, Rogen was back at work rehearsing for a role in Danny Boyle's *Steve Jobs* by January. In 2021, he marveled, "I'm still allowed to work. People still pay me to make my films. People still finance them."

That's all true. But it's also true that while Rogen has starred in numerous movies since 2014, and he and Goldberg have created a diverse array of television projects through their Point Grey production company, it's now been a dozen years since they directed a feature film.

That says more about the state of movie comedies in general than the industry's feelings about these two specific filmmakers. Sony shunted *The Interview* to a home-first release out of necessity, but the incident became the canary in the comedy coal mine. It was almost unheard of in 2014 for a movie with major stars and tons of publicity to bypass theaters and debut online. Now it's routine.

"My goal in my career was to try to write comedies that would come out in theaters," says *Old School* and *Starsky & Hutch* cowriter Scot Armstrong. "I was worried that *I* wouldn't succeed. It never occurred to me that the whole business would go away. It never occurred to me that movies would not be released in theaters. So to have built a career, and then have that go away, is really wild."

So what the hell happened to theatrical movie comedies? The wave of movies that inundated theaters in the mid-2000s didn't shut off like a faucet; more like a hose that gradually lost water pressure. Or maybe in this context it was more like a frat party that never gets shut down by the cops and slowly loses steam as the night wears on, people get tired, and the guests head home, one by one.

"Looking back with a little distance, you can see that it was a moment," Judd Apatow wrote in his 2025 memoir, *Comedy Nerd*. "We were all working with each other and when we weren't, we were going to each other's table reads and preview screenings—it was an unofficial comedy collective, connected by our friendships and a shared sensibility. As we got older, people drifted apart and had different visions for their careers, so slowly that moment ended."

That process seemed to begin soon after the publication of the *USA Today* article that anointed the group in the first place. Armstrong says the first time he heard the phrase he knew it was going to "be bad for business" because "it seemed like the perfect thing for everyone to hate."

The members of the Frat Pack certainly hated it. In 2004, Will Ferrell dismissed the notion that he belonged to any sort of organized group of movie comedians, saying, "It's not like there's a hotline—we're not calling each other saying, 'What are we gonna do next?' It's that we're friends, like-minded people, and we think each other's funny." Vince Vaughn chimed in two years later, saying that while he loved working with "those guys . . . the whole Rat Pack–Frat Pack thing that came out is overblown. It was really Ben Stiller giving opportunities to people." Stiller himself was even more blunt in his criticism, saying in 2010, "That stupid bullshit Frat Pack name . . . that never really existed." Decades later, *Wedding Crashers* director David Dobkin says he's still "annoyed" that his movie sparked the term. ("I hate fraternities. I hate dudeness and male toxicity. To me, there's none of that in my movies," he adds.)

Given the way these filmmakers recoil at the mere mention of the Frat Pack, it's easy to attribute the group's slow dissolution to the showbiz equivalent of the observer effect, the principle in quantum physics that states the very act of observing a phenomenon inherently alters it. Recognizing and naming this very real movement in 2000s Hollywood seemed to change it on a cellular level.

But in truth there were more practical reasons for their gradual split. The success of the Frat Pack's collaborations raised the profiles of all the group's stars, which in turn raised their salaries on subsequent projects. At the start of the twenty-first century, DreamWorks could make a movie like *Old School* on a budget of $24 million, which was more than enough to afford Will Ferrell, Vince Vaughn, and Luke Wilson. In a world where Jim Carrey got $20 million to make *The Cable Guy*, that was a hell of a deal. A few years and hits later, Ferrell and Vaughn each commanded salaries in the Carrey range, making it almost impossible to put them opposite one another in a single film without enormous financial risk.

Victims of their own success, the Frat Pack essentially priced themselves out of making the ensemble-driven comedies that had made them so popular in the first place. While they were all talented enough to carry their own movies, they also were at their best bouncing ideas off one another and plussing up each other's jokes. By the late 2000s, even when a film *could* afford more than one of these stars, they were each so busy with their own individual projects it became nearly impossible to contribute to one another's films. Will Ferrell wanted Steve Carell to appear in *Talladega Nights*, just as he had in *Anchorman*. Carell had to turn him down; he had gotten so hot off *The 40-Year-Old Virgin* and *The Office* that when Jim Carrey didn't want to make a sequel to *Bruce Almighty*, Universal reconfigured the franchise around Carell's minor character from the first movie and rechristened the follow-up *Evan Almighty*. The Carell-fronted sequel, budgeted at around $175 million, became a massive flop. *Talladega Nights* moved on without him.

"It doesn't happen anymore really, but there was a time when we *would* go and do read-throughs of each other's scripts," Ferrell admitted a few years later. "I went and read on a script for Ben, I remember Ben came and read. There was communication, there was a sense of camaraderie, and actually appreciation of everyone's work. And then everyone became huge and too busy."

With each star generating their own material, instead of one Frat Pack movie every six months there was closer to six movies starring one member of the Frat Pack every month. Though Susan Wloszczyna's 2004 article in *USA Today* initially identified just six members of the Pack, her piece led to the creation of a "Frat Pack Tribute website" that kept meticulous tabs on the group's productions all through their heyday, partly via a massive bull's-eye–style graphic charting all of their frequent costars and affiliates. Within a few years of *Wedding Crashers*, this "Frat Pack Circle of Trust," named after a memorable Ben Stiller quote from *Meet the Parents*, had ballooned to the point that it included 132 different actors, actresses, and filmmakers, and encompassed such disparate screen presences as Melissa McCarthy, Jason Bateman, Emma Stone, Jackie Chan, cycling and doping legend Lance Armstrong, and Democratic strategist James Carville. (For some reason, Carville made cameos in both *Old School* and *Wedding Crashers*.)

That many people is not a pack. It's an army—one that generated an enormous quantity of films. From 2006 to 2016, Judd Apatow alone produced twenty-one movies. New adult-oriented comedies appeared at such a frequent clip that what had seemed so novel and edgy just a few years earlier now began to feel familiar. And familiarity can be comedy Kryptonite.

Seth MacFarlane, the creator of *Family Guy*, *American Dad!*, and the massive R-rated comedy franchise and subsequent TV series *Ted*, says that while there isn't a single factor that defines a great comedy, "the same thing that makes a dramatic twist work, the same thing that makes something like *The Sixth Sense* work, is the same thing that makes a great comedy work: It's surprise. If you can surprise your audience, whether surprise them with a laugh they weren't expecting, or surprise them with a plot twist, then you are on the road to making something that's great." Comedies like *Old School*, *Wedding Crashers*, *Anchorman*, and *The 40-Year-Old Virgin* surprised audiences with their gross-out gags, surreal set pieces, and boundary-pushing humor. But it's awfully hard to surprise an audience with a comedy when a new one opens in theaters almost every weekend of the year. When everyone is trying to shock people, nothing seems all that outrageous.

Still, while a glut of edgy comedies battling for space in a crowded marketplace didn't help matters, the true turning point came on January 16, 2007—a couple months after *Talladega Nights* debuted and a few months before Judd Apatow had his biggest hit as a director with *Knocked Up*—when a company called Netflix that sent customers DVDs through the mail in little red envelopes launched a sister service that delivered movies directly to its customers over their broadband internet connections.

In 2007, Netflix's streaming service debuted as a perk to its existing subscribers; those who used the company's movies-by-mail business could instantly access roughly one thousand movies and television shows online at no extra cost. The selection was minuscule compared to the seventy thousand DVDs Netflix offered via mail. At launch, Netflix was so cautious about the future of their streaming plan that company CEO Reed Hastings told *The New York Times* that he considered the market for online movies "microscopic."

"DVD," he added, "is going to be a very big market for a very long time."

Maybe not. By the summer of 2011, while *Bridesmaids* and *The Hangover Part II* were dominating the box office charts, Netflix's streaming service had grown popular enough that the company announced plans to split it off into a separate entity with its own monthly subscription fee. And they felt so strongly about the future of online movies at that point that they dubbed their streaming service Netflix while rebranding their lucrative DVD business "Qwikster," a name that's funnier than several of the films covered in this book. Netflix maintained both divisions until the fall of 2023, when they finally shuttered their physical rental business. At that point, Netflix had a little over 1 million DVD subscribers remaining—and over 230 million streaming subscribers worldwide.

It's impossible to overstate the impact Netflix and other streaming services had on the movie business as a whole, and comedy films in particular. For one thing, it accelerated the decline of the DVD business that Hastings felt so bullish about just a few years earlier. In 2007, the same year that Netflix launched its streaming service, the six major movie studios grossed $50 billion, with a combined profit margin of 10.5 percent. Nearly half of that gross came from DVDs. Just a few years later, with Netflix on the rise and the DVD business in free fall, that overall margin decreased to 8.1 percent. Studios counted on DVD sales and rentals as a financial backstop; even a film that flopped in theaters could be expected to recoup most of its investment on home video. Not anymore—something that hit comedies much harder than other genres.

"DVDs used to be half the money a comedy made," Judd Apatow said. "So if a movie made $30 million at the box office, it usually would make $30 million on DVD. So if that money disappears, suddenly the studios think you need to make that money at the box office, which they usually don't. And so they go, 'We can make a horror movie for $4 million, it'll play in Romania'—the way comedy usually can't. And so the bets change, and that's why there's less [comedies]."

Netflix's rise impacted theaters as well. Instant on-demand high-definition movies at the push of a button reconfigured the mental calculus every moviegoer made when they debated whether it was worth the time, the hassle, and especially the money to venture to the multiplex. Why bother when you can watch something on Netflix without leaving your house? The explosion of streaming movies also coincided with all sorts of other technological innovations: bigger and higher-resolution televisions, smaller and more advanced cell phones, and an endless array of apps and social media offering countless options for entertainment and distraction.

That hit comedies particularly hard, too, because they had been dominated for so long by the Frat Pack, a group whose target audience was primarily young men, among the earliest adopters of all those technologies.

Suddenly, says Erica Huggins, former president of Imagine Entertainment and current president of Fuzzy Door Productions, "there were too many things that were vying for the attention of teenagers and twenty-year-olds. You had gaming, which was huge, you had streaming, which was huger, and movies became a different animal. And I think comedies got relegated to streaming, and IP became the only way to make a movie that was going to open."

For that reason, IP—intellectual property—and concepts with built-in name value designed to attract the widest possible audience became the watchword around the movie business during this period. But attracting the widest possible audience meant crafting movies that could play to every single person, young and old, liberal and conservative. And that meant R-rated comedies' caustic humor would no longer fly.

"When we used to schedule our movies' release dates," said Seth Rogen, "the idea was always that we didn't want to come out near another R-rated comedy. And now there's only like three big R-rated comedies a year, and sometimes we produce two of them."

"People want choices. When you look at a movie theater now, there's the one or two movies every weekend, and then there's some other shit. We killed our own industry," says *Wedding Crashers* director David Dobkin. "We got killed the minute we got involved with Wall Street. If [the studios] don't think a movie can make a billion, they don't want to make it. It's like going to the $5 table in Vegas. They're not interested in winning $150. That's a waste of their time."

In large part, the films of the Frat Pack succeeded specifically because they were safe bets for the movie studios (at least when they did not involve the extremely graphic death of the supreme leader of the Democratic People's Republic of Korea). Their jokes were daring at times, but in terms of scale, their ambitions were otherwise modest. They didn't cost a ton of money; the lower budgets and lower financial risk directly translated to their creators' ability to take greater creative risks, which in turn translated to wilder and funnier jokes. But as Netflix began drawing customers away from theaters, the traditional studios decided the best way to compete was to offer larger and larger spectacles that played better on the big screen than at home. The more studios invested in blockbusters, the less they focused on smaller productions—including comedies.

"What drives people to theaters are events. A movie about some people hanging out or doing their thing, or a guy gets someone pregnant—'Eh, I can see that at home and just be on my couch.' We used to just go to the movies a lot more and it didn't have to be this massive event," says *I Love You, Man* director John Hamburg.

As a result, Huggins says, "comedies became a sort of streaming business. Very early into the Netflix world, after it became clear that people were going less to the movies, you had to take bigger swings. You needed events, as everybody's calling them. And a comedy felt like you could see it anywhere. They didn't need to look good; they just had to be funny."

According to Michael H. Weber, cowriter of *(500) Days of Summer* and *The Disaster Artist*, comedy didn't just become a streaming business; Netflix actively made it one.

"Years ago, Scott [Neustadter] and I made a movie with Robert Redford and Jane Fonda," Weber recalls. "We were in an early meeting when we first set up that project with Netflix. I can't say enough good things about how Netflix was to that movie and to all of us. But we were in a meeting, and [Netflix co-CEO] Ted Sarandos said their first deal with Adam Sandler [in 2014, for four Netflix-exclusive comedies] was the most important deal creatively in the history of Netflix. And he said it was because Sandler is a movie star on every continent. Those movies transcend language barriers and borders."

The more studios doubled down on big bland movies, the more they ceded the world of smart adult entertainment (and Adam Sandler comedies) to streaming and television—the very same medium that had previously handcuffed or discarded talents like Stiller, Apatow, and Feig. Netflix's groundbreaking streaming service launched a few weeks before the final season of HBO's *The Sopranos*, the foundational cornerstone of a new generation of high-quality shows that rose to prominence on cable television in parallel with the Frat Pack's ascendance in cinemas.

This new era of TV emphasized complex characters, serialized stories, dynamic visuals, weighty themes, and heaping doses of the profanity and sexuality that also defined the Frat Pack's movie comedies. Plus, series on cable or Netflix might only release ten installments or less every year or two; stars could now appear in an eight-episode miniseries for Apple's streaming service—as Will Ferrell and Paul Rudd did in 2021 with Apple TV+'s *The Shrink Next Door*—and immediately move on to their next gig before the show had even aired.

As a result, pretty much every single person affiliated with the Frat Pack, either in front of or behind the camera, has made one or two (or many) TV shows as the years wore on. The movie comedy became an endangered species—although Seth MacFarlane is quick to note that comedy is not the only genre suffering.

"As far as today, comedies are just a piece of it," he says. "It's hard to get *any* movie made in Hollywood today. It's a weird time to sell anything 'cause people are just so terrified of a million different things. Comedies are just one thing that gets swept up in that."

Can big comedies make a comeback? While it's a long shot, some of the creators of those movies are cautiously optimistic.

Judd Apatow says, "People got out of the habit of going to see comedies, because they're not making that many of them. [But] something will happen. Someone will do something amazing. There will be a breakthrough of some kind, 'cause these things are cyclical. But as of right now, we're fucked."

John Hamburg doubts we'll ever return to the days where "every week you could go to the theater to see an Adam McKay movie or a Judd Apatow movie." But he also says he still holds out hope for the future of comedies because they can still create something Netflix or cell phones or TikTok cannot provide: a communal experience.

"People love getting together and laughing communally—having any experience communally. Some of my best moments, both as an audience member and as a filmmaker, are when I've been sitting with four hundred other people and we're all laughing. There's just nothing better." That might explain why Hamburg is currently writing and directing a new sequel to *Meet the Parents* with Ben Stiller and Robert De Niro, the first in the franchise in over fifteen years. As he assembled his cast and crew, he says he's been struck by how many of them have said things to him like, "God, they don't make those movies anymore!"

"When you go to a comedy," adds Huggins, "that feeling in an audience when it's packed and everybody's waiting for that movie—and it happens! There's something . . . I don't know, it's ecstatic. It makes you joyful. And that's what the movies were always about for me."

Michael H. Weber, who's currently working on a biopic about the life of *SNL* star Chris Farley, cautions that while comedies could return, he wonders whether the next generation of comedians will even want to make them. "A young comic in the '80s would see Eddie Murphy and go, 'I'm funny. I hope one day I get to star in a really funny movie,'" he notes. "I don't know if that's the dream anymore. Chris Farley worshipped [John] Belushi. He wanted to be in comedy movies like his heroes. He loved *Caddyshack*, he loved *The Blues Brothers*, he loved *Animal House*. We don't know what the downriver of this dearth of a healthy comedy film system is going to look like. An entire generation of funny young people are not growing up on comedy movies."

Rodney Rothman, a writer on comedies like *22 Jump Street* and the Oscar-winning codirector of *Spider-Man: Into the Spider-Verse*, notes that "making a good movie is so hard and time-consuming and can be so expensive that I get why it's more appealing for lots of people to make shorter stuff, or going on tour with no overhead. And you make a very good living, and have a direct connection to the audience that way. There's less incentive to make feature comedies. But all that said, I don't think it's done as a format. There *could* be massive comedies now. But people need to invest in them, and invest in comedy creators. You need to oxygenate these things."

But the dearth of movie comedies could also create the exact conditions needed for the genre's revival. After all, the R-rated comedy died once before, when *Animal House*'s imitators so inundated the marketplace that people finally had their fill of wild men misbehaving. A few years later, Ben Stiller getting his dick caught in his zipper felt fresh again. A decade or so after the Frat Pack's apex, their volatile brand of movie comedy is so rare that the release of any funny movie might qualify as a big enough "event" to get people back into theaters. Scot Armstrong says he believes "the pendulum is swinging back" already.

Just look at the reaction to *The Naked Gun*, 2025's reboot of the classic spoof franchise of the 1980s and '90s. Produced by Seth MacFarlane and Erica Huggins, and directed by *SNL* alum Akiva Schaffer, *The Naked Gun* earned the sort of rapturous reviews typically reserved for Best Picture contenders, not a movie where Liam Neeson says of a beautiful woman "she had a bottom that would make any toilet beg for the brown." I witnessed an audience's reaction to the film firsthand at a packed theater in New York City. The laughs were so big, they drowned out many of the jokes. You'd think these people hadn't seen a movie comedy in years—probably because they hadn't.

"We haven't had [a big movie comedy] in so long," Huggins concurs. "And times are so fucked-up right now. It was like, 'Oh, I get to forget for eighty-five minutes about what's out there right now?' That was fun."

That's what these comedies represent. They may not be perfect. They may not age well. (Admittedly, some didn't age well within days of their release.) But when they work, they drag us away from whatever else is bothering us and invite us along to crash the party with them.

"Look at these movies," Huggins notes. "*Zoolander*, *Old School*, *Starsky & Hutch*, *Dodgeball*, *Anchorman*, *Wedding Crashers*, *40-Year-Old Virgin*, *Talladega Nights*, *Borat*, *Bridesmaids*, *Pineapple Express*, *The Hangover*, *Step Brothers*, *Superbad*, *Tropic Thunder*. This was like in a ten-year period. Those are a lot of great movies. And we took 'em for granted."

TODD PHILLIPS, who owed his career to a documentary that HBO refused to air, is the only major comedy figure of this period who's yet to return to the world of television. For a while, he didn't need to. The three *Hangover* movies grossed $1.4 billion, and thanks to the deal he signed on the first film, he earned tens of millions of dollars directing the trilogy. In 2019, he became the first member of this motley comedy crew to figure out how to successfully translate his sensibility to superheroes, when he transformed the most famous villain in the history of comics into a mentally ill outcast who lashes out at a world that has mistreated him. Phillips's *Joker*, starring Joaquin Phoenix in the title role, more closely resembled Martin Scorsese dramas like *Taxi Driver* and *The King of Comedy* than most Batman comics. But it also bore plenty of Phillips's distinctive DNA; Phoenix's Arthur Fleck is basically Zach Galifianakis's eccentric misfit from *The Hangover* with fewer friends and a worse sense of humor.

Though *Joker*'s bleak depiction of modern life attracted some controversy around the question of whether the film endorsed its psychotic antihero's nihilistic worldview, it generated far more revenue. It ultimately earned more than $1 billion worldwide, eclipsing all the Frat Pack's earlier efforts along the way to becoming the biggest R-rated movie in history at that time. The film proved so successful that Phillips and Phoenix were coaxed back for a sequel in 2024; in typically confrontational fashion, Phillips made this one a courtroom drama where the Joker (and, by extension, the first movie's divisive content) is put on trial. *Joker: Folie à Deux* was also a musical, with dreamlike song and dance numbers featuring Lady Gaga as the Joker's girlfriend, Harley Quinn. But *Folie à Deux* became as colossal a flop as the first film had been a shocking smash. By one industry estimate, *Folie à Deux* cost Warner Bros. $144 million—almost $60 million more than Phillips's *Old School* had earned worldwide during its entire theatrical run.

ADAM MCKAY never directed another Will Ferrell movie after *Anchorman 2*. Although they continued Gary Sanchez Productions for several more years, the two longtime collaborators drifted apart during the second half of the 2010s, as McKay's work got more overtly political. In 2015 he directed *The Big Short*, based on the nonfiction book about the 2008 financial crisis, and won an Academy Award for Best Adapted Screenplay. He then directed the pilot of the Gary Sanchez TV series *Succession*, a more serious treatment of *Anchorman 2*'s cable news satire, this time as a family drama about the various heirs fighting for control of a media company. The show went on to earn seventy-five Emmy nominations and nineteen wins across four seasons. McKay followed it with the Dick Cheney biopic *Vice*, which was not nearly as successful with audiences, critics, or the Academy, but was, if nothing else, a fascinating companion piece to all those *Saturday Night Live* sketches he wrote for Will Ferrell's bumbling impression of President George W. Bush.

McKay and Ferrell's breakup became official in 2019 when they ended Gary Sanchez and launched two separate production companies, McKay's Hyperobject Industries and Ferrell's Gloria Sanchez Productions. By that point, McKay had already quit their humor website, Funny or Die, after the company accepted a sponsorship from Shell Oil, a decision he found untenable with his increasing concern about climate change. (McKay later tackled the subject of global warming head-on in his 2021 dark comedy, *Don't Look Up*, about scientists trying to warn humanity about an impending comet strike; the film bypassed theaters and premiered on Netflix.) McKay told *Vanity Fair* he and Ferrell finalized the dissolution of their creative partnership with a single, brief phone call. Afterward, McKay thought to himself, "Fuck, Ferrell's never going to talk to me again."

Somehow things got even messier from there. In Gary Sanchez's final days, McKay began developing a TV series about the glory days of the Los Angeles Lakers. A huge Lakers fan, Ferrell wanted to play team owner Jerry Buss, but "was good" with McKay's initial choice of actor Michael Shannon for the role. But when Shannon dropped out a week before shooting was set to begin, McKay asked John C. Reilly to play Buss rather than Ferrell. Before Reilly accepted the role, he called Ferrell, who was "very hurt" that McKay wasn't the one to deliver the news. ("And I should have," McKay admitted. "I fucked up.")

During an interview promoting *Don't Look Up* in 2021, McKay was asked what inspired his turn toward more serious material and away from the "empty-suit white guys" comedies that defined the first chapter of his film career.

"You started to see the ravages of that culture," he explained, "and it wasn't so funny anymore." Amid so many major issues affecting our society, from income inequality to the ongoing climate crisis, McKay said, he felt it was "almost bizarre to do those old-school comedies."

But, he added, "I love Ferrell. Always will. I had the best, most fun run of my life with him."

* * *

WILL FERRELL saw the split with McKay as a matter of differing priorities. McKay wanted "growth and a sphere of influence." To Ferrell, "that sounds like a lot that I have to keep track of . . . At the end of the day we just have different amounts of bandwidth." So far, no reconciliation has materialized—but if Ferrell and McKay's movies have taught us anything, it's that the bonds between longtime coworkers, whether at a local news station or a NASCAR track, are surprisingly strong, and a reunion is always possible, no matter how unlikely.

Despite Ferrell's stated disinterest in presiding over a sphere of influence, Gloria Sanchez Productions has produced plenty of worthy films in the last few years, including Kristen Wiig and Annie Mumolo's *Bridesmaids* follow-up *Barb and Star Go to Vista Del Mar*, Jessica Yu's *Quiz Lady*, and Todd Haynes's *May December*. Ferrell continues to use the rest of his bandwidth to star in new old-school comedies, although most of his movies these days tend to premiere on streaming platforms rather than in theaters. In recent years, his repertoire of overconfident, overmatched white dudes has grown to include an Icelandic musician in Netflix's *Eurovision Song Contest: The Story of Fire Saga* and the ineffectual CEO of Mattel in Greta Gerwig's *Barbie*.

In contrast to his old writing partner, Ferrell sees no conflict between the state of society and his taste for broad humor, saying in 2021, "there's just so much going on in the world, and sometimes it's nice to turn your brain off." He compared his approach to Steve Martin's back in his stand-up heyday.

"Steve was like, 'Everyone's doing message comedy, and I just want to walk out with an arrow shooting through my head,' and that's kind of how I feel right now."

* * *

For a man who never set out to be an actor, OWEN WILSON sure has made a lot of movies. Though he almost always plays some variation of the same easygoing charmer, Wilson's default onscreen mode has proven surprisingly malleable, capable of fitting into everything from action thrillers (*No Escape*) to frothy romantic comedies (*Marry Me*) to the kid-friendly exploits of talking automobiles; his vehicular alter ego, Lightning McQueen, has driven Pixar's *Cars* franchise to a collective $1.4 billion at the worldwide box office and countless billions more in merchandise sales. All these years later, he still works with the guy who put him onscreen in the first place, his old college buddy Wes Anderson. Although they haven't written a movie together since 2001's *The Royal Tenenbaums*, Wilson has appeared in Anderson's *The Life Aquatic with Steve Zissou*, *Fantastic Mr. Fox*, *The Grand Budapest Hotel*, and *The French Dispatch*.

Unlike the other members of the Frat Pack, he even found a way to adapt his signature style to the top-grossing film franchise of the day, the Marvel Cinematic Universe. In 2021, he played the character of Mobius M. Mobius, a quirky middle manager at the Time Variance Authority, the bureaucratic organization in charge of policing Marvel's convoluted timeline. On two seasons of Marvel's *Loki*, he generated the same sort of oil-and-water buddy chemistry with series star Tom Hiddleston that powered so many of his classic 2000s films.

Like so many of his contemporaries from that era, Wilson now finds a lot of work on television, not just on *Loki* but also on the Apple TV+ series *Stick*, where he played a washed-up former golf pro who finds a renewed sense of purpose as the mentor to a talented golf prodigy. Promoting the show in the summer of 2025, Wilson was asked what about his character resonated with him some thirty years into a prolific Hollywood career.

"I think back to the times in my life where somebody has believed in me, or given me confidence, where maybe I didn't have much," he replied. "I just think that's so important for people: to have someone who is a mentor, or who gives you some help, or gives you a break." Prompted to name the mentor in his life like that, Wilson cited James L. Brooks, who liked the original *Bottle Rocket* short, brought Wilson and Wes Anderson out to Hollywood, and guided them through the process of making a feature film version.

"His belief," Wilson added, "changed my life! And I think Wes and my brothers would say the same thing."

VINCE VAUGHN tried a few times to re-create the vibes of the old Frat Pack in the 2010s. In addition to *The Internship*, he also starred in 2012's *The Watch* with Ben Stiller, Jonah Hill, and Richard Ayoade as a bunch of friends from the suburbs who form a neighborhood watch group and uncover an alien invasion. With its ensemble cast, surprisingly graphic violence, and an R rating to match, *The Watch* looked in most ways like Vaughn's biggest hits from the decade prior. But audiences didn't show up this time. (It probably didn't help that the movie, originally titled *Neighborhood Watch*, opened in theaters a few months after the killing of Trayvon Martin by George Zimmerman, a member of his community's neighborhood watch. That was perhaps not the ideal moment to release a goofy movie about a bunch of unruly neighborhood watchers shooting aliens.)

When audiences stopped showing up for his typical comic fare, Vaughn tried a variety of other genres including action (*Term Life*), war (*Hacksaw Ridge*), sports (*Fighting with My Family*), crime (*Dragged Across Concrete*), and even horror (*Freaky*—a slasher-movie twist on *Freaky Friday* in which a teenage girl swaps bodies with a serial killer. You can probably figure out which one Vaughn played). Most of those films struggled to find audiences in theaters as well.

He had more luck reinventing himself on television, including stints on the gritty HBO police drama *True Detective* in 2015, and a recurring role on *Curb Your Enthusiasm.* A few years later, he starred in a well-received adaptation of Carl Hiaasen's comic crime novel *Bad Monkey* for Apple TV+. He recently reunited with Owen Wilson for their first project together in many years—a commercial, fittingly, for Xfinity cable TV service. *Wedding Crashers* director David Dobkin shot it.

BEN STILLER took his own stab at a full-blown Frat Pack revival in 2016. Looking to rebound from the tepidly received *The Secret Life of Walter Mitty* in 2013, Stiller reteamed with Owen Wilson and Will Ferrell for *Zoolander 2.* But instead of spoofing the fashion world, 2016's *Zoolander 2* mostly just made fun of *Zoolander 1*, with characters constantly mocking Derek and Hansel for being old and out of touch. Late in the film, Ferrell's Mugatu throws a knife at Stiller's Zoolander, who tries to use his magical Magnum look to stop the weapon in midair, just as he had in the climax of the first movie fifteen years earlier. This time, the trick doesn't work; Derek gets stabbed in the face. "It just doesn't hold up, does it?" Mugatu says, chuckling. It was a funny meta gag, and a perfect metaphor for the ways Frat Pack alumni tried and mostly failed to recapture their old magic in the years since their biggest triumphs.

When *Zoolander 2* tanked, grossing a dismal $28.8 million in U.S. theaters, Stiller took a break from starring roles for seven years. (He still hasn't directed another fiction feature.) Instead, he pivoted back to television for the first time since the failed *Heat Vision and Jack* pilot—and for the first time ever, finally fulfilled his childhood ambitions and began directing things other than comedies.

In 2018, he helmed all seven episodes of Showtime's prison-break drama *Escape at Dannemora*, which garnered strong reviews from critics and earned six Primetime Emmy nominations, including one for

Outstanding Directing for Stiller. He followed that with an even bigger TV triumph as the producer and director—and notably *not* the star—of the Apple TV+ mystery series *Severance*, which follows the lives of tech employees who willingly submit themselves to a brain-altering surgery. Once they go through this "severance" procedure, they do not remember their activities at home when they are on the job, and vice versa. In its first two seasons, *Severance* has been nominated for forty-one Emmys and won ten. If the show is a comedy at all, it's an extremely dark one.

After the deaths of his parents, Stiller also uncovered his father's trove of family photographs and home movies. He used those materials to create *Stiller & Meara: Nothing Is Lost*, a look back at his parents' marriage and partnership. In the doc's most compelling moment, a journalist interviewing the Stiller family asks young Ben whether he will cast his parents in the movies he makes when he grows up.

"I would hire someone else," Stiller replies. "The movie I was gonna make, they wouldn't be right for it," he adds. "I'll be making adventure or a murder or something like that, but never comedy. I don't like comedy."

As a high school dropout and a man who seemingly has never gone more than a few hours without getting stoned in his entire adult life, SETH ROGEN does not necessarily strike the figure of a Hollywood mogul. But that's what he's become. Through his Point Grey production company with Evan Goldberg, he's produced many of the best comedy films of the last decade, including *The Disaster Artist*, *Blockers*, and *Good Boys*. On television, Point Grey also carved out a niche making faithful adaptations of graphic novels like *Preacher*, *The Boys*, and *Invincible*. Rogen even launched his own weed and weed accessory company, Houseplant, in 2019.

All the while, Rogen maintained an impressive level of output as an actor. His singular voice and laugh have rumbled through animated movies like *Kung Fu Panda*, 2019's *Lion King* remake, and *Sausage Party*, which Rogen also cowrote and coproduced, and then spun off into an absolutely filthy streaming television series. (Parents, I cannot stress this enough: Even if your children love Rogen's work in *Kung Fu Panda* and *The Lion King*, do *not* let them near *Sausage Party*.) He also wooed Charlize Theron in the rom-com *Long Shot* and costarred in a Steven Spielberg movie, 2022's *The Fabelmans*, where he did not seem the slightest bit out of place or overmatched in a cast that also included acting heavyweights Michelle Williams and Paul Dano.

Ironically, after a career as a writer and director entirely consumed with movies about the power of enduring friendships, Rogen publicly ended his relationship with his most frequent costar, James Franco. The duo had worked together since *Freaks and Geeks* and became a popular big-screen tandem thanks to *Pineapple Express* and *This Is the End*—until multiple women accused Franco of sexual misconduct, including several of his former acting students. Although Rogen initially defended Franco, he said in 2021, "I also look back to that interview in 2018 where I comment that I would keep working with James, and the truth is that I have not and I do not plan to right now." (In 2024, Franco told *Variety* the two hadn't spoken in years, "and not for lack of trying" on his part.)

Rogen became a Hollywood mogul onscreen as well. On *The Studio*—which Rogen co-created, cowrites, and codirects—he stars as Continental Studios chief Matt Remick, whose genuine love of cinema constantly butts up against the realities of running a film company in a time when all anyone cares about is IP. (Matt's big new movie is an "adaptation" of the Kool-Aid Man.) The show is simultaneously one of the funniest things Rogen has ever done and the most technically complex; each episode is shot in a series of Steadicam long takes that require pinpoint-precision timing from the actors and crew members to nail every scripted line and movement perfectly. Aesthetically, it's about as far from a shaggy Judd Apatow riff fest as you can get.

Where Rogen goes from here, and what worlds he tries to conquer next, remains to be seen. But he holds a clear-eyed perspective on his career thus far.

"I have accepted that a lot of what I do just won't age well, but the thing is, nothing ages well," he said in 2018. "*Animal House* is one of the best comedies of all time and you watch it today and it's appalling. There's tons of shit in that movie that back then was 'edgy' and today feels categorically wrong. That's just part of comedy."

JUDD APATOW still makes movies and TV shows, and continues to serve as a comedy conduit, discovering untapped talent and finding appropriate outlets for their voices. After *This Is 40*, he started directing screenplays written by other comedians. In 2015, he made *Trainwreck* with Amy Schumer; five years later, he helmed *The King of Staten Island* starring and cowritten by *Saturday Night Live*'s Pete Davidson. After so many unhappy experiences on broadcast television in the 1990s and early 2000s, he found the cable and streaming TV landscape of the 2010s far more receptive to his dirty-but-heartfelt brand of humor. He admired indie writer/director Lena Dunham's 2010 feature, *Tiny Furniture*, and invited her to collaborate on a television show that became the six-season HBO series *Girls*. Apatow also produced *Love* for Netflix and *Crashing* for HBO.

In recent years, Apatow has also refocused his attention on his first love: stand-up comedy. He began performing again for the first time in decades and released his first hour-long special, *Judd Apatow: The Return*, on Netflix in 2017. He also directed a series of documentaries about great comedians like Garry Shandling and George Carlin. It was a full-circle moment—a return to chronicling the lives of stand-up comedians just as he had in his high school days on WKWZ at Syosset High School. He recently told *The Atlantic* that with funny films in shorter supply "he would be content as the Elvis Costello of comedy:

not the person who sells out Madison Square Garden but the person who makes great art for its own sake, for an audience who appreciates it, even if that audience is smaller."

Given how so much of his career sprouted from a chance encounter at an Elvis Costello concert, that would only be fitting. Maybe someone waiting in line to see Apatow's next movie will strike up a conversation with a stranger and they will make the comedy that brings the genre roaring back to life.

APPENDIX

Buried Treasures of the Frat Pack Era

While the stars and directors that became known as the Frat Pack only worked closely together for a handful of years, their individual careers span more than three decades of movies, television shows, talk show appearances, YouTube videos, at least one board game that I'm aware of, and even a couple of podcasts. (Go out of your way to find *Owen & TJ Read the News*, the short-lived audio series where Adam McKay played "a cell phone case salesman and aspiring hip hop artist" from Jacksonville named TJ, who for some reason weighs in on current events with his uptight sidekick, Owen Burke. It will change your life forever.)

Many of this group's creations became generational pop culture milestones and require no advocacy on their behalf. (You guys ever see *Anchorman*? It's pretty funny, I think!) But these comedians also made a fair number of obscurities over the last thirty years. To that end, I compiled this appendix of twenty lesser-known and underappreciated creations from the members of this esteemed film fraternity.

Although it focuses primarily on their movie work, it also includes TV pilots that were never officially released, DVD commentary tracks that are largely unavailable in the world of streaming, and assorted other comedy curios. Some predate *USA Today*'s original "Frat Pack" article from 2004; others came out in the last few years, after these artists had largely drifted apart. If you're looking for something to watch and you're not in the mood for a seventieth viewing of *Step Brothers*, these recommendations offer some alternatives. (Or just watch *Step Brothers* for the seventieth time. No one on Earth has ever regretted doing that.)

ANACONDA (1997)

Directed by Luis Llosa

This book covers some terrific comedies, but I'm not sure any of them contain anything half as funny as Jon Voight with his face contorted into a lizard-man sneer as he hisses, "Eh, he gonna be all right" half a second after jabbing a dirty drinking straw into the side of Eric Stoltz's neck in *Anaconda*. (Stoltz's character needed help breathing after an allergic reaction to a wasp sting, you see.) The rest of this supposed horror film is about a documentary film crew (including a young Owen Wilson, fresh off of *Bottle Rocket*) hunting for a lost Amazonian tribe; instead, they find a giant snake and Voight's Paraguayan hunter. But Voight's performance is so absurd it tips *Anaconda* over from creature feature to unintentional laugh riot through sheer force of will. (No wonder Jack Black and Paul Rudd remade *Anaconda* in 2025 as a full-blown comedy.) Wilson, still a relative rookie actor, can't hold a candle to Voight's slithery antics, but his enormous potential is right there on the screen in the heroic way he sells lines like "Just remember: You don't know shit about the shit we're in out here!"

ZERO EFFECT (1998)

Directed by Jake Kasdan

The same year Ben Stiller cemented his comic leading-man status in *There's Something About Mary*, he also had one of the best supporting roles in *Zero Effect*, playing a modern day Dr. Watson to Bill Pullman's eccentric Holmesian detective Daryl Zero. Hired to find a blackmailer, Zero quickly uncovers the criminal's identity—a beautiful woman played by Kim Dickens, who puts all of Zero's beliefs about the importance of professional detachment to the test. The film marked the auspicious debut of writer/director Jake Kasdan, who provided a witty script and guided Pullman, Stiller, and Dickens to three superb performances. But viewers were almost as mystified by *Zero Effect* as Zero's clients were by his unusual methods of deduction, and the movie struggled to find an audience in theaters. Unfortunately, that's a fate shared by several of Kasdan's projects through the years, including his singular musical biopic spoof, *Walk Hard: The Dewey Cox Story*, and another title coming up later in this list.

HEAT VISION AND JACK (1999)
Directed by Ben Stiller

An astounding compilation of comic talent—including director Ben Stiller, creators Dan Harmon and Rob Schrab, and stars Jack Black and Owen Wilson—collaborated on this unaired Fox pilot, a genial spoof of campy TV series of the 1970s and '80s like *The Six Million Dollar Man* and *Knight Rider*. Black played an astronaut who becomes the smartest man alive after exposure to excessive levels of solar energy; Wilson voices his best friend, a sentient talking motorcycle. Each week (or it *would* have been each week if they'd ever gotten a second episode) Heat Vision and Jack wandered America, helping people they encounter and evading the evil head of NASA, Ron Silver (as himself, sort of). "We just went off and did it and then it didn't get picked up. Like, it *very* quickly didn't get picked up," Stiller joked in 2010. Years after Fox passed on *Heat Vision and Jack*, the pilot leaked online, where it's been watched by millions of appreciative fans of the various artists who converged on this one-of-a-kind project.

MADE (2001)

Directed by Jon Favreau

The closest Jon Favreau and Vince Vaughn ever got to a *Swingers* sequel was this 2001 comedy about a pair of blue-collar joes who agree to serve as hired muscle for a local Mafia boss (Peter Falk). But anyone who bought a ticket to *Made* expecting another movie about Vaughn as a smooth-talking charmer was in for a big disappointment. Just like Trent from *Swingers*, Vaughn's Ricky from *Made* never shuts up—but where Trent was funny and entertaining, Ricky is an obnoxious imbecile who drives everyone around him crazy every time he opens his mouth. As a result, Favreau and Vaughn's follow-up to one of the great hangout movies of the 1990s was the cinematic equivalent of getting trapped in an elevator with an asshole for forty-five minutes. It's such an unusual hook for a comedy—and such an obvious rebuke to fans who took their love of Trent's oily charisma too far—it's hard not to respect it.

SHANGHAI KNIGHTS (2003)

Directed by David Dobkin

Before they teamed on *Wedding Crashers*, director David Dobkin and star Owen Wilson first collaborated on *Shanghai Knights*, the sequel to Wilson and martial artist Jackie Chan's 2000 comic Western, *Shanghai Noon*. Few onscreen teams in film history were more amusingly mismatched than Chan and Wilson; the former supplied inexhaustible kinetic energy, while the latter lazed around the edges of the frame, cracking laconic jokes. The plot, something about Chan avenging his father's death in 1880s London, is mostly an excuse for a series of Chan action set pieces and Wilson quips. But *what* action set pieces and quips! Chan tussles with fellow action master Donnie Yen and sprinkles in homages to his cinematic heroes, including Gene Kelly and Harold Lloyd. Meanwhile, Wilson interacts with Sir Arthur Conan Doyle

(Tom Fisher) and chases a pickpocket, who turns out to be a young Charlie Chaplin (played by a pre-fame Aaron Taylor-Johnson?!). Of all the hit 2000s franchises that got legacyquels in the last few years, how has there never been a *Shanghai Afternoon*?

WAKE UP, RON BURGUNDY: THE LOST MOVIE (2004)

Directed by Adam McKay

Adam McKay's directorial emphasis on improvisation produced so much material he sometimes wound up with more jokes than he could cram in a single film. For the DVD release of *Anchorman*, McKay compiled ninety minutes of alts into a second feature titled *Wake Up, Ron Burgundy*. The structure is undeniably odd; a narration by Bill Kurtis treats the film as if it is a sequel to *Anchorman* when it's obviously a collection of deleted scenes, alternate punch lines, and a cut subplot about a terrorist group called the Alarm Clock. Given that *Wake Up, Ron Burgundy* is comprised of jokes that weren't good enough to make the theatrical release, the fact that it's not as funny as *Anchorman* is not a shock. But it's a testament to McKay and his cast's ingenuity that it's still far funnier than many other comedies released in theaters during this period. The highlight may be a sequence where the News Team enjoys their lunch at the station's cafeteria, and Steve Carell's dim-witted Brick Tamland tucks into what he describes as "one of those delicious falafel hot dogs with cinnamon and bacon on top." "What do you mean 'one of those'?" Ron replies. "*Those* don't exist. That's a used coffee filter with cigarette butts on it." Undeterred, Brick gamely continues stuffing his face until Carell's mouth is overflowing with old coffee grounds.

THE BREAK-UP (2006)

Directed by Peyton Reed

Vince Vaughn parlayed his early 2000s hot streak into this one-of-a-kind unromantic comedy that he also cowrote and produced. It contains an appealingly oxymoronic concept: a rom-com about the end of a love story. It begins with a classic movie meet-cute, when sparks fly between Gary (Vaughn) and Brooke (Jennifer Aniston) over some hot dogs at a Chicago Cubs game. Then the film takes an unexpected path, bypassing their happy years together to depict the couple's ugly dissolution. Instead of snappy banter, the duo trade passive-aggressive insults and argue about why Gary doesn't want to do the dishes. ("Why would I *want* to do the dishes?" he groans.) So many of Vaughn's movies of this period feature men who refuse to grow up, settle down, or accept adult responsibility—usually with few negative consequences. *The Break-Up* is a rare example where his character's immaturity actually costs him something he cares about. The movie's downbeat conclusion makes it both less conventionally satisfying and a lot more interesting than a typical Hollywood romance.

TALLADEGA NIGHTS' "25 YEARS LATER" DVD COMMENTARY (2006)

Featuring Adam McKay and Will Ferrell

Almost every major motion picture of the 2000s got a "special edition" DVD release loaded with bonus features, including at least one commentary. A dryly informative track about lighting and sound design wasn't really Adam McKay and Will Ferrell's style, so instead they created a "25 Years Later" commentary for *Talladega Nights*, where they pretend they're recording their thoughts on the movie a quarter century into the future—with McKay playing his adult son, "Darnell," who notes at the start of the commentary that he's there to fill in for his dad after he "was eaten by a hammerhead shark off the coast of Catalina." (R.I.P.) Costars like John C. Reilly, David Koechner, and Jack McBrayer pop in as well, each playing absurd versions of themselves from the future. (Michael Clarke Duncan, for example, is the leader of his own religion that supposedly has 8 million followers all over the world.) The track amounts to an astounding improv the cast manages to sustain for 105 hilarious minutes. (For further audio lunacy, check out the *Anchorman* commentary, with contributions from Christina Applegate, Paul Rudd, Andy Richter, and, for reasons no one can explain, R&B legend Lou Rawls.)

THE TV SET (2006)

Directed by Jake Kasdan

Judd Apatow served as an executive producer of this wry lampoon of the TV industry. Given David Duchovny's portrayal of a flannel-clad producer buried beneath a mountain of nonsensical notes from his network bosses, it's pretty clear Apatow also served as one of writer/director Jake Kasdan's inspirations for the lead character. Apatow and Kasdan previously collaborated on both *Freaks and Geeks* and *Undeclared*, so they had plenty of material to work with; *The TV Set* reveals the way good television pilots are turned into slop by heavy-handed executives who use the word "smart" as an insult. In this case, Duchovny's Mike Klein wrote a seriocomic script about a man who returns home after his brother's suicide. Sigourney Weaver as the head of the network wonders: Does it *have* to be suicide? Or a brother? What if their mom, an annoying character she openly hates, died instead? Klein must choose whether to stick to his principles—and thus threaten the financial security of his young family—or suffer an artistic death by a thousand compromises. With all the changes in the movie and television worlds in the last twenty years, *The TV Set*'s use of the indie film medium to mock the idiocy of mainstream TV now plays a little like a Bizarro World version of Seth Rogen's *The Studio*.

BLADES OF GLORY (2007)

Directed by Will Speck and Josh Gordon

It's hard to pick the greatest Will Ferrell character name. From Jacobim Mugatu to Damien Weebs to Lance DeLune to Federal Wildlife Marshal Willenholly, he's had a lot of good ones. But the best of the best may be Chazz Michael Michaels, his libidinous figure skater from *Blades of Glory.* In this stupendously silly sports movie, Michaels and his chief rival (*Napoleon Dynamite*'s Jon Heder) get banned from skating for life after a physical altercation during an event. Ah, but there's a loophole in the rules: They were banned from men's skating, not from pairs. If they can set aside their mutual contempt for one another, they could become partners and return to the ice. The looming, oversexed Ferrell's and the shrimpy, repressed Heder's energies are so different they were born to costar in a buddy comedy, and they're matched note for over-the-top note by the reigning pairs-skating champs, a couple of incestuous siblings played by Will Arnett and Amy Poehler. The film concludes with possibly the funniest chase scene of the twenty-first century, when Arnett tries to keep Ferrell from making it to the final competition while the two men can barely stay on their feet as they awkwardly stumble through the lobby of a hockey arena on ice skates.

DAN IN REAL LIFE (2007)

Directed by Peter Hedges

Despite inspiring one of the worst posters in the history of cinema—Steve Carell's smirking, weightless head resting awkwardly atop a large plate of syrupy pancakes, an image that has no connection to the film whatsoever—*Dan in Real Life* is actually one of Carell's stronger post–*40-Year-Old Virgin* projects. He plays a widower who returns home to Rhode Island for a family reunion, where sparks fly when he encounters a beautiful and charming stranger (Juliette Binoche) at a local bookstore. Of course, there wouldn't be much of a movie if they just lived happily ever after, so when Dan arrives at his family's house overlooking the Atlantic, he discovers Binoche's character is his younger brother's new girlfriend. As *The 40-Year-Old Virgin* previously proved, few actors are as good at mining a character's discomfort for simultaneous laughs and melancholy as Carell, something he does with aplomb here as well. *Dan in Real Life* also makes lovely use of its small-town New England locations, adding a rustic texture to a story that occasionally creeps into sitcom territory. It's just a shame about that poster.

ROLE MODELS (2008)
Directed by David Wain

Although Paul Rudd will forever be linked with Judd Apatow—that'll happen when you repeatedly cast an actor to play the husband of your real-life wife and the father of your real-life kids—he's actually appeared in more movies directed by David Wain, the former member of the sketch comedy troupes the State and Stella turned director of *Wet Hot American Summer*, *The Ten*, *Wanderlust*, *They Came Together*, and this film. While most of Wain's work veers into willfully bizarre territory, *Role Models* was designed as a more mainstream effort in the bromance mold, with Rudd and *American Pie*'s Seann William Scott as a pair of miscreants sentenced to 150 hours of community service in lieu of prison time. They wind up as big brothers to a pair of wayward youths, one played by *Superbad*'s Christopher Mintz-Plasse, the other by foulmouthed twelve-year-old Bobb'e J. Thompson. Although the storyline is totally predictable, Wain's off-kilter humor elevates the material, like the extended subplot about egomaniacal live-action role players, and the surprisingly sweet finale, where Rudd's character wins back his ex-girlfriend Beth (Elizabeth Banks) by serenading her with Kiss's famous ballad of the same name, updated with lyrics he's rewritten to reflect their relationship. ("We don't have to get married, but I'm still in love with you / We can just be together like Tim Robbins and Susan Sarandon, Tim and Sue.")

TROPIC THUNDER: RAIN OF MADNESS (2008)
Created by Justin Theroux and Steve Coogan

To get a sense of just how lucrative the DVD market was in this period, look no further than *Rain of Madness*, an elaborate thirty-minute mockumentary featured on *Tropic Thunder*'s various home video releases. It stars *Thunder* cowriter Justin Theroux as a heavily accented Werner Herzog–esque documentarian named Jan Jürgen, who chronicles the troubled making of the film-within-a-film of *Tropic Thunder*, and profiles its overmatched director (played by Steve Coogan, who co-created the short with Theroux). To sum up: This is a fake documentary directed by a fake filmmaker about the making of a fake war movie based on a fake memoir written by a fake Vietnam veteran and containing clips of other fake movies and the fake backstories of the fake stars of the fake movie whose creation is chronicled in the fake documentary. Got it? (The *Tropic Thunder* Blu-ray also contains a commentary by Ben Stiller, Jack Black, and Robert Downey Jr.—who, true to one of his lines of dialogue in the film, stays in character as Lincoln Osiris right until the end of the track.)

MARLEY & ME (2008)
Directed by David Frankel

Sick of movies about taming poorly behaved men yet? How about taming a poorly behaved dog instead? *Marley & Me* adapted the bestseller about a newspaper columnist and his lovably incorrigible Labrador retriever, with Owen Wilson as the writer and Jennifer Aniston as his wife. Despite the presence of two A-list comedy actors, most of the biggest laughs belong to the pooch and his outrageous antics. In fact, for a mainstream comedy about a raucous canine, *Marley & Me* is surprisingly well observed—and, in its final act, as Marley succumbs to old age, quite moving—in a way that now makes it feel like a fossil dug up from some prehistoric era of Hollywood. When was the last time you saw a mainstream movie with famous stars and solid production values about a happily married couple dealing with relatable problems like crummy jobs and cranky babies? When was the last time you saw one that dealt with heavy concepts like loss and grief? These days that sort of studio film feels as rare as an obedient puppy.

THE GOODS: LIVE HARD, SELL HARD (2009)

Directed by Neal Brennan

Two of the funniest minutes of Will Ferrell's entire movie career are buried in this obscure comedy about a cocky used-car salesman named Don Ready (*Entourage*'s Jeremy Piven) hired by a struggling dealership to move hundreds of cars over a single weekend. Late in the film, we learn Don's tragic backstory: On a previous job he accidentally killed his best friend, McDermott (Ferrell), when he convinced him to skydive onto a car lot dressed as Abraham Lincoln. Unfortunately, Don was so distracted by a horny customer that he mistakenly swapped McDermott's parachute for his own bag of "sexual accoutrements" filled with condoms, dildos, and French ticklers. That's where Ferrell comes in, as he leaps out of a plane and then plummets to the earth surrounded by sex toys. While in free fall, he recounts the list of things he's most proud of in his life ("Number one: Full-length back tattoo of the Hawaiian Punch guy. Ten percent real fruit juice, motherfuckers!") and then tries to survive the oncoming impact by getting into an "aerodynamic tuck" and using a dildo to absorb his momentum. It's one of the most inspired feats of comic lunacy you'll find in this era.

THE FIVE-YEAR ENGAGEMENT (2012)
Directed by Nicholas Stoller

Throughout his career, Judd Apatow's critics have knocked his movies for their excessive length. Most are over two hours; a few creep toward the 150-minute mark. But their shagginess reflects one of Apatow's central themes: that life is rarely as straightforward as a formulaic movie plot, an idea expressed in the Apatow-produced *The Five-Year Engagement*. Its synopsis is succinctly encapsulated by its title: Chef Tom (Jason Segel) and psychologist Violet (Emily Blunt) get engaged before the film's opening credits, but one problem after another delays their wedded bliss. Relatives die, new jobs take them across the country, and at least one character loses a toe in an accident. *The Five-Year Engagement* followed Stoller, Segel, and Apatow's *Forgetting Sarah Marshall*, which was a more conventional romantic comedy filled with broad set pieces. By design, *The Five-Year Engagement* is messier and more ambitious, and it's very long by the standards of its genre. But it *needs* to be long to explore how the passage of time impacts a relationship, and to show how some bonds are strong enough to endure almost anything.

WAR DOGS (2016)
Directed by Todd Phillips

In between his *Hangover* and *Joker* franchises, Todd Phillips made this effectively small-scale biopic about a greedy massage therapist (Miles Teller) who forms a partnership with an old buddy who works as a low-level arms dealer (Jonah Hill, giving one of his most convincingly sleazy performances). Their company is a little fish in the big pond of the munitions industry, but their cut-any-corner business practices eventually land them a huge contract with the U.S. military. Unfortunately, the deal violates a trade embargo, which forces the men to engineer an elaborate scheme to disguise their illicit Chinese bullets. *War Dogs* itself employs a similar bit of subterfuge, with Phillips smuggling one of his signature investigations of male friendship into a *Goodfellas*-style historical caper picture. *War Dogs* was one of Phillips's least financially successful films—it's the second-lowest grossing title of his entire career—but it's an interesting counterpoint to a filmography otherwise filled with stories about macho doofuses absolved (if not outright rewarded) for their willful misbehavior.

THE HOUSE (2017)

Directed by Andrew Jay Cohen

The plot of this underrated late-career Will Ferrell vehicle is patently absurd: Ferrell and Amy Poehler play a married couple who team up with their gambling-addicted best friend (Jason Mantzoukas) to open an illegal casino and fund their daughter's college education. And yet beneath the gags about underground fight clubs and Will Ferrell accidentally setting Jeremy Renner on fire, there's a surprisingly mature story about middle-age, middle-class malaise. Ferrell's and Poehler's characters have nominally achieved the American dream, with a solid marriage, a nice house, and a smart, well-adjusted kid. They're also bored, unhappy, and can't afford their only child's tuition. Also, the local government is nakedly corrupt, and the only way to get ahead is by becoming a criminal and exploiting their neighbors. It's an extremely bleak vision of modern life sugarcoated with some very funny comic sequences. (See: Will Ferrell accidentally setting Jeremy Renner on fire.)

BARB AND STAR GO TO VISTA DEL MAR (2021)

Directed by Josh Greenbaum

It took ten years for Kristen Wiig and Annie Mumolo to write a follow-up to *Bridesmaids*, but it was worth the wait. In *Barb and Star Go to Vista*

Del Mar, they play cloistered middle-aged buddies who get laid off from their jobs and travel to Florida for a vacation. Rather than try to compete with their own carefully observed comedy about a close friendship jeopardized by jealousy, Wiig and Mumolo instead crafted a wildly preposterous comedy about a close friendship jeopardized by jealousy, as Barb and Star get mixed up in a madwoman's plot to kill everyone in Vista Del Mar with deadly mosquitoes. (Wiig also plays the villain under pasty white makeup and a severe wig.) *Barb and Star*'s delightful flights of fancy include lavish musical numbers, talking crabs, a magical woman from the sea named Trish, and more references to culottes than any other motion picture in history. Wiig and Mumolo better not wait ten more years to make their next comic masterpiece.

YOU'RE CORDIALLY INVITED (2025)

Directed by Nicholas Stoller

Somehow, Will Ferrell and Reese Witherspoon never made a movie together until 2025's *You're Cordially Invited*, a peppy little rom-com from *Forgetting Sarah Marshall* and *The Five-Year Engagement* director Nicholas Stoller. They play the squabbling father and mother of two brides whose weddings were both booked in the same tiny hotel on the same weekend. The stars make an exemplary odd couple; Ferrell with his enormous beta energy, and Witherspoon as the tiny alpha refusing to give an inch to his absurd demands and claims of superiority. Their battle for control of the venue escalates until Ferrell is wrestling an alligator, a gag that would have killed on the big screen . . . if only *You're Cordially Invited* had gotten a theatrical release. In a sign of the times, it went straight to Amazon's Prime Video service instead.

ACKNOWLEDGMENTS

The first movies I loved were comedies.

I didn't discover Kurosawa until college. I wasn't introduced to Bresson until grad school. The films that made me a cinephile were all comedies: *Ghostbusters*, *Spaceballs*, *Wayne's World*, the original *Naked Gun*. I saw that one at Movie City 5 in East Brunswick, New Jersey, where I laughed so hard at Leslie Nielsen ruining a press conference by going to the bathroom while wearing a wireless microphone that I fell out of my seat.

So first of all my thanks go out to the people who make comedy movies, then, now, and (hopefully) in the future. Comedies have always been undervalued by critics, who generally do not take silly films seriously. I hope this book helps to balance the scales in some small way.

I can't possibly overstate the importance of good research. Everyone goes through life dropping crumbs. If you can recognize the crumbs, you can trace a path all the way back from your death certificate to the dinner and a movie that resulted in you in the first place. But research is an art, not a science, because anyone who knows what they're doing can find the crumbs, the wheres, whats, and whos. The art is in the whys: the ability to read between the crumbs, not to mix metaphors.

All right, so I did not invent that last paragraph. It first appeared in the 1998 comic mystery film *Zero Effect*, as a speech delivered by Bill Pullman as Daryl Zero, the world's greatest private detective. Zero hates to leave his house and has some curious ideas about dieting; his fridge contains nothing but Tab soda and his pantry is stocked with hundreds of cans of tuna. But when it comes to research, he's right on the money. I speak from experience; I have done a lot of it over the course of writing this book. Thank you to the filmmakers and film experts who spoke to me as part of that research, and also to the kind and helpful staff of the New York Public Library for the Performing Arts for enduring my countless requests for materials.

If you followed the crumbs I've dropped throughout my own life, you'd find that my why starts with my parents, Howie and Sandy Singer, two extremely sensible people who made the extremely irrational decision to nurture and encourage their dorky son's passions, and never made him feel like trying to become the next Roger Ebert was a pipe dream, even though it absolutely was. I have always appreciated their support and love. Also, during the outlining stage of this book, my mother gave me a pack of colored note cards on the condition that she receive a mention in the acknowledgments. So here you go, Mom. I acknowledge you. *Are you happy now???*

I also need to acknowledge my agent, Peter Steinberg, who didn't give me colored note cards, but who has twice found a literary venue for me to explore my personal passions. And I'm so lucky that both of those books landed at Putnam, whose staff is so smart and collaborative, and who work tirelessly for their authors. That's especially true of editors Michelle Howry and Ashley Di Dio, who immediately responded to the ideas behind *Funny Business* from its earliest stages.

My parents' first date was a trip to the movies to see Mel Brooks's *The Producers*, a film where two hucksters try to defraud their investors by mounting an intentionally dreadful Broadway musical about the life and times of Adolf Hitler, a concept that's arguably more politically incorrect than any of the films discussed in this book. If that's where a fifty-plus-year relationship starts, it shouldn't be too much of a shock that it produced a kid who loves movie comedies.

That love of comedies was fostered from a very early age watching countless films with my brother, Doug, who I want to thank for being a terrific brother, and also for agreeing with me that it was funny when Leslie Nielsen peed loudly. These days, I watch a lot of comedies with my daughters, Eloise and Riley. I would like to thank them both for inspiring our ritual of regular family movie nights, and for enduring (and occasionally laughing at) my terrible Dad jokes. Now go spackle the den, both of you.

Sifting through more of my crumbs, I see that my movie education really started at home, where I stayed up late as a teenager to watch episodes of *Siskel & Ebert*, and then continued at Syracuse University. While it certainly did not feel that way at the time, the most important decision of my entire life was the choice to attend a screening in the spring of 1999 at UU Cinemas, the on-campus film society at Syracuse. The movie itself was not particularly memorable. But before the feature began, the students who ran UU Cinemas happened to mention they were looking for new members. My personal life at the time closely resembled Daryl Zero's, so I gave it a shot.

By the fall semester I wasn't just helping at UU Cinemas, I was running it: programming movies, hosting screenings, designing advertising, splicing 16mm film reels . . . you name it, I did it. It was an enormous amount of work, all of it unpaid, but the people in this group, including Becky, Flora, Reid, Heather, Jen, Neil, Jason, MK, Robin, Len, and more, gave me a feeling of community I didn't experience anywhere else at Syracuse. I remain indebted to all of them, and to anyone else who ever volunteered at UU Cinemas over the years. (Somehow, despite all the hand-wringing over the death of the theatrical experience, UU Cinemas still shows films regularly at Syracuse University. Maybe they'll invite me up to host a screening of *Zoolander* or something.)

My colleagues at UU Cinemas introduced me to a lot of movies, but none were as important as one particular person I never would have met without the organization. In the fall of 1999, two UU members,

Pete Thomas and Nikki Bramley, noticed that I constantly quoted the *Austin Powers* movies. (Shut up, it was 1999, everyone quoted *Austin Powers*.) They thought I might hit it off with one of Nikki's friends, who *also* quoted *Austin Powers*, and arranged a meeting at a Syracuse bowling alley.

That friend turned out to be Melissa Vacca—now Melissa Singer, my wife. Ironically, she doesn't quote movies that much; the *Austin Powers* thing was a total fluke. (I told you; *everyone* quoted *Austin Powers* in 1999!) That lucky break led to more than twenty-five amazing years together. She's a great dinner date, a great mom, a great first reader, and a great partner. Everything good I have done and made in the last quarter century is because of her. That is why this book is dedicated to her. (I probably should have dedicated it to Mike Myers, too, though, come to think of it.)

Finally and sincerely, I want to thank you, whoever you are, for reading. Remember to keep looking for the art in the whys. While you're at it, try to find some of the whys in the art as well. That's what this book is all about.

NOTES

Introduction: Leaders of the Pack

1 **"of their career":** Judd Apatow, "Elvis Costello Talks to Judd Apatow About *Wise Up Ghost*, His Album with the Roots, and His Musical with Burt Bacharach," *Vanity Fair*, October 28, 2013, https://www.vanityfair.com/culture/music/2013/10/elvis-costello-wise-up-ghosts-burt-bacharach.

2 **"'kick one around'":** Apatow, "Elvis Costello Talks."

2 **"for two weeks":** Bruce Bennett, "Offshoots of a Comedy of Darers," *Wall Street Journal*, November 9, 2012, A22.

4 **Dwight D. Eisenhower:** Jasper Drake, "Wedding Crashers Shot in 7 Different Locations and Even Used a Writer's House: 'It Was a Lego Set,'" Showbiz Cheat-Sheet, January 8, 2021, https://www.cheatsheet.com/news/wedding-crashers-shot-in-7-different-locations-and-even-used-a-writers-house-it-was-a-lego-set.html/.

4 **"from a chair":** Susan Wloszczyna, "Wilson and Vaughn: Leaders of the 'Frat Pack,'" *USA Today*, June 15, 2004, https://usatoday30.usatoday.com/life/movies/news/2004-06-15-frat-pack_x.htm.

5 **"the same wavelength":** Wloszczyna, "Wilson and Vaughn: Leaders of the 'Frat Pack.'"

6 **"Pack Checks Zeitgeist":** Dennis Harvey, "Frat Pack Checks Zeitgeist," *Variety*, February 17–23, 2003, 39.

6 **"done my job":** Devin Mitchell and Mark Lieberman, "*The M&M Report*: A Conversation with Film Critic Susan Wloszczyna," *The Eagle*, April 15, 2014, https://www.theeagleonline.com/article/2014/04/the-mm-report-a-conversation-with-rogerebert-com-film-critic-susan-wloszczyna.

Chapter 1: The Less-Bad Guys

9 **"power booting":** Chris Miller, *The Real Animal House: The Awesomely Depraved Saga of the Fraternity That Inspired the Movie* (Little, Brown, 2006), 88.

10 **"Technicolor yawn":** Chris Miller, "Return to Animal House," *Playboy*, October 1989, https://dartreview.com/this-is-long/.

10 **Board of Trustees:** Miller, *The Real Animal House*, 145.

10 **"Vanilla Fudge":** Miller, *The Real Animal House*, 46.

11 **"my basic training":** Mark Leffler, "House Rules: Chris Miller Takes Us Back to the Real Animal House," *Review*, November 16, 2006, https://www.review-mag.com/article/house-rules-chris-miller-takes-us-back-to-the-real-animal-house.

11 **"It's so rare":** John Landis, author interview, Brooklyn, NY, June 27, 2025.

12 **"change a thing":** Tony Schwartz, "College Humor Comes Back," *Newsweek*, October 23, 1978, 91.

12 **"the United States":** *Drunk Stone Brilliant Dead*, directed by Douglas Tirola (2015: Magnolia Pictures), Tubi.

13 **"extraordinary national appeal":** *Unseen & Untold: National Lampoon's Animal House*, produced by Paul Nihipali Jr. (2003: Spike TV), YouTube.

13 **"I said, 'Alright'":** Adam Pockross, "Ivan Reitman Talks *Meatballs*, How Bill Murray Took Pity on Him, and Why It Just Doesn't Matter," Yahoo! Movies, June 11, 2012, https://ca.movies.yahoo.com/blogs/this-week-dvd-blu-ray/ivan-reitman-talks-meatballs-bill-murray-took-pity-015951346.html.

14 **"Ramis for $2,500":** Matty Simmons, *Fat, Drunk & Stupid: The Inside Story Behind the Making of Animal House* (St. Martin's Press, 2012), 33.

14 **"'make a movie!'":** Simmons, *Fat, Drunk & Stupid*, 32.

14 ***Laser Orgy Girls*:** Miller, *The Real Animal House*, 5.

14 **"'Make it college!'":** Landis, author interview.

15 **"*Peace* on speed":** Simmons, *Fat, Drunk & Stupid*, 41.

16 **"*they're* the heroes?!":** Simmons, *Fat, Drunk & Stupid*, 50.

17 **"toilet gags":** "G Is for Golden: The MPAA Film Ratings at 50," Motion Picture Association, October 29, 2018, https://www.motionpictures.org/research-docs/g-is-for-golden-the-mpaa-film-ratings-at-50/.

18 **"basic bad taste":** *M*A*S*H*, directed by Robert Altman (Fox Home Entertainment, 2004), DVD.

18 **"just hated me":** Landis, author interview.

18 **"follow your lead":** Landis, author interview.

19 **"classic college comedy":** Elvis Mitchell, "Critic's Notebook; Revisiting Faber College (Toga, Toga, Toga!)," *New York Times*, August 25, 2003, https://www.nytimes.com/2003/08/25/movies/critic-s-notebook-revisiting-faber-college-toga-toga-toga.html.

19 **"not particularly likable":** *Unseen & Untold: National Lampoon's Animal House*, YouTube.

20 **"skilled it was":** Landis, author interview.

20 **$2.3 million:** Landis, author interview.

20 **"super-grossers":** William Bates, "Hollywood in the Era of the 'Super-Grosser,'" *New York Times*, December 24, 1978, https://www.nytimes.com/1978/12/24

/archives/hollywood-in-the-era-of-the-supergrosser-hollywood-enters-the-era .html.

20 **"the main reason":** Landis, author interview.

20 **"language and behavior":** Simmons, *Fat, Drunk & Stupid*, 84.

21 **"went crazy over":** *Unseen & Untold: National Lampoon's Animal House*, YouTube.

22 **"'that in movies?'":** Christopher Borrelli, "Farrelly Brothers Are Serious About Comedy," *Toledo Blade*, August 12, 1998, https://www.southcoasttoday.com /story/entertainment/local/1998/08/12/farrelly-brothers-are-serious-about /50548815007/.

22 **their inspiration:** "We Are the Farrelly Brothers. Ask Us Anything," Reddit, November 11, 2014, https://www.reddit.com/r/IAmA/comments/2lztn5/we_are_the_farrelly_brothers_ask_us_anything/.

Chapter 2: The Hustler of Money

24 **"y'know, *something* here":** "Ben Stiller Wins the Emmy for 'The Ben Stiller Show,'" September 19, 1993, posted July 30, 2020, by Television Academy, YouTube, https://www.youtube.com/watch?v=pCtY7oQJqk4.

24 **"really funny person":** Dennis Lim, "The Able Guy," *Village Voice*, August 4, 1998, 102.

24 **"really? What scene?":** Tad Friend, "Funny Is Money," *New Yorker*, June 18, 2012, https://www.newyorker.com/magazine/2012/06/25/funny-is-money.

24 **"out of here!":** Conan O'Brien, host, *Conan O'Brien Needs a Friend*, podcast, episode 326, "Ben Stiller Returns," Earwolf, January 26, 2025, https://www .earwolf.com/episode/ben-stiller-returns/.

25 **the Pips:** Rachel Abramowicz, "His Style? Pretty Goofy," *Newsday*, September 30, 2001, D9.

25 **instead of turkey:** David Hochman, "Stiller: Crazy After All These Years," *New York Daily News*, February 22, 2004, 6.

25 **"hours at a time":** John Milward, "Ben Stiller Finds 'Reality' Is in the Genes," *New York Times*, February 13, 1994, https://www.nytimes.com/1994/02/13 /movies/film-ben-stiller-finds-reality-is-in-the-genes.html.

25 **"seemed very comforting":** Friend, "Funny Is Money."

25 **"child of television":** Franz Lidz, "Cornering the Market on Creeps and Nerds," *New York Times*, September 20, 1998, https://www.nytimes.com/1998/09/20 /movies/film-cornering-the-market-on-creeps-and-nerds.html.

25 **"20 trillion times":** Edward Margulies, "Beyond Parody," *Movieline*, March 1994, 60.

26 ***Murder in the Park*:** Margulies, "Beyond Parody."

26 **"'Stiller's kid sucks'":** Joe Neumaier, "Ben Stiller's Serious About Being Funny," *New York Daily News*, September 24, 2003, 42.

26 **"way you can":** Meredith Berkman, "Jerry's Kid," *New York*, April 3, 1989, 26.

27 **"'This is good'":** Hilary de Vries, "It's No Mystery," *Newsday*, August 8, 1999, D4.

28 **"making short films":** David Marchese, "The Interview: Ben Stiller on 'Severance,' Selling Out and Being Jewish Today," *New York Times Magazine*, January 11, 2025, https://www.nytimes.com/2025/01/11/magazine/ben-stiller-interview.html.

28 **"comedy freak":** Judd Apatow, *Sick in the Head: Conversations About Life and Comedy* (Random House, 2016), ix.

29 **"speaking to me":** Graham Bensinger, "Judd Apatow: Tricking Jay Leno and Jerry Seinfeld," *In Depth with Graham Bensinger*, November 2, 2016, YouTube, https://www.youtube.com/watch?v=U1qg9nPJHwQ.

29 **"Your Friend, Steve Martin":** Judd Apatow, "A Note from Comedy Issue Guest Editor Judd Apatow: The Death of an Anecdote," *Vanity Fair*, December 4, 2012, https://www.vanityfair.com/hollywood/2012/12/note-from-judd-apatow-comedy-issue?srsltid=AfmBOopJOLErw1cfmEAOG1Yu7u2HX_I7aOXsTReVXy34GEnW1XDonx3X.

30 **"and stayed buddies":** Paul Feig, author interview, Brooklyn, NY, September 9, 2025.

30 **"'so hooked up?'":** Feig, author interview.

30 **"'a good performer'":** Nathan Rabin, "Judd Apatow," A.V. Club, March 1, 2011, https://www.avclub.com/judd-apatow-1798224447.

30 **"should think about":** Rabin, "Judd Apatow."

31 **lead a staff:** David Handelman, "The Ambivalent-About-Prime-Time Players," *New York Times Magazine*, December 28, 1997, https://www.nytimes.com/1997/12/28/magazine/the-ambivalent-about-prime-time-players.html.

31 **"'now what happens?'":** Judd Apatow, *Comedy Nerd: A Lifelong Obsession in Stories and Pictures* (Random House, 2025), 60.

32 **"'We're doing it'":** Joel Stein, "Taking Judd Apatow Seriously," *Time*, July 30, 2009, https://time.com/archive/6689113/taking-judd-apatow-seriously/.

32 **"on the air":** Marc Maron, host, *WTF with Marc Maron*, podcast, episode 79, "Ben Stiller," WTF+, June 7, 2010, https://www.wtfpod.com/podcast/episodes/episode_79_ben_stiller.

32 **"anything from Ben":** MW Staff, "Judd Apatow, Seth Rogen, and Romany Malco Talk *The 40 Year Old Virgin*," MovieWeb, August 18, 2005, https://movieweb.com/judd-apatow-seth-rogan-and-romany-malco-talk-the-40-year-old-virgin/.

32 **"Ben do those":** Ryan D'Agostino, "Ben Stiller Sees the World Differently Now," *Esquire*, February 22, 2022, https://www.esquire.com/entertainment/tv/a39139152/ben-stiller-severance-profile/.

33 **"my own experience":** Gene Seymour, "Ben Stiller Gets Real," *Fanfare*, February 13, 1994, 14.

34 **"connect with it":** Robert Dominguez, "Stiller & Mirror: Reflections on 'Reality,'" *New York Daily News*, February 16, 1994, 41.

34 **"in terms of directing":** Maron, "Ben Stiller."

34 **"to do both":** Seymour, "Ben Stiller Gets Real."

34 **"get rid of":** Bernard Weinraub, "How a Sure Summer Hit Missed," *New York Times*, June 27, 1996, https://www.nytimes.com/1996/06/27/movies/how-a-sure-summer-hit-missed.html.

34 **"or *Cape Fear*":** Manohla Dargis, "Ben Stiller," *Interview*, April 1996, 40.

35 **"a big leap":** *The Cable Guy*, directed by Ben Stiller (Sony Pictures Home Entertainment, 2011), Blu-ray.

36 **"also a nightmare":** Rob Tannenbaum, "Natural Born Stiller," *Details*, August 1996, 102.

37 **"Summer Hit Missed":** Weinraub, "How a Sure Summer Hit Missed."

37 **"line than his":** Merle Ginsberg, "Stiller's Crossing," *W*, June 1996, 88.

Chapter 3: The Silent Assassin

39 **"It's Over. Please Die":** Newsweek Staff, "Dear *Saturday Night Live*: It's Over. Please Die," *Newsweek*, October 16, 1994, https://www.newsweek.com/dear-saturday-night-live-its-over-please-die-189670.

40 **"be Chevy Chase":** Lynn Hirschberg, "A Wild and Uncrazy Guy," *New York Times Magazine*, November 12, 2006, https://www.nytimes.com/2006/11/12/magazine/12ferrell.html.

40 **"garbled the lines":** *SNL50: Beyond Saturday Night*, "More Cowbell," directed by Neil Berkeley, aired January 16, 2025, on NBC, Peacock.

40 **"best possible way":** Sharon Waxman, "Will Ferrell: The Incredible Growing Elf," *New York Times*, May 9, 2004, https://www.nytimes.com/2004/05/09/movies/summer-movies-will-ferrell-the-incredible-growing-elf.html.

41 **"talented he is":** Hirschberg, "A Wild and Uncrazy Guy."

41 **"Isn't that wrong?":** Dan Jewel and Anthony Duignan Cabrera, "Night Moves," *People*, April 6, 1998, 143.

41 **"by being normal":** Marc Peyser, "Comedian in Chief," *Newsweek*, February 18, 2001, https://www.newsweek.com/comedian-chief-155541.

41 **"The Silent Assassin":** Jenelle Riley, "Gary Sanchez at 10: Pair Helm Antic Empire," *Variety*, May 24, 2016, 59.

42 **"had two meetings":** Jewell and Cabrera, "Night Moves."

42 **"with that idea":** Tim Adams, "Funny Face," *Observer*, December 20, 2015, 17.

42 **"'What's *his* problem?'":** Dave Itzkoff, "A Night Out with Will Ferrell: Give Me a W!" *New York Times*, January 5, 2003, https://www.nytimes.com/2003/01/05/style/a-night-out-with-will-ferrell-give-me-a-w.html.

42 **all the money:** Marc Maron, host, *WTF with Marc Maron*, podcast, episode 450, "Will Ferrell," WTF+, December 9, 2013, https://www.wtfpod.com/podcast/episodes/episode_450_-_will_ferrell.

43 **"theatrical graduate school":** Gerri Hirshey, "All I Wanted Was to Be Normal," *Parade*, October 19, 2003, 4.

43 **"'just by myself'":** Maron, "Will Ferrell."
45 **"or leave it":** James Andrew Miller and Tom Shales, *Live from New York: An Uncensored History of* Saturday Night Live (Little, Brown, 2002), 446.
45 **"pull the trigger":** Maron, "Will Ferrell."
45 **"Most Annoying Newcomer":** Ken Tucker, "Saturday Night Fever," *Entertainment Weekly*, October 13, 1995, https://ew.com/article/1995/10/13/saturday-night-fever-2/.
46 **"being so painful":** David Edelstein, "Butts Below the Border," *New York*, March 26, 2012, 53.
46 **"guy at heart":** Maron, "Will Ferrell."
46 **"inappropriate behavior really funny":** Susan Stewart, "Fast Chat: Will Ferrell," *Newsday*, November 16, 2003, D3.
47 **"as he did":** Alan Sepinwall, author interview, Brooklyn, NY, May 2, 2025.
47 **"in the cast":** Waxman, "Will Ferrell: The Incredible Growing Elf."
47 **"done the show":** Peyser, "Comedian in Chief."
48 **"into another club":** Anthony Breznican, "Will Do Anything," *New York Post*, February 20, 2003, 78.
48 **"that was it":** Maron, "Will Ferrell."

Chapter 4: Through a Constant Regimen of Activities We Begin to Learn a Craft

50 **a single screening:** *Bottle Rocket*, directed by Wes Anderson (Criterion Collection, 2008), Blu-ray.
50 **a "serious" child:** Nancy Mills, "Owen Wilson Gets Hot," *New York Daily News*, November 20, 2001, 47.
51 **an "obnoxious" person:** Marshall Sella, "Boyish Wonder," *New York Times Magazine*, December 2, 2001, https://www.nytimes.com/2001/12/02/magazine/boyish-wonder.html.
51 **the other students:** Pamela Colloff, "The New Kids," *Texas Monthly*, May 1998, 112.
51 ***A Night in Tunisia*:** Richard Brody, "Wild, Wild Wes," *New Yorker*, October 26, 2009, https://www.newyorker.com/magazine/2009/11/02/wild-wild-wes.
52 **"aloud was froufrou":** James L. Brooks, "Bottle Rocket," Criterion, November 23, 2008, https://www.criterion.com/current/posts/886-bottle-rocket?srsltid=AfmBOoomNCHvvvnELKgOzshFt-Nzb_mHv9lGhSb_rTe4gyOtAam_S1J_.
53 **"more legitimate movie":** *Rushmore*, directed by Wes Anderson (Criterion Collection, 2000), DVD.
53 **"dramatic chops, too":** John Hamburg, author interview, Brooklyn, NY, June 11, 2025.
54 **a unique talent:** Nathan Rabin, "Judd Apatow," A.V. Club, March 1, 2011, https://www.avclub.com/judd-apatow-1798224447.

Chapter 5: Beans Before Franks

55 **"in movie jail":** Tad Friend, "Funny Is Money," *New Yorker*, June 18, 2012, https://www.newyorker.com/magazine/2012/06/25/funny-is-money.

56 **"not studio executives":** Simon Bland, "The Problematic, Jizz-Soaked Legacy of 'There's Something About Mary,'" *Daily Beast*, September 30, 2023, https://www.thedailybeast.com/theres-something-about-mary-farrelly-brothers-on-its-problematic-jizz-soaked-legacy/.

56 **"'going to do here?'":** Bland, "The Problematic, Jizz-Soaked Legacy."

57 **"have her for himself":** *There's Something About Mary*, directed by Peter and Bobby Farrelly (20th Century Fox, 1999), DVD.

57 **"what motivated us":** Donald Liebenson, "*There's Something About Mary* at 20: Its Creators and Actors Share Memories of Risky Scenes (Hello, Hair Gel)," *Los Angeles Times*, August 16, 2018, https://www.latimes.com/entertainment/movies/la-ca-mn-something-about-mary-anniversary-20180816-story.html.

57 **"to untangle himself":** Bland, "The Problematic, Jizz-Soaked Legacy."

58 **"'in any minute'":** Griffin Newman and David Sims, hosts, *Blank Check with Griffin and David*, podcast, "*The Big Lebowski* with Seth Rogen," Blank Check, August 23, 2025, https://blankcheck.beam.ly/episode/the-big-lebowski-with-seth-rogen.

59 **"just ego free":** *There's Something About Mary*, DVD.

60 **derail her career:** Susan King, "*There's Something About Mary* at 20: Cameron Diaz, the Farrelly Brothers on 'Hair Gel' Scene and Other Raunchy Gags," *Variety*, July 14, 2018, https://variety.com/2018/film/news/theres-something-about-mary-20th-anniversary-cameron-diaz-hair-gel-scene-1202871227/.

60 **"Turns out, nobody cared":** Dennis Hensley, "There's Something About Ben," *The Advocate*, September 11, 2001, 43.

60 **"is individually loaded":** "These Were the Free Samples of 'Something About Mary' Hair Gel the Studio Sent My Theater . . . ," Reddit, October 24, 2017, https://www.reddit.com/r/movies/comments/78k5f4/these_were_the_free_samples_of_something_about/.

61 **"my whole career":** David Dobkin, author interview, Brooklyn, NY, November 17, 2025.

61 **"in a zipper!":** Annabel Vered, "There's Something About Ben," *TV Guide Insider*, September 5, 1998, 3.

61 **"people find funny":** Hilary de Vries, "It's No Mystery," *Newsday*, August 8, 1999, D4.

62 **"good thing, I guess":** Franz Lidz, "Cornering the Market on Creeps and Nerds," *New York Times*, September 20, 1998, https://www.nytimes.com/1998/09/20/movies/film-cornering-the-market-on-creeps-and-nerds.html.

62 **"can you do?":** Hensley, "There's Something About Ben."

Chapter 6: The Most Personal Thing I've Ever Done

64 **"misanthropy and contempt":** Janet Maslin, "The Cable Guy," *New York* Times, June 14, 1996, https://archive.nytimes.com/www.nytimes.com/library/filmarchive/cable_guy.html.

64 **"and take chances":** John Sellers, "Judd Apatow Tells Us the Legend of *The Cable Guy*, the Bomb That Wasn't," Vulture, March 1, 2011, https://www.vulture.com/2011/03/cable_guy_judd_apatow.html.

64 **"horse in *Blazing Saddles*":** Adrienne LaFrance, "The Invention of Judd Apatow," *The Atlantic*, September 15, 2025, https://www.theatlantic.com/magazine/archive/2025/10/judd-apatow-comedy-career/683975/.

65 **a "weird education":** "Judd Apatow and Seth Rogen on *Knocked Up*," moderated by David Denby, October 7, 2007, posted July 22, 2014, by *New Yorker*, YouTube, https://www.youtube.com/watch?v=BB80Fm4pwgo.

65 **"imaginative, broader comedy":** Alan Siegel, "Comedy in the '90s, Part 6: Judd Apatow and the Decade That Followed," The Ringer, October 23, 2019.

65 **"a year anyway":** Judd Apatow, "How I Got Kicked Out of High School," in *I Found This Funny: My Favorite Pieces of Humor and Some That May Not Be Funny at All*, ed. Judd Apatow (McSweeney's, 2011), 41.

66 **"show that side":** Robert Lloyd, "2 Good 2 Be 4Gotten: An Oral History of *Freaks and Geeks*," *Vanity Fair*, December 6, 2012, https://www.vanityfair.com/hollywood/2013/01/freaks-and-geeks-oral-history.

66 **"just never happens":** Lloyd, "2 Good 2 Be 4Gotten."

67 **"usually are enough":** Apatow, "How I Got Kicked Out of High School," 41.

67 **"stories I know":** Paul Feig, author interview, Brooklyn, NY, September 9, 2025.

68 **"water it down":** John Bowe, "The Trouble with Paul Feig," *New York Times Magazine*, September 26, 2008, https://www.nytimes.com/2008/09/28/magazine/28feig-t.html.

68 **"experiencing this life":** Nathan Rabin, "Judd Apatow," A.V. Club, March 1, 2011, https://www.avclub.com/judd-apatow-1798224447.

68 **"the best thing":** Marc Maron, host, *WTF with Marc Maron*, podcast, episode 103, "Judd Apatow Part 1," WTF+, August 29, 2010, https://www.wtfpod.com/podcast/episodes/episode_103_-_judd_apatow_part_1.

70 **"'at all costs'":** *Cultureshock*, episode 4, "*Freaks and Geeks*: The Documentary," directed by Brent Hodge, aired July 16, 2018, on A&E, https://www.dailymotion.com/video/x8yo982.

70 **"work together again?":** *Cultureshock*, episode 4.

Chapter 7: Mr. Creepy

72 **"it to happen":** viceuk, "Todd Phillips's Frat House," *Vice*, October 13, 2010, https://www.vice.com/en/article/todd-phillips-frat-house/.

72 **"to a group":** Todd Gilchrist, "The Mostly Comedic Road Trip of Todd Phillips," *Variety*, January 2, 2020, https://variety.com/2024/film/features/todd-phillips-joker-2-movie-interview-1236111122/.

73 **"bonding that happens":** Stephen Mooallem, "Interview: Todd Phillips," *Interview*, October 12, 2010, https://www.interviewmagazine.com/film/todd-phillips.

73 **"at least mine are":** Anne S. Lewis, "Rush Hour," *Austin Chronicle*, September 8, 2000, https://www.austinchronicle.com/screens/2000-09-08/78582/.

73 **"thought of him":** Mooallem, "Interview: Todd Phillips."

74 **he raised $15,000:** Stefanie Fluty-Hall, "Todd Phillips on GG Allin," *Stefanie's Rock Show*, June 9, 2010, YouTube, https://www.youtube.com/watch?v=9In4SB8DxE0.

74 **"attracted to mayhem":** Erik Hedegaard, "How *The Hangover* Director Took on the Military Industrial Complex," *Rolling Stone*, August 11, 2016, https://www.rollingstone.com/tv-movies/tv-movie-features/how-the-hangover-director-took-on-the-military-industrial-complex-111504/.

76 **"for airing documentaries":** Steve Daly, "Frat's Entertainment," *Entertainment Weekly*, August 7, 1998, 48.

77 **"were subjected to":** Leo Reisberg, "Film Promoted as Inside Look at Hazing Is Attacked for Including Staged Scenes," *Chronicle of Higher Education*, February 12, 1999, A43.

77 **Phillips's own idea:** Reisberg, "Film Promoted as Inside Look."

77 **"hundred and five":** Steve Daly, "Hazed and Confused," *Entertainment Weekly*, January 8, 1999, 20.

77 **"when they're drunk":** Mooallem, "Interview: Todd Phillips."

77 **"thing to do":** Hedegaard, "How *The Hangover* Director Took on the Military Industrial Complex."

78 **"heat for it":** viceuk, "Todd Phillips's *Frat House.*"

78 **"and underage drinking":** Eleanor Yang, "HEC News: Alpha Tau Omega Members Linked to Fights, Hazing, and More," Higher Education Center, June 24, 2000, https://web.archive.org/web/20090213065215/http://archives.higheredcenter.org/hecnews/events/000630.html#1.

79 **"a terrible student":** David A. Keeps, "Brothers from Another Planet," *Details*, March 1999, 76.

80 **"telling you about":** Josh Horowitz, *The Mind of the Modern Moviemaker: 20 Conversations with the New Generation of Filmmakers* (Plume, 2006), 247.

80 **"kind of funny":** Dave Karger and William Keck, "Highway to Heck," *Entertainment Weekly*, May 26, 2000, 32.

81 **"talking about comedy":** Scot Armstrong, author interview, Brooklyn, NY, August 14, 2025.

81 **"the funny parts":** Armstrong, author interview.

82 **"to other 15-year-olds":** Karger and Keck, "Highway to Heck."

82 **"*Silence of the Lambs*":** Karger and Keck, "Highway to Heck."

Chapter 8: So Hot Right Now

86 **"out of that":** *Zoolander*, directed by Ben Stiller (Paramount, 2016), Blu-ray.

86 **"in the world,"** *Zoolander*, Blu-ray.

86 **"'it won't air'":** Andrew Buss, "'But Why Male Models?': An Oral History of *Zoolander*," *Vanity Fair*, September 30, 2021, https://www.vanityfair.com/hollywood/2021/09/zoolander-20th-anniversary-oral-history.

87 **"For like $30,000":** Travis Andrews, "The *Meet the Parents* Movie You've Never Seen," *Washington Post*, December 24, 2024, https://www.yahoo.com/entertainment/meet-parents-movie-youve-never-150008990.html.

88 **"worked on was *Zoolander*":** John Hamburg, author interview, Brooklyn, NY, June 11, 2025.

88 **"comedy nerd kid":** Brock Swinson, "'Relax into Your Perspective': John Hamburg on *Me Time*, *Zoolander*, *Meet the Parents*, and *I Love You, Man*," Creative Screenwriting, September 14, 2022, https://www.creativescreenwriting.com/relax-into-your-perspective-john-hamburg-on-me-time-zoolander-meet-the-parents-and-i-love-you-man/.

88 **"caring about Derek":** Buss, "'But Why Male Models?'"

88 **"'a male model?'":** Hamburg, author interview.

89 **"emphasize that aspect":** *Meet the Parents*, directed by Jay Roach (Universal, 2015), DVD.

89 **"having it go wrong":** *Meet the Parents*, DVD.

89 **"be just right":** Hamburg, author interview.

92 **a baseball umpire:** Dennis Hensley, "There's Something About Ben," *The Advocate*, September 11, 2001, 38.

92 **"worse than PG-esque?":** Buss, "'But Why Male Models?'"

92 **"was one victory":** Hensley, "There's Something About Ben."

92 **"context for it":** Buss, "'But Why Male Models?'"

93 **"Do Blue Steel!":** Deanna Kizis, "Be Still Our Hearts, Ben," *Cosmopolitan*, January 2002, 138.

93 **"they're worth it":** Joe Neumaier, "Ben Stiller's Serious About Being Funny," *New York Daily News*, September 24, 2003, 42.

93 **"I regret that":** Tad Friend, "Funny Is Money," *New Yorker*, June 18, 2012, https://www.newyorker.com/magazine/2012/06/25/funny-is-money.

Chapter 9: The Movie Star Superstar Guy

95 **"idea for a movie":** Ryan Gajewski, "Old School Sweet 16 Reunion: The Oral History of *Old School*," *Playboy*, February 23, 2019, https://web.archive.org/web/20210126192110/https://www.playboy.com/read/old-school-oral-history.

96 **"wasn't really great":** Gajewski, "Old School Sweet 16 Reunion."

96 **"stuff to connect":** Scot Armstrong, author interview, Brooklyn, NY, August 14, 2025.

96 **even *do* comedy?:** Jenelle Riley, "Vince Vaughn: Big Fan of 'Adult Storytelling,'" *Variety*, March 3, 2015, 61.

97 **and emotional problems:** Holly Sorensen, "Is This the Face of a Psycho Killer?" *Time Out New York*, August 13–20, 1998, 10.

97 **"'she's gonna play!'":** Wendy Jenson, "Vince Charming," *Cosmopolitan*, October 1997, 206.

97 **"get involved professionally":** Fred Schruers, "Vince Vaughn," *Rolling Stone*, June 12, 1997, 76.

98 **"Improv is writing":** Marc Maron, host, *WTF with Marc Maron*, podcast, episode 501, "Vince Vaughn," WTF+, May 29, 2014, https://www.wtfpod.com/podcast/episodes/episode_501_-_vince_vaughn.

99 **"the whole thing":** Josh Horowitz, *The Mind of the Modern Moviemaker: 20 Conversations with the New Generation of Filmmakers* (Plume, 2006), 34.

99 **"a fucking movie":** Maron, "Vince Vaughn."

99 **gave him the part:** Alex French and Howie Kahn, "So Money," *Grantland*, January 22, 2014, http://grantland.com/features/an-oral-history-swingers/.

101 **"play character parts":** Schruers, "Vince Vaughn."

101 **"movie star superstar guy":** Stephen Schaefer, "The Other 'Swinger,'" *New York Post*, October 14, 1996, 33.

101 **"'are about something'":** Maron, "Vince Vaughn."

102 **"top of that list":** Riley, "Vince Vaughn: Big Fan of Adult Storytelling."

102 **"to create in":** Gajewski, "Old School Sweet 16 Reunion."

102 **"went with it":** Gajewski, "Old School Sweet 16 Reunion."

103 **"indebted to Todd":** Gajewski, "Old School Sweet 16 Reunion."

103 **"will be successful":** Armstrong, author interview.

103 **"in the beginning":** Armstrong, author interview.

104 **"letting him inside":** Armstrong, author interview.

104 **"doing that now?":** Gajewski, "Old School Sweet 16 Reunion."

105 **"I was ripped":** Lynn Hirschberg, "A Wild and Uncrazy Guy," *New York Times Magazine*, November 12, 2006, https://www.nytimes.com/2006/11/12/magazine/12ferrell.html.

105 **"I was amazed":** Gajewski, "Old School Sweet 16 Reunion."

105 **"wear the thing":** *Old School*, directed by Todd Phillips (Paramount, 2008), Blu-ray.

105 **"a comedy artist":** Armstrong, author interview.

Chapter 10: A Bold Strategy

108 **"sharp, like razors":** "Chin Chomper," *New York Post*, December 20, 2003, 10.

108 **"to do it?":** Tad Friend, "Funny Is Money," *New Yorker*, June 18, 2012, https://www.newyorker.com/magazine/2012/06/25/funny-is-money.

108 **"making him uncomfortable":** John Hamburg, author interview, Brooklyn, NY, June 11, 2025.

109 **"Owen Wilson. *Starsky & Hutch*":** Sharon Waxman, "They're in on the Joke: Hollywood's Funniest Clique," *New York Times*, March 27, 2005, https://www.nytimes.com/2005/03/27/movies/theyre-in-on-the-joke-hollywoods-funniest-clique.html.

110 **"become really close":** Scot Armstrong, author interview, Brooklyn, NY, August 14, 2025.

110 **"to the show":** Josh Horowitz, *The Mind of the Modern Moviemaker: 20 Conversations with the New Generation of Filmmakers* (Plume, 2006), 249.

110 **"those same beats":** *Starsky & Hutch*, directed by Todd Phillips (Warner Bros., 2006), DVD.

110 **"make that a scene":** Raymond Fiore, "Sensitive Issue," *Entertainment Weekly*, March 12, 2004, 19.

111 **"on his face":** Armstrong, author interview.

111 **"for his life":** Armstrong, author interview.

111 **"dream to work with":** Ryan Gajewski, "Old School Sweet 16 Reunion: The Oral History of *Old School*," *Playboy*, February 23, 2019, https://web.archive.org/web/20210126192110/https://www.playboy.com/read/old-school-oral-history.

112 ***and Iron Face*:** Conan O'Brien, host, *Late Night with Conan O'Brien*, "Ben Stiller / Owen Wilson / Meredith Vieira / Cee-Lo," directed by Allan Kartun, aired March 5, 2004, on NBC, YouTube, https://www.youtube.com/watch?v=e04RnonhhEY.

113 **"want to make it":** "*Dodgeball: A True Underdog Story*," *Entertainment Weekly*, April 30, 2004, 59.

113 **"movies at DreamWorks":** Jake Kring-Schreifels, "Go Balls Deep: The Oral History of 'Dodgeball: A True Underdog Story,'" The Ringer, June 18, 2024, https://www.theringer.com/2024/06/18/movies/dodgeball-true-underdog-story-movie-oral-history-vince-vaughn.

114 **"a pillow":** Kring-Schreifels, "Go Balls Deep."

114 **"uniform came back":** Kring-Schreifels, "Go Balls Deep."

114 **back, and groin:** *Dodgeball: A True Underdog Story*, directed by Rawson Marshall Thurber (Fox, 2014), DVD.

115 **"but it worked":** Kring-Schreifels, "Go Balls Deep."

116 **"comfortable, remunerative rut":** Lou Lumenick, "Ben There, Done That," *New York Post*, March 17, 2004, 43.

116 **"reflexive and self-indulgent":** David Edelstein, "America's Favorite Seething Man-Child," *New York Times*, June 20, 2004, https://www.nytimes.com/2004/06/20/movies/film-america-s-favorite-seething-man-child.html.

116 **"wants the camera":** David Denby, "The Current Cinema: The Contender," *New Yorker*, January 17, 2005, 99.

116 **a "jerk":** Daniel Saney, "Owen Wilson Defends Ben Stiller," Digital Spy, February 7, 2005, https://www.digitalspy.com/showbiz/a19073/owen-wilson-defends-ben-stiller/.

117 **"up a hill":** Logan Hill, "Billion-Dollar Ben," *New York*, March 18, 2005, https://nymag.com/nymetro/movies/features/11543/.

Chapter 11: Keep Going, Only Bigger

119 **"Virtual Reality . . . *No Joke*":** Tracy Swartz, "Adam McKay Talks Faking Suicide in a '90s Chicago Performance," *Chicago Tribune*, December 10, 2015, https://www.chicagotribune.com/2015/12/10/adam-mckay-talks-faking-suicide-in-a-90s-chicago-performance/.

120 **"Jump! Jump!":** Mike Sacks, "Adam McKay on What He Learned from Working with Improv Guru Del Close," Vulture, June 30, 2014, https://www.vulture.com/2014/06/adam-mckay-on-what-he-learned-from-working-with-improv-guru-del-close.html.

121 **"end of our show":** Mike Sacks, "Adam McKay Talks Improvising His Own Suicide and Other Early Career Stunts," The Occasional, June 25, 2014, https://www.theoccasional.com/content/adam-mckay-talks-improvising-his-own-suicide-and-other-early-career-stunts.

121 **infielder Randy Ready:** Sam Schubert, "Adam McKay Has Become the Grown-Up in the Room. He's as Surprised as You Are," *GQ*, December 24, 2021, https://www.gq-magazine.co.uk/culture/article/adam-mckay-interview.

121 **"the frat world":** Terry Gross, host, *Fresh Air*, "*Anchorman* Director Adam McKay," July 8, 2004, https://freshairarchive.org/segments/anchorman-director-adam-mckay.

121 **"'out there, hold on'":** Marc Maron, host, *WTF with Marc Maron*, podcast, episode 119, "Adam McKay," WTF+, November 1, 2010, https://www.wtfpod.com/podcast/episodes/episode_119_-_adam_mckay.

122 **"teachers would suggest":** Sacks, "Adam McKay on What He Learned."

123 **"funny ha-ha":** *Saturday Night Live in the '90s: Pop Culture Nation*, directed by Kenneth Bowser, aired May 5, 2007, on NBC, https://www.bilibili.com/video/BV1gM4y1w7Hn/.

123 **"car dealership guys":** Charles Barfield, "Will Ferrell Talks *August Blowout*, His First Adam McKay Collab Which Caught the Eye of Paul Thomas Anderson," The Playlist, January 13, 2021, https://theplaylist.net/will-ferrell-august-blowout-adam-mckay-paul-thomas-anderson-20210113/.

123 **"we wrote *Anchorman*":** Barfield, "Will Ferrell Talks *August Blowout*."

124 **"male chauvinist pig":** Lorne Manly, "Good News! He's Back!" *New York Times*, November 27, 2013, https://www.nytimes.com/2013/12/01/movies/will-ferrell-returns-as-ron-burgundy.html.

124 **"went from there":** Manly, "Good News! He's Back!"
125 **"telling her, 'Wrong!'":** Bill Simmons, host, *The Bill Simmons Podcast*, episode 226, "Will Ferrell on His Favorite Movie, *SNL*, and LeBron on the Lakers," Apple Podcasts, June 16, 2017, https://podcasts.apple.com/is/podcast/will-ferrell-on-his-favorite-movie-snl-and-lebron-on/id1043699613?i=1000386636839.
125 **single twenty-four-hour period:** Rachel Abramowicz, "It's Fast Cars, Hot Women and Dumb Guys," *Newsday*, August 3, 2006, B6.
125 **during the meeting:** Sharon Waxman, "Will Ferrell: The Incredible Growing Elf," *New York Times*, May 9, 2004, https://www.nytimes.com/2004/05/09/movies/summer-movies-will-ferrell-the-incredible-growing-elf.html.
125 **"'this can make sense?'":** Judd Apatow, *Comedy Nerd: A Lifelong Obsession in Stories and Pictures* (Random House, 2025), 238.
126 **"It's too crazy":** Saul Austerlitz, *Kind of a Big Deal: How* Anchorman *Stayed Classy and Became the Most Iconic Comedy of the Twenty-First Century* (Dutton, 2023), 49.
126 **"then *Old School* hit":** Maron, "Adam McKay."
126 **"'nervous about him'":** Dave Itzkoff, "A Night Out with Will Ferrell: Give Me a W!" *New York Times*, January 5, 2003, https://www.nytimes.com/2003/01/05/style/a-night-out-with-will-ferrell-give-me-a-w.html.
127 **"That's not me":** Joe Neumaier, "The Biggest Dope in Hollywood," *New York Daily News*, July 4, 2004, 2.
129 **"to give Will":** Gross, "*Anchorman* Director Adam McKay."
131 **"buffoonery for [comedy]":** Jay Carr, "Bad News for *Anchorman*," *amNewYork*, July 9, 2004.

Chapter 12: Smart-Dumb Comedy

134 **"'something for Vince and Owen'":** David Dobkin, author interview, Brooklyn, NY, November 17, 2025.
134 **"a cool movie":** Kate McCallum, "THE GREAT IDEA: Steve Faber and Bob Fisher on Big Screen Comedy," *Script*, November 18, 2015, https://scriptmag.com/features/great-idea-steve-faber-bob-fisher-big-screen-comedy.
134 **food and booze:** Hugh Hart, "Lifelong Friends Write a Buddy Pic," *SFGate*, July 10, 2005, https://www.sfgate.com/entertainment/article/LIFELONG-FRIENDS-WRITE-A-BUDDY-PIC-2656318.php.
135 **"for Vince and Owen":** Dobkin, author interview.
136 **"get into it":** Jeff Otto, "Interview: Vince Vaughn and Owen Wilson," IGN, July 11, 2005, https://www.ign.com/articles/2005/07/11/interview-vince-vaughn-and-owen-wilson?page=3.
136 **"absolutely" intentional:** Dobkin, author interview.
136 **down to PG-13:** Dobkin, author interview.

136 **"people really talk":** Tim Grierson, "The Oral History of *Wedding Crashers*," *MEL*, June 23, 2017, https://medium.com/mel-magazine/the-oral-history-of-wedding-crashers-6936866f100b.

137 **"a little subtler":** Grierson, "The Oral History of *Wedding Crashers*."

137 **"best weddings ever":** Dobkin, author interview.

138 **"go through and change":** Logan Hill, "The Player," *New York*, July 18, 2005, 61, https://nymag.com/nymetro/movies/features/12192/.

138 **"some frat guys":** Hill, "The Player."

138 **"a guy movie":** Dobkin, author interview.

138 **"like a breakup":** Dobkin, author interview.

139 **"or leave it":** Sharon Waxman, "They're In on the Joke: Hollywood's Funniest Clique," *New York Times*, March 27, 2005, https://www.nytimes.com/2005/03/27/movies/theyre-in-on-the-joke-hollywoods-funniest-clique.html.

139 **"smart-dumb comedy":** Waxman, "They're In on the Joke."

140 **"dirtier than that":** MW Staff, "Judd Apatow, Seth Rogen, and Romany Malco Talk *The 40 Year Old Virgin*," MovieWeb, August 18, 2005, https://movieweb.com/judd-apatow-seth-rogan-and-romany-malco-talk-the-40-year-old-virgin/.

Chapter 13: Wax Philosophical

142 **"Merry Christmas, Judd":** Judd Apatow, *Comedy Nerd: A Lifelong Obsession in Stories and Pictures* (Random House, 2025), 127.

142 **"make a movie":** NPR Staff, "From Early Failures to New *Trainwreck*, Judd Apatow Gets Serious," NPR, July 5, 2015, https://www.npr.org/2015/07/05/419254922/from-early-failures-to-new-trainwreck-judd-apatow-gets-serious.

143 **"out on it":** "Steve Carell Career Retrospective," moderated by Jenelle Riley, SAG-AFTTRA Foundation, January 4, 2015, YouTube, https://www.youtube.com/watch?v=jh9djS-e6W4.

143 **"understood the issue":** "Judd Apatow and Seth Rogen on *Knocked Up*," moderated by David Denby, October 7, 2007, posted July 22, 2014, by *New Yorker*, YouTube, https://www.youtube.com/watch?v=BB80Fm4pwgo.

143 **"passed him by":** "Steve Carell Career Retrospective."

143 **"might be true":** Denby, "Judd Apatow and Seth Rogen on *Knocked Up*."

143 **"greenlit it on Monday":** Riley, "Steve Carell Career Retrospective."

143 **"not going to happen":** Carole Cadwalladr, "Steve Carell Interview," *The Guardian*, August 21, 2010, https://www.theguardian.com/film/2010/aug/22/steve-carell-interview-dinner-for-schmucks.

144 **"he entertained us":** Tad Friend, "First Banana," *New Yorker*, June 28, 2010, https://www.newyorker.com/magazine/2010/07/05/first-banana.

144 **"'give it a shot'":** Riley, "Steve Carell Career Retrospective."

144 **"out of fear":** Riley, "Steve Carell Career Retrospective."

145 **"not going to happen":** *Too Funny to Fail: The Life & Death of the Dana Carvey Show*, directed by Josh Greenbaum, October 21, 2017, Hulu.

145 **"'on the show'":** Greenbaum, *Too Funny to Fail.*

146 **"on the map":** Greenbaum, *Too Funny to Fail.*

148 **"during the shoot":** Ryan Gajewski, "*The 40 Year Old Virgin* Turns 20: Judd Apatow on Controversial Scenes and the Studio Shutting Down Production, *Hollywood Reporter*, August 25, 2025, https://www.hollywoodreporter.com/movies/movie-features/40-year-old-virgin-20th-anniversary-judd-apatow-interview-1236351083/.

148 **"more personal than that":** Tim Appelo, "Judd Apatow Reveals His Penis Rule—'5 Seconds Yes, 20 Seconds No'—and Talks About 'Girls' Sex Scenes Banned by HBO," *Hollywood Reporter*, March 18, 2014, https://www.hollywoodreporter.com/news/general-news/judd-apatow-reveals-his-penis-689436/.

149 **"out the window?":** Marc Maron, host, *WTF with Marc* Maron, podcast, episode 104, "Judd Apatow Part 2," WTF+, September 1, 2010, https://www.wtfpod.com/podcast/episodes/episode_104_-_judd_apatow_part_2.

150 **"when people connected":** Rodney Rothman, author interview, Brooklyn, NY, December 3, 2025.

150 **"to his style":** Clayton Townsend, author interview, Brooklyn, NY, October 15, 2025.

150 **"do it again":** MW Staff, "Judd Apatow, Seth Rogen, and Romany Malco Talk *The 40 Year Old Virgin*," MovieWeb, August 18, 2005, https://movieweb.com/judd-apatow-seth-rogan-and-romany-malco-talk-the-40-year-old-virgin/.

150 **"too creepy-looking":** Townsend, author interview.

151 **"to kill someone?":** Riley, "Steve Carell Career Retrospective."

151 **"we did improvisations":** Appelo, "Judd Apatow Reveals His Penis Rule."

152 **"people liked it":** Maron, "Judd Apatow Part 2."

152 **"seemed really annoyed":** MW Staff, "Judd Apatow, Seth Rogen, and Romany Malco Talk."

152 **"call 'a movie'":** *The 40-Year-Old Virgin*, directed by Judd Apatow (Universal, 2011), Blu-ray.

153 **"meant as compliments":** Gajewski, "*The 40 Year Old Virgin* Turns 20."

153 **"actually laughing at":** Caroline McCloskey, "Seth Rogen and the Science of Rogenomics," *GQ*, May 21, 2019, https://www.gq.com/story/seth-rogen-cover-profile-june-july-2019.

153 **"I still do":** Alonso Duralde, author interview, Brooklyn, NY, September 22, 2025.

154 **"the turning point":** NPR Staff, "From Early Failures to New *Trainwreck*."

Chapter 14: If You Ain't First, You're Last

155 **Team for Halloween:** Marc Maron, host, *WTF with Marc Maron*, podcast, episode 119, "Adam McKay," WTF+, November 1, 2010, https://www.wtfpod.com/podcast/episodes/episode_119_-_adam_mckay.

156 **"could ever pick?":** Rachel Abramowicz, "It's Fast Cars, Hot Women and Dumb Guys," *Newsday*, August 3, 2006, B6.

156 **"'shooting race cars'":** Abramowicz, "It's Fast Cars, Hot Women and Dumb Guys."

157 **"soliciting my ideas":** Devin Faraci, "Interview: John C. Reilly (*Talladega Nights*)," CHUD.com, August 2, 2006, https://chud.com/7294/interview-john-c-reilly-talladega-nights/.

158 **"He's a monster":** Maron, "Adam McKay."

158 **"'getting to riff'":** Faraci, "Interview: John C. Reilly."

158 **"for dear life":** Lauren Huff, "Will Ferrell Reveals the Time John C. Reilly Made Him Break Character in *Talladega Nights*," *Entertainment Weekly*, March 4, 2025, https://ew.com/will-ferrell-reveals-time-john-c-reilly-made-him-break-character-11690976.

159 **"placements per frame":** A. O. Scott, "*Talladega Nights*: The Men Are Rowdy, the Cars Are Fast and the Product Placement Is Extreme," *New York Times*, August 4, 2006, https://www.nytimes.com/2006/08/04/movies/talladega-nights-the-men-are-rowdy-the-cars-are-fast-and-the-product.html.

159 **"integrity came from":** Maron, "Adam McKay."

159 **"backend promotions":** Gail Schiller, "*Talladega* in High Gear with Brands," *Hollywood Reporter*, August 3, 2006, https://link.gale.com/apps/doc/A151054333/ITOF?u=nysl_me_bpl_cent&sid=bookmark-ITOF&xid=8ef79ab8.

159 **"'get real products'":** Maron, "Adam McKay."

160 **"in good fun":** Martin Miller, "Film Sponsors: Spoof Me, Please," *Los Angeles Times*, August 4, 2006, https://www.latimes.com/archives/la-xpm-2006-aug-04-et-talladega4-story.html.

161 **"would hate it":** Marc Maron, host, *WTF with Marc Maron*, podcast, episode 683, "Sacha Baron Cohen," WTF+, February 22, 2016, https://www.wtfpod.com/podcast/episodes/episode_683_-_sacha_baron_cohen.

161 **"'Booyakasha!'":** Neil Strauss, "The Man Behind the Mustache," *Rolling Stone*, November 30, 2006, https://www.rollingstone.com/tv-movies/tv-movie-news/sacha-baron-cohen-the-man-behind-the-mustache-249539/.

161 **"a real situation":** Strauss, "The Man Behind the Mustache."

163 **were not amused:** "*Borat* Turns 10: Real Stories Behind the Making of the Satirical Documentary," ABC News, November 3, 2016, https://abcnews.go.com/Entertainment/borat-turns-10-real-stories-making-satirical-documentary/story?id=43138286.

163 **"they were doing":** "*Borat* Turns 10," ABC News.

163 **he disappeared:** Maron, "Sacha Baron Cohen."
164 **"sue this Jew":** Steven Lee Myers, "Kazakhs Shrug at Borat While the State Fumes," *New York Times*, September 28, 2006, https://www.nytimes.com/2006/09/28/movies/kazakhs-shrug-at-borat-while-the-state-fumes.html.
164 **"this ex-Soviet backwater":** Strauss, "The Man Behind the Mustache."
164 **"their own prejudice":** Strauss, "The Man Behind the Mustache."
165 **on a Jet Ski:** *Vanity Fair*, "Sacha Baron Cohen Rewatches Borat, Talladega Nights, Da Ali G Show & More," November 12, 2024, YouTube, https://www.youtube.com/watch?v=a8d-Xj2V4Zg.
165 **"like forty-five seconds":** *GQ*, "Sacha Baron Cohen Breaks Down His Most Iconic Characters," November 21, 2024, YouTube, https://www.youtube.com/watch?v=Ha_cHQxGFMI.
166 **"stuff that's bullshit":** Maron, "Adam McKay."
167 **"Which I *hate*":** Maron, "Adam McKay."

Chapter 15: Revenge of the Nerds

170 **"awful":** Andrew Buss, "'It's Either Going to Be Really Funny, or They're Going to Be Horrified': An Oral History of *Superbad*," *Vanity Fair*, August 17, 2022, https://www.vanityfair.com/hollywood/2022/08/superbad-oral-history.
170 **"a lot of ways":** Marc Maron, host, *WTF with Marc Maron*, podcast, episode 396, "Seth Rogen and Evan Goldberg," WTF+, June 10, 2013, https://www.wtfpod.com/podcast/episodes/episode_396_-_seth_rogen_and_evan_goldberg.
171 **"people will stop":** Caroline McCloskey, "Seth Rogen and the Science of Rogenomics," *GQ*, May 21, 2019, https://www.gq.com/story/seth-rogen-cover-profile-june-july-2019.
171 **"not fucking stand?!":** Seth Rogen, *Yearbook* (Crown, 2021), 4.
171 **"it was impossible":** Maron, "Seth Rogen and Evan Goldberg."
172 **"'guy is hilarious'":** Paul Feig, author interview, Brooklyn, NY, September 9, 2025.
173 **"'a movie star'":** "Judd Apatow and Seth Rogen on *Knocked Up*," moderated by David Denby, October 7, 2007, posted July 22, 2014, by *New Yorker*, YouTube, https://www.youtube.com/watch?v=BB80Fm4pwgo.
173 **"about eight seconds":** "*Undeclared / Freaks and Geeks* Reunion," moderated by Judd Apatow, March 12, 2011, posted January 26, 2021, by ChinaCat Sunflower, YouTube, https://www.youtube.com/watch?v=cv1GFOY-WVg.
173 **"literally laughed":** Denby, "Judd Apatow and Seth Rogen on *Knocked Up*."
174 **"would be amazing":** Rodney Rothman, author interview, Brooklyn, NY, December 3, 2025.
174 **pasta, cheese, and hot dogs:** Tim Ferriss, host, *The Tim Ferriss Show*, podcast, episode 108, "Seth Rogen, Evan Goldberg," Tim Ferriss, September 29, 2015, https://tim.blog/2015/09/29/seth-rogen-and-evan-goldberg/.

174 **"head of the studio!":** Buss, "'It's Either Going to Be Really Funny.'"
174 **"in this thing?":** Denby, "Judd Apatow and Seth Rogen on *Knocked Up*."
175 **"'handsome *and* funny!'":** Denby, "Judd Apatow and Seth Rogen on *Knocked Up*."
175 **"'go for it'":** Griffin Newman and David Sims, hosts, *Blank Check with Griffin and David*, podcast, "*The Big Lebowski* with Seth Rogen," Blank Check, https://blankcheck.beam.ly/episode/the-big-lebowski-with-seth-rogen.
176 **"lame it was":** Denby, "Judd Apatow and Seth Rogen on *Knocked Up*."
176 **"people still remember":** *GQ*, "Seth Rogen Breaks Down His Most Iconic Characters," May 21, 2019, YouTube, https://www.youtube.com/watch?v=6Db_8Oyy09w.
176 **"say it right now":** *The 40-Year-Old Virgin*, directed by Judd Apatow (Universal, 2011), Blu-ray.
177 **"a girl pregnant":** Rachel Abramowicz, "The King of Geeks," *Los Angeles Times*, May 13, 2007, https://www.latimes.com/archives/la-xpm-2007-may-13-ca-apatow13-story.html.
177 ***at some point*:** Scott Myers, "How Judd Apatow Used Email to Write *Knocked Up*," Medium, September 6, 2023, https://gointothestory.blcklst.com/how-judd-apatow-used-email-to-write-knocked-up-c4ea8b0449cd.
178 ***Knocked Up*'s climax:** Stephen Rodrick, "Judd Apatow's Family Values," *New York Times*, May 27, 2007, https://www.nytimes.com/2007/05/27/magazine/27apatow-t.html.
178 **"treats you in the movie":** *Knocked Up*, directed by Judd Apatow (Universal, 2010), Blu-ray.
178 **"'something from it'":** Scott Meslow, "How Judd Apatow Bounced Back with *The 40-Year-Old Virgin*," *GQ*, January 28, 2022, https://www.gq.com/story/from-hollywood-with-love-40-year-old-virgin-excerpt.
178 **"thousands of years!":** Robert Capps, "Writer-Director (and Geek God) Judd Apatow Invites You into His Mind Test," *Wired*, May 30, 2007, https://www.wired.com/2007/05/writer-director-and-geek-god-judd-apatow-invites-you-into-his-mind-test/.
179 **"I hate Judd!":** *GQ*, "Paul Rudd Breaks Down His Most Iconic Characters," February 9, 2023, YouTube, https://www.youtube.com/watch?v=WYIW5P4q5fM.
180 **"thought to write":** Tim Appelo, "Judd Apatow Reveals His Penis Rule—'5 Seconds Yes, 20 Seconds No'—and Talks About 'Girls' Sex Scenes Banned by HBO," *Hollywood Reporter*, March 18, 2014, https://www.hollywoodreporter.com/news/general-news/judd-apatow-reveals-his-penis-689436/.
180 **"having to see that":** Rodrick, "Judd Apatow's Family Values."
180 **"sensibility would play":** Maron, "Seth Rogen and Evan Goldberg."
181 **long-awaited green light:** Buss, "'It's Either Going to Be Really Funny.'"
181 **"brightly lit, palatable comedies":** Buss, "'It's Either Going to Be Really Funny.'"

181 **“leagues funnier”:** *GQ*, “Seth Rogen Breaks Down.”

182 **upward of 150 candidates:** Denby, “Judd Apatow and Seth Rogen on *Knocked Up*.”

182 **“‘makeup and hair’”:** Buss, “‘It’s Either Going to Be Really Funny.’”

182 **the new Seth:** *GQ*, “Seth Rogen Breaks Down.”

182 **“This is you!”:** Denby, “Judd Apatow and Seth Rogen on *Knocked Up*.”

182 **Seth and McLovin:** Fan Expo, “Jonah Hill Hated McLovin’,” March 1, 2025, YouTube, https://www.youtube.com/shorts/FSNpxNYtxRA.

183 **“over the years”:** *GQ*, “Seth Rogen Breaks Down.”

183 **“her adult life”:** Buss, “‘It’s Either Going to Be Really Funny.’”

184 **“shit’ll happen also”:** Denby, “Judd Apatow and Seth Rogen on *Knocked Up*.”

185 **“Seth was wrong”:** *Superbad*, directed by Greg Mottola (Sony, 2007), DVD.

185 **“of your movies?”:** Denby, “Judd Apatow and Seth Rogen on *Knocked Up*.”

Chapter 16: Action!

188 **“apparent suicide attempt”:** *LA Times*, “Owen Wilson Ducks Publicity for New Film,” *HuffPost*, March 28, 2008, https://www.huffpost.com/entry/owen-wilson-ducks-publici_n_92499.

188 **“history of depression”:** Paula Froelich and Marianne Garvey, “‘O.D.’ Try by Owen,” *New York Post*, August 28, 2007, https://nypost.com/2007/08/28/owen-in-suicide-attempt/.

188 **“this difficult time”:** Sarah Kliff, “Owen Wilson: Battling Depression,” *Newsweek*, October 13, 2007, https://www.newsweek.com/owen-wilson-battling-depression-103931.

189 **“‘go to war?’”:** Edward Douglas, “Ben Stiller Feels the Tropic Thunder,” ComingSoon.net, March 17, 2008, https://www.comingsoon.net/movies/features/42984-ben-stiller-feels-the-tropic-thunder.

189 **“actual Vietnam veterans”:** Josh Horowitz, “Ben Stiller & Seth Rogen Talk *Severance*, *The Studio*, Scorsese, Tom Cruise, *Zoolander*,” August 21, 2025, YouTube, https://www.youtube.com/watch?v=0Gtg-Gwf-30.

190 **“the plot holes”:** Alex French and Howie Kahn, “The Making of Les Grossman: An Oral History,” Grantland, July 30, 2015, https://grantland.com/features/the-making-of-les-grossman-an-oral-history/.

190 **“Grossman role yet”:** French and Kahn, “The Making of Les Grossman.”

191 **“‘I’m gonna dance’”:** Team Coco, “Tom Cruise Brings Les Grossman to #ConanCon,” July 18, 2019, YouTube, https://www.youtube.com/watch?v=mveeFrDGm_4.

191 **“Owen Wilson and Vince Vaughn”:** Mickey Rapkin, “Funnyman of the Year: Danny McBride,” *GQ*, November 17, 2008, https://www.gq.com/story/funnyman-of-the-year-danny-mcbride.

192 **“the whole movie”:** Douglas, “Ben Stiller Feels the Tropic Thunder.”

192 **"could be disastrous":** CBS, "Robert Downey Jr. on *Thunder*," YouTube, August 18, 2008, https://www.youtube.com/watch?v=-EU_vi6QgeY.

192 **"Comedy Death Camp":** Chris Lee, "Looking for Action, He Got It," *Los Angeles Times*, August 10, 2008, https://www.latimes.com/archives/la-xpm-2008-aug-10-ca-stiller10-story.html.

193 **$15 million over budget:** Tad Friend, "Funny Is Money," *New Yorker*, June 18, 2012, https://www.newyorker.com/magazine/2012/06/25/funny-is-money.

193 **"to win awards":** "Ben Stiller: Taking Chances with *Tropic Thunder*," ABC News, August 12, 2008, https://abcnews.go.com/Nightline/story?id=5567544&page=1.

194 **"'Cheech and Chong movies?'":** *Pineapple Express*, directed by David Gordon Green (Sony, 2009), DVD.

194 **"where we started":** Steven Weintraub, "Comic-Con 2008: *Pineapple Express*," Collider, August 6, 2008, https://collider.com/comiccon-2008-pineapple-express-interviews/.

194 **"'stupid version of it'":** *GQ*, "Seth Rogen Breaks Down His Most Iconic Characters," May 21, 2019, YouTube, https://www.youtube.com/watch?v=6Db_8Oyy09w.

195 **"'probably more interesting'":** *GQ*, "Seth Rogen Breaks Down."

195 **"the emotional stories":** *GQ*, "Seth Rogen Breaks Down."

197 **"create a comedy":** BAFTA Guru, "Will Ferrell on Creating *Step Brothers* with John C. Reilly," January 7, 2019, YouTube, https://www.youtube.com/watch?v=5A3YRFp3ky0.

197 **"'to have that?'":** Alan Siegel, "Unadulterated Joy: An Oral History of *Step Brothers*," The Ringer, July 10, 2018, https://www.theringer.com/2018/07/10/movies/step-brothers-oral-history-will-ferrell-john-c-reilly-adam-mckay.

197 **$10,000 to make:** Dan Patrick, host, "Will Ferrell on the Dan Patrick Show (Full Interview)," *Dan Patrick Show*, June 10, 2014, YouTube, https://www.youtube.com/watch?v=6H7_56bsGhQ.

198 **"arc of the movie":** Terry Gross, host, *Fresh Air*, "A Band of 'Brothers' and a Barrel of Laughs," NPR, July 23, 2008, https://www.npr.org/2008/07/23/92794521/a-band-of-brothers-and-a-barrel-of-laughs.

199 **"let us do this":** Marc Maron, host, *WTF with Marc Maron*, podcast, episode 119, "Adam McKay," WTF+, November 1, 2010, https://www.wtfpod.com/podcast/episodes/episode_119_-_adam_mckay.

199 **"of our civilization":** Roger Ebert, "The Feel-Bad Comedy of the Year!" Roger Ebert.com, July 23, 2008, https://www.rogerebert.com/reviews/step-brothers-2008.

Chapter 17: Where No Man Has Gone Before

202 **"hurt the movie":** Erik Hedegaard, "How *The Hangover* Director Took on the Military Industrial Complex," *Rolling Stone*, August 11, 2016, https://www

.rollingstone.com/tv-movies/tv-movie-features/how-the-hangover-director-took-on-the-military-industrial-complex-111504/.

202 **"spoke to me":** Diane Garrett and Tatiana Siegel, "Warner Weds Phillips Film," *Variety*, October 4, 2007, https://variety.com/2007/scene/markets-festivals/warner-weds-phillips-film-1117973450/.

203 **"built it around that":** Stephen Mooallem, "Interview: Todd Phillips," *Interview*, October 12, 2010, https://www.interviewmagazine.com/film/todd-phillips.

203 ***not good at auditions*:** Matthew Belloni and Lacey Rose, "The Uncensored Oral History of *The Hangover*," *Hollywood Reporter*, May 1, 2013, https://www.hollywoodreporter.com/movies/movie-news/hangover-uncensored-oral-history-449046/.

203 **"'at the premiere'":** Belloni and Rose, "The Uncensored Oral History."

204 **"the next half-hour?":** Belloni and Rose, "The Uncensored Oral History."

204 **"stepped in, thank God":** Dave Itzkoff, "Finding the Fun in Eternal Frat Boys," *New York Times*, May 28, 2009, https://www.nytimes.com/2009/05/31/movies/31itz.html.

205 **$70 million:** Belloni and Rose, "The Uncensored Oral History."

206 **"with *Funny People*":** David Marchese, "In Conversation: Judd Apatow," Vulture, August 7, 2017, https://www.vulture.com/2017/08/judd-apatow-on-his-legacy-feminism-and-republicans.html.

208 **"fun to watch":** Pbadmin, "Funny People Set Visit: Judd Apatow," Coming Soon.net, April 7, 2009, https://www.comingsoon.net/extras/news/54255-funny-people-set-visit-judd-apatow.

Chapter 18: God's Great Miracles

209 **"in the world":** Associated Press, "Remarks About Women Elicit No Laughs for Lewis at Comedy Arts Festival," *Deseret News*, February 14, 2000, https://www.deseret.com/2000/2/14/19491107/remarks-about-women-elicit-no-laughs-for-lewis-at-comedy-arts-festival/.

210 **"misinterpreted":** Glenn Collins, "Public Lives," *New York Times*, February 18, 2000, https://www.nytimes.com/2000/02/18/nyregion/public-lives.html.

210 **"make a baby":** Michele Orecklin, "People: February 28, 2000," *Time*, February 28, 2000, https://time.com/archive/6740477/people-feb-28-2000/.

211 **"a 12-year-old boy":** Natalie Abrams, "*The Sweetest Thing* Writer Nancy Pimental Sets Recor Straight on Film's True Inspiration," *Entertainment Weekly*, March 30, 2018, https://ew.com/movies/2018/03/30/the-sweetest-thing-writer-nancy-pimental-sequel/.

211 **"behind her tonsils":** Abrams, "*The Sweetest Thing* Writer."

211 **"penis song went away":** Abrams, "*The Sweetest Thing* Writer."

212 **"walked in the door":** Amy Wallace, "I Have a Great Idea, Maybe Like the Best Idea I've Ever Had," *GQ*, December 20, 2012, https://www.gq.com/story/judd-apatow-profile-gq-january-2013-video.

213 **"a little too accurate":** Liane Hansen, "From Funnyman Judd Apatow, a Few Solid Laughs," NPR, October 31, 2010, https://www.npr.org/transcripts/130915010.

213 **"love the movie":** Leslie Bennett, "Heigl's Anatomy," *Vanity Fair*, January 2008, https://archive.vanityfair.com/article/2008/1/heigls-antomy.

213 **"warranted much reflection":** Marchese, "In Conversation: Judd Apatow."

214 **"You're mocking immaturity":** Wallace, "I Have a Great Idea."

214 **"a young idiot":** Amy Nicholson, "Judd Apatow's Second Act," *Village Voice*, May 27, 2015, 8.

214 **"weren't good yet":** Anna Peele and Judd Apatow, "The Judd Apatow Profile, Annotated by Judd Apatow," *Esquire*, June 2, 2015, https://www.esquire.com/entertainment/interviews/a35389/judd-apatow-profile/.

214 **"any movie ideas?":** Tim Appelo, "Judd Apatow Reveals His Penis Rule—'5 Seconds Yes, 20 Seconds No'—and Talks About 'Girls' Sex Scenes Banned By HBO," *Hollywood Reporter*, March 18, 2014, https://www.hollywoodreporter.com/news/general-news/judd-apatow-reveals-his-penis-689436/.

215 **"want to try acting":** Marc Maron, host, *WTF with Marc Maron*, podcast, episode 734, "Kristen Wiig," WTF+, August 18, 2016, https://www.wtfpod.com/podcast/episode-734-kristen-wiig.

215 **"thought of you":** Scott Feinberg, host, *Awards Chatter*, "Kristen Wiig—*Saturday Night Live*," *Hollywood Reporter*, August 27, 2017, https://www.hollywoodreporter.com/news/general-news/awards-chatter-podcast-kristen-wiig-saturday-night-live-1032943/.

215 **"'find this theater'":** Maron, "Kristen Wiig."

216 **"become very different":** Megan Angelo, "Tossing the Bouquet Out of the Genre," *New York Times*, May 6, 2011, https://www.nytimes.com/2011/05/08/movies/bridesmaids-with-kristen-wiig-opens-friday.html.

216 **"'the other one'":** Kim Masters, host, *The Business*, "*Bridesmaids* Co-Writers Kristen Wiig and Annie Mumolo," KCRW, May 12, 2014, https://www.kcrw.com/shows/the-business/stories/bridesmaids-co-writers-kristen-wiig-and-annie-mumolo-1.

217 **"[Apatow] was like, 'What?'":** Masters, "*Bridesmaids* Co-Writers Kristen Wiig and Annie Mumolo."

217 **"be annoyed by":** Paul Feig, author interview, Brooklyn, NY, September 9, 2025.

218 **"close to home":** Feig, author interview.

219 **"didn't love the idea":** Feinberg, "Kristen Wiig—*Saturday Night Live*."

219 **wouldn't use it:** Sara Stewart, "Girls Will Be Boys," *New York Post*, May 8, 2011, 8.

219 **"think that way":** Feinberg, "Kristen Wiig—*Saturday Night Live*."

220 **"the written stuff":** Masters, "*Bridesmaids* Co-Writers Kristen Wiig and Annie Mumolo."

221 **"done in Vegas":** David Canfield, "'We Didn't Want to Wallow in Grossness': An Oral History of *Bridesmaids*," *Entertainment Weekly*, February 4, 2019, https://ew.com/movies/2019/02/04/bridesmaids-rom-com-oral-history/.

221 **"no deeper meaning":** Feinberg, "Kristen Wiig—*Saturday Night Live*."

221 **"a sobering moment":** Feig, author interview.

221 **"in the trailer":** Feig, author interview.

222 **"fuck you":** Gregg Kilday, "Jerry Lewis Drew Ire over His Comments About Female Comedians," *Hollywood Reporter*, August 23, 2017, https://www.hollywoodreporter.com/news/general-news/jerry-lewis-drew-ire-his-comments-female-comedians-1031730/.

Chapter 19: This Is the End

224 **a disappointment:** Bilge Ebiri, "You're Only as Good as Your Last Film," Vulture, August 13, 2025, https://www.vulture.com/article/ron-howard-in-conversation.html.

224 **"we ever had":** Marc Maron, host, *WTF with Marc Maron*, podcast, episode 396, "Seth Rogen and Evan Goldberg," WTF+, June 10, 2013, https://www.wtfpod.com/podcast/episodes/episode_396_-_seth_rogen_and_evan_goldberg.

225 **"type of thing":** Maron, "Seth Rogen and Evan Goldberg."

225 **"fish to fry":** Caroline McCloskey, "Seth Rogen and the Science of Rogenomics," *GQ*, May 21, 2019, https://www.gq.com/story/seth-rogen-cover-profile-june-july-2019.

225 **"'we doing here?'"** McCloskey, "Seth Rogen and the Science of Rogenomics."

225 **called the film "deadly":** Lou Lumenick, "*Hornet* Stink Is Deadly," *New York Post*, January 14, 2011, https://nypost.com/2011/01/14/hornet-stink-is-deadly/.

226 **"not understanding why":** Amy Wallace, "I Have a Great Idea, Maybe Like the Best Idea I've Ever Had," *GQ*, December 20, 2012, https://www.gq.com/story/judd-apatow-profile-gq-january-2013-video.

227 **"start with darkness":** *Wolfpack Only: The Hangover Retrospective*, directed by Joseph Garner (Warner Bros., 2013), Blu-ray.

229 **"portrayed its products":** Ronald Grover and Alexei Oreskovic, "Google Goes Hollywood with *The Internship*," Reuters, May 28, 2013, https://www.reuters.com/article/2013/05/28/entertainment-us-google-movie-idUSBRE94R0XY20130528/.

230 **on their own:** McCloskey, "Seth Rogen and the Science of Rogenomics."

232 **"cut their price substantially":** Russ Fischer, "*Anchorman 2* Much Closer to Happening Than Previously Thought," Slashfilm, April 27, 2010, https://www

.slashfilm.com/508803/anchorman-2-much-closer-to-happening-than-previously-thought/.

Epilogue: No Laughing Matter

235 **"liking the guy":** Seth Rogen, *Yearbook* (Crown, 2021), 178.

236 **"we'll make it":** Rogen, *Yearbook*, 178.

237 **"they don't like":** "Remarks by the President in Year-End Press Conference," ObamaWhiteHouse.archives.gov, December 19, 2014, https://obamawhitehouse.archives.gov/the-press-office/2014/12/19/remarks-president-year-end-press-conference.

238 **"and move on":** Rogen, *Yearbook*, 194.

238 **"still finance them":** Stuart McGurk, "Seth Rogen and the Year That Went to Pot," *GQ*, May 26, 2021, https://www.gq-magazine.co.uk/culture/article/seth-rogen-interview-2021.

238 **"is really wild":** Scot Armstrong, author interview, Brooklyn, NY, August 14, 2025.

239 **"that moment ended":** Judd Apatow, *Comedy Nerd: A Lifelong Obsession in Stories and Pictures* (Random House, 2025), 181.

239 **"everyone to hate":** Armstrong, author interview.

239 **"each other's funny":** Joe Neumaier, "The Biggest Dope in Hollywood," *New York Daily News*, July 4, 2004, 2.

239 **"opportunities to people":** Susan Wloszczyna, "'Frat Pack' Splits," *USA Today*, July 13, 2006, link.gale.com/apps/doc/A148161457/AONE?u=nysl_oweb&sid=bookmark-AONE&xid=36953a28.

239 **"never really existed":** Marc Maron, host, *WTF with Marc Maron*, podcast, episode 79, "Ben Stiller," WTF+, June 7, 2010, https://www.wtfpod.com/podcast/episodes/episode_79_ben_stiller.

239 **"in my movies":** David Dobkin, author interview, Brooklyn, NY, November 17, 2025.

241 **"huge and too busy":** Marc Maron, host, *WTF with Marc Maron*, poscast, episode 450, "Will Ferrell," WTF+, December 9, 2013, https://www.wtfpod.com/podcast/episodes/episode_450_-_will_ferrell.

242 **"something that's great":** Seth MacFarlane, author interview, Brooklyn, NY, October 8, 2025.

242 **"a very long time":** Miguel Helft, "Netflix to Deliver Movies to the PC," *New York Times*, January 16, 2007, https://www.nytimes.com/2007/01/16/technology/16netflix.html.

243 **streaming subscribers worldwide:** Associated Press, "Netflix to End DVD-by-Mail Service That Changed Video Rental Industry," PBS, April 18, 2023, https://www.pbs.org/newshour/arts/netflix-to-end-dvd-by-mail-service-that-changed-video-rental-industry.

243 **to 8.1 percent:** Tad Friend, "Funny Is Money," *New Yorker*, June 18, 2012, https://www.newyorker.com/magazine/2012/06/25/funny-is-money.

243 **"there's less [comedies]":** Judd Apatow, "Judd Apatow, Comedy Nerd," public lecture, New York, NY, October 29, 2025.

244 **"going to open":** Erica Huggins, author interview, Brooklyn, NY, September 9, 2025.

244 **"two of them":** David Marchese, "In Conversation: Seth Rogen," Vulture, April 30, 2018, https://www.vulture.com/2018/04/seth-rogen-in-conversation.html.

244 **"waste of their time":** Dobkin, author interview.

245 **"this massive event":** John Hamburg, author interview, Brooklyn, NY, July 11, 2025.

245 **"had to be funny":** Huggins, author interview.

246 **"barriers and borders":** Michael H. Weber, author interview, Brooklyn, NY, October 30, 2025.

246 **"swept up in that":** MacFarlane, author interview.

247 **"right now, we're fucked":** Apatow, "Judd Apatow, Comedy Nerd."

247 **"just nothing better":** Hamburg, author interview.

247 **"those movies anymore!"** Hamburg, author interview.

247 **"about for me":** Huggins, author interview.

248 **"on comedy movies":** Weber, author interview.

248 **"oxygenate these things":** Rodney Rothman, author interview, Brooklyn, NY, December 3, 2025.

248 **"pendulum is swinging back":** Armstrong, author interview.

249 **"That was fun":** Huggins, author interview

249 **"took 'em for granted":** Huggins, author interview.

250 **entire theatrical run:** Anthony D'Alessandro, "Four Fanboy Flicks Bomb Out in Deadline's 2024 Most Valuable Blockbuster Tournament," Deadline, April 30, 2025, https://deadline.com/2025/04/biggest-box-office-bombs-2024-lowest-grossing-movies-1236381446/.

251 **"talk to me again":** Joe Hagan, "'Who the Fuck Cares About Adam McKay?' (We Do, and with Good Reason)," *Vanity Fair*, November 29, 2021, https://www.vanityfair.com/hollywood/2021/11/who-the-fuck-cares-about-adam-mckay.

251 **"I fucked up":** Lacey Rose, "How HBO's Lakers Series Ticked Off the NBA, Ended a Friendship and Became the Most Anticipated Show in Decades," *Hollywood Reporter*, February 23, 2022, https://www.hollywoodreporter.com/tv/tv-features/winning-time-adam-mckay-john-c-reilly-hbo-laker-series-1235097468/.

251 **"life with him":** Pamela McClintock, "Adam McKay on His Enduring Love for Will Ferrell and the 'Insane' State of the World: 'I'm Fully Freaked Out,'" *Hollywood Reporter*, December 8, 2021, https://www.hollywoodreporter.com/movies/movie-features/adam-mckay-interview-dont-look-up-will-ferrell-1235058377/.

252 **"amounts of bandwidth":** Lacey Rose, "Will Ferrell Just Wants to Entertain You (and Himself)," *Hollywood Reporter*, October 28, 2021, https://www.hollywoodreporter.com/feature/will-ferrell-shrink-next-door-christmas-carol-spirited-1235037010/.

252 **"turn your brain off":** Rose, "Will Ferrell Just Wants."

252 **"feel right now":** Rose, "Will Ferrell Just Wants."

254 **"the same thing":** Evan Romano, "Owen Wilson Leans Into His Sports Obsession with *Stick*," *Men's Health*, June 5, 2025, https://www.menshealth.com/entertainment/a64979851/owen-wilson-interview-stick-apple-tv/.

256 **"don't like comedy":** *Stiller & Meara: Nothing Is Lost*, directed by Ben Stiller, October 24, 2025, Apple TV+.

257 **"plan to right now":** Decca Aitkenhead, "Seth Rogen on Fame, Smoking Weed, and Why His Films Have Not Aged Well," London *Sunday Times*, May 9, 2021, https://www.thetimes.com/culture/tv-radio/article/seth-rogen-on-fame-smoking-weed-and-why-his-films-have-not-aged-well-ksm8pvtvl.

257 **"lack of trying":** Nick Vivarelli, "James Franco on New Movie *Hey Joe*, Being 'Grateful' for His Fall from Grace and the End of Seth Rogen Friendship: 'I Guess It's Over,'" *Variety*, October 25, 2024, https://variety.com/2024/film/global/james-franco-new-movie-hey-joe-lawsuit-seth-rogen-friendship-1236190559/.

258 **"part of comedy":** Marchese, "In Conversation: Seth Rogen."

259 **"audience is smaller":** Adrienne LaFrance, "The Invention of Judd Apatow," *The Atlantic*, September 15, 2025, https://www.theatlantic.com/magazine/archive/2025/10/judd-apatow-comedy-career/683975/.

Appendix: Buried Treasures of the Frat Pack Era

263 **"didn't get picked up":** Marc Maron, host, *WTF with Marc Maron*, podcast, episode 79, "Ben Stiller," WTF+, June 7, 2010, https://www.wtfpod.com/podcast/episodes/episode_79_ben_stiller.

PHOTO CREDITS

INDEX

INDEX

INDEX

INDEX

INDEX

Photo © Clayton Rathiel

Matt Singer is the editor and film critic of ScreenCrush.com and a member of the New York Film Critics Circle. He won a Webby Award for his work on the Independent Film Channel's website, IFC.com, and is the author of *Marvel's Spider-Man: From Amazing to Spectacular* and *Opposable Thumbs: How Siskel & Ebert Changed Movies Forever.* He lives in Brooklyn, New York, with his wife and two daughters.

VISIT MATT SINGER ONLINE

mattsinger.bsky.social

SuperPulse